THE HUMAN DEVELOPMENT RACE

Since 1985 the International Center for Economic Growth, a nonprofit international policy institute, has contributed to economic growth and human development in developing and post-socialist countries by strengthening the capacity of indigenous research institutes to provide leadership in policy debates. To accomplish this the Center sponsors a wide range of programs—including research, publications, conferences, seminars, and special projects advising governments—through a network of over 250 correspondent institutes worldwide.

The Center is affiliated with the Institute for Contemporary Studies and is headquartered in Panama with the administrative office in San Francisco, California.

For further information, please contact the International Center for Economic Growth, 720 Market Street, San Francisco, California 94102, USA. Phone (415) 981-5353; fax (415) 986-4878.

ICEG Board of Overseers

THE HUMAN DEVELOPMENT RACE
IMPROVING THE QUALITY OF LIFE
IN DEVELOPING COUNTRIES

Marc M. Lindenberg

An International Center for Economic Growth Publication

PRESS

San Francisco, California

Publication signifies that the International Center for Economic Growth believes a work to be a competent treatment worthy of public consideration. The findings, interpretations, and conclusions of a work are entirely those of the author and should not be attributed to ICEG, its affiliated organizations, its Board of Overseers, or organizations that support ICEG.

Inquiries, book orders, and catalog requests should be addressed to ICS Press, Institute for Contemporary Studies, 720 Market Street, San Francisco, California 94102 USA. Telephone: (415) 981-5353; fax (415) 986-4878; book orders within the continental United States: **(800) 326-0263.**

Publication of this book was made possible by support from the Ford Foundation, the William and Flora Hewlett Foundation, and the Starr Foundation.

Editor: Heidi Fritschel
Indexer: Shirley Kessel
Cover designer: Ben Santora
Cover photos courtesy of CARE

Library of Congress Cataloging-in-Publication Data
Lindenberg, Marc M.
    The human development race : improving the quality of life in
developing countries / Marc M. Lindenberg.
        p.   cm.
    ''An International Center for Economic Growth publication.''
    Includes bibliographical references and index.
    ISBN 1-55815-277-6 (cloth). — ISBN 1-55815-278-4 (pbk.)
    1. Quality of life—Developing countries. 2. Developing
countries—Economic policy. 3. Developing countries—Social policy.
4. Economic development—Social aspects. I. Title.
HN980.L54   1993
                                                      93-14619

To Cathy, Robbie, and Anni,
whose patience and supportiveness
during this long process
I have greatly appreciated

CONTENTS

PREFACE

Although economists spend a great deal of time studying, measuring, and trying to understand economic growth, they still know little about how to improve the quality of people's lives in developing countries. What strategies work best for improving access to education and health care? How can people's lives be made as long, healthy, and productive as possible? *The Human Development Race* addresses these questions.

Some developing countries have succeeded in improving the human development level of their population: Chile, Costa Rica, Singapore, and South Korea, to name a few. But many others are still struggling with widespread illiteracy, poor health care, and low incomes. To understand why such wide differences in human development exist, Marc Lindenberg examines the countries with the best human development performance to see what the ingredients have been. Have they been characterized by high or low state spending on social services? Have they been the lucky beneficiaries of beneficial world economic cycles and well-endowed with natural resources, or have policies been more important? He looks not only at economic factors, but at political factors as well. Have democracies or authoritarian systems been more successful at stimulating human development?

The most successful countries, Lindenberg discovers, are those that have used their policy tools wisely over long periods of time to invest in the well-being of their people. Such policy commitments have been possible only in countries that enjoy some measure of political stability. His conclusions offer sobering lessons to the many countries now attempting to pursue both economic and political liberalization.

If the true goal of development is not simply to raise growth rates by several percentage points but rather to improve the lives of people, then the issues raised in this book are central to every student of economic policy. The International Center for Economic Growth is pleased to publish this important work.

Nicolás Ardito-Barletta
General Director
International Center for Economic Growth

Panama City, Panama
September 1993

ACKNOWLEDGMENTS

The idea for this book came out of my attempt to put the intense experience of economic and political collapse in Central America in the 1980s into a broader context of global human development. The effort to develop a deeper understanding of this period of turmoil would not have happened without a series of helpful conversations with and strong encouragement from Robert Klitgaard, a valued friend and colleague. These conversations began in Costa Rica and continued in places like Nicaragua, Equatorial Guinea, and Boston. The ideas were expanded with help and useful insights from Jack Montgomery. Shantayana Devarajan helped deepen my understanding of the relationship between economic growth and democracy. Chapter 2 is a longer version of ideas that we published together in an article called ''Prescribing Strong Economic Medicine,'' *Comparative Politics* 25, no. 2 (January 1993). Jorge Domínguez and Forrest Colburn's ideas were invaluable in helping get at the underlying trends in Central America and in keeping me motivated to finish what I began. These insights about Central American political transitions were deepened through a series of workshops that Jorge and I coordinated at Harvard with support from Richard Bloomfield and the World Peace Foundation.

Many colleagues contributed useful ideas along the way, among them: Graham Allison, William Ascher, Jim Austin, Nicolás Ardito-Barletta, Ricardo Castañeda, Silvio De Franco, Jorge Manuel Dengo, John Ickis, Ray Goldberg, Mark Moore, Jay Patel, Rodolfo Paíz, Dwight Perkins, Roger Quant, Dani Roderik, Edith Stokey, Harry Strachan, Eduardo Vallarino, Louis Wells, Richard Zeckhauser, and Andrew Zimbalist.

I could not have completed this book without the special help of the Ford Foundation and an individual author's grant from their Mexico and

Central America Office. Steve Cox was particularly supportive throughout the entire period. Special thanks to Tom Trebat as well.

A number of research assistants helped to prepare data analysis during this project. I am particularly grateful to Antonio Colindres, Rodrigo Valvarde, Veronica Marseillan, and María Joaquina Larraz de Quant. Special thanks go to Laura Maderos, Jolie Maldonado, and Ileana Ramírez, who helped prepare parts of the manuscript.

While many friends and colleagues helped to make this project happen, I take full responsibility for the errors and oversights.

THE HUMAN DEVELOPMENT RACE

PART I

INTRODUCTION

The Human
Development Dilemma

The 1980s were bitter years for most developing countries. The world economy experienced its worst collapse since the Great Depression of the 1930s. This global turmoil was accompanied by economic crisis and political instability in much of the developing world.[1] The battle to raise living standards through the economic medicine of industrial import substitution and a strong interventionist state suffered dramatic setbacks. According to the World Bank, living standards plummeted to the levels of the early 1970s in much of Africa, South Asia, and Latin America.[2] The life chances of an entire generation of the world's population were compromised along the way.[3]

At the same time a small group of developing countries—the four Asian tigers, Singapore, Hong Kong, Korea, and Taiwan—came to be viewed as heros, first by a small group of academics[4], later by the World Bank, the International Monetary Fund (IMF), and the U.S. Agency for International Development (USAID), and still later by a widening circle of policy makers. Finally they, along with Japan, were elevated to the status of folk heros by the media.[5]

According to those enamored with their performance, these little dynamos adopted a different medicine—outwardly oriented, export-led economic strategies—and achieved sustained high levels of economic growth accompanied by improved income distribution in the 1960s and

1970s. They weathered the shocks of the 1980s with less economic hardship and political turmoil than their unfortunate neighbors.[6]

Although there was considerable tactical diversity among the tigers, the essential ingredients in their success were outwardly oriented policies pursued in a consistent fashion over a twenty- to thirty-year period, fostered by a state whose size decreased during the period but whose dynamism did not. These were states that encouraged the development of a strong private sector in an environment of political continuity.[7]

As the 1970s drew to a close, policy makers from crisis-plagued developing countries as well as the World Bank and the IMF became increasingly convinced that at least one part of the message—outwardly oriented economic strategies like those employed by the tigers—might provide the basis of economic recovery and takeoff in developing nations.[8] But because of the need for quick responses to the economic crisis in the 1980s and the popularization of the Asian tiger story, other essential ingredients got lost in the shuffle. This complex and subtle story somehow got translated into evidence for rapid, often simultaneous economic and political liberalization with a drastically reduced role for the state. As a result the 1980s and 1990s have become the decades of experimentation with this new quick fix for underdevelopment.

In Latin America some countries, like Mexico, Costa Rica, and Chile, continued with relatively successful experiments to open their economies. Costa Rica maintained its democratic traditions, while Chile edged toward political opening after years of pursuing an outward economic orientation. But Bolivia and twelve other Latin American countries began the more difficult task of simultaneous economic and political liberalization later and with differing levels of success. By the end of the 1980s only a few "museum pieces" like Paraguay and Panama continued under authoritarian rule.[9] As the 1990s began these countries started to liberalize as well. Similar openings began in Asia, the fifteen republics of the former Soviet Union, and Eastern Europe. In Africa the curtain rose on the struggle for multiparty democracy.

Some observers view the rising tide of rapid economic and political liberalization as an irreversible step along the path of human progress. For example, Milovan Djilas, a keen observer of and participant in post–World War II developments in Eastern Europe, commented recently:

> The ruling class has been dissolving [in Eastern Europe]. It is no longer capable of government by the old ideology and methods. . . . The prolonged inefficiency of monopolistic government and restricted freedom of ownership have brought about the present situation. With the former and without the latter, further development of the forces of production is not possible.[10]

Others who tend to popularize such ideas place liberalization on the same plane as the smallpox vaccine. They treat the astonishing reversal of economic and political strategy in countries like Hungary, Poland, Nicaragua, Ghana, and Mozambique as confirmation of this viewpoint. Politicians from the industrial countries frequently express these views. For example, former U.S. president George Bush commented:

> A new breeze of freedom is gaining strength around the world. In man's heart, if not in fact, the day of the dictator is over. The totalitarian era is passing, its old ideas blown away like leaves from an ancient leafless tree.[11]

Britain's former prime minister was a bit more cautious:

> Mrs. Thatcher told Commonwealth leaders that communism was in crisis. But she warned that while the "secular religion" of communism had been discredited and had lost its inner faith it retained its outer power. Thus, the West had to maintain secure defenses.[12]

More than fifty years ago Rudyard Kipling counseled even greater caution to those inclined to jump too quickly onto the bandwagon with politicians who look for simple solutions.

> I could not dig: I dared not rob:
> Therefore, I lied to please the mob.
> Now all my lies are proved untrue
> And I must face the men I slew.
> What tale shall serve me here among
> Mine angry and defrauded young?[13]

If we heed Kipling's warning, we might conclude that it is still early to draw conclusions about the implications of the wave of rapid economic and political liberalization that took place in the 1980s for the developing world. In a generation or two the plans for immediate, radical privatization in the former Soviet Union may seem as naive as the rapid collectivization of agriculture there after the Russian Revolution or the Great Leap Forward in China. Development is just not that easy. There is no quick fix.

Kipling's counsel might be to step back and take a more careful look at the lessons of successful development performance from the past three decades. Such a perspective brings new dilemmas into focus. For example, one must look beyond the Asian tigers and ask what the other top developing-country economic and social performers did to achieve their progress. Perhaps there are deeper common threads that led to improved human development—the process by which people expand their life choices by gaining greater access to economic resources, improving their ability to acquire knowledge and increasing their chances of a long and healthy life. Second, as I noted earlier, many politicians assume that rapid, simultaneous economic and political liberalization and a quick reduction in the size of the state are indivisible parts of the remedy. Yet it is not at all clear that the developing-country high performers took their medicine exactly this way. Finally, those who see history as either cyclical or dialectical remind us that today's medicine often becomes tomorrow's poison.[14] They argue that strong counterforces in most developing societies are waiting in the wings for the first signs of failure to reverse the process. One need only remember the drama of Tiananmen Square in the People's Republic of China, which was the first major illiberal counterrevolution of the 1980s, the internal conflicts in the new republics of the former Soviet Union, or the resilience of some of the African authoritarian regimes to find evidence for the fragility of the new processes.[15] Instead of making irreversible advances along the path of human progress, some nations may tumble into a decade or two of real chaos.

The Search for Solutions

The search for strategies of development in poor countries in the 1990s poses new problems for scholars and policy makers alike, particularly those who step back from the temptation of quick fixes and try to put several decades of development experience in perspective. According to some students of the subject, there is a growing consensus that well-implemented policies have made a difference in country performance.[16] Yet others suggest that policy makers in developing countries have been no more than prisoners of world economic forces.[17] Still others argue that country performance is paralyzed by internal factors such as small country size and poor natural resource endowments.[18] What does recent development experience tell us about the relative importance of good policies, sound implementation, and strong social support, as opposed to other factors? Finally, those charged with the responsibility of improving the immediate well-being of their nation's population rightfully ask, does the post–World War II experience tell us anything about potentially successful development strategies for poor countries in the next twenty years? If so, how might these insights be most effectively transmitted?

The Purpose of This Book

The primary objective of this book is to shed light on the key questions about post–World War II development. These questions are:

1. What have been the characteristics of developing-country high human development performers?

2. Is there evidence that policy choice and implementation have been as important as external factors like world economic cycles or internal contextual factors like size or natural resource endowments in performance?

3. What role has the state played, and how important have regime type and political and civil rights been in this process?

4. How much of a wave of rapid economic and political liberalization has really taken place in developing countries in the 1980s?

5. Have countries that have ridden this wave achieved higher rates of growth and performance or is it too soon to tell?

6. Finally, what lessons if any might be drawn for development policy for the next decade?

A second important purpose of this book is to provide an integrative methodology for studying development. The questions will be addressed through two different research approaches: (1) an analysis of ninety developing countries as a group and in cross sections, and (2) a deeper historical study of six Central American countries. Each of these methods can be thought of as a lens that permits a different focus—unfortunately, at the expense of others.

Another objective is to help in the search for paths to development in one group of small poor countries where I spent almost one quarter of my life and about which I care deeply. Perhaps a greater understanding of the options open to them will shed particular light on choices for other small developing countries as well as for developing nations in general. My final objective is to present the results in a way that is accessible to policy makers. I have dropped as much technical discussion as possible into notes and appendixes to emphasize readability.

The book is organized as follows. Part II (Chapters 2-4) provides a global analysis of human development performance in developing countries between 1965 and 1990. Part III (Chapters 5-7) looks at the same issues in one region, Central America. Chapter 2 identifies high human development performers and the factors underlying their achievements between 1965 and 1987. It uses the first lens described earlier—cross-sectional and longitudinal analysis of a large data set. Chapter 3 continues with this lens to explore the role of political and institutional factors like regime type in human development. It also assesses the performance of nations that attempted rapid economic and political liberalization in the 1980s. Chapter 4 concludes the global analysis with a look at the role of overall governance structures and human development performance. Chapters 5 and 6 treat the same issues using the second lens—deeper but longer historical analysis—for six Central American countries from 1930 through 1988. Chapter 7 looks at the roots of differences in human development performance among the Central American countries. The final chapter briefly summarizes some of the lessons of human development performance for development practitioners.

PART II

A GLOBAL VIEW OF HUMAN DEVELOPMENT

2

Measuring Human Development

In 1965 the Republic of Korea and Liberia continued their race for economic and social development in the middle of the pack. Korea ranked fifty-sixth (US\$687) and Liberia fifty-eighth (US\$642) in per capita gross national product (GNP) among the 120 countries for which the World Bank has collected data since 1965.[1]

By 1987 Korea had become one of the world's highest-performing developing countries. Its average annual growth rates in per capita GNP were among the highest in the world between 1965 and 1987. In 1987 both its GNP per capita (US\$2,690) and its physical quality of life index (a composite index of literacy, life expectancy, and infant mortality) placed it among the forty most prosperous nations and in the top five developing-country high performers.[2] Its score on the United Nations' human development index (a combination of real GNP per capita, literacy, and life expectancy) placed it among the top thirty nations of the world.[3]

In contrast, Liberia's performance plummeted between 1965 and 1987. Its per capita GNP fell to US\$450, and its relative position declined from fifty-eighth to seventy-seventh. In the same two decades Liberia became one of the world's forty economically poorest nations. Its low levels of literacy and life expectancy and high level of infant mortality combined to place it on the social casualty list as well, among the thirty countries with the lowest physical quality of life and human development index scores.

What accounts for such differences in performance? One might argue that oil and mineral exporters have been among the highest developing-country performers since 1965. This makes sense when one looks at the advances of Saudi Arabia or Ecuador. Yet Korea's oil and mineral exports dropped from 15 percent of its total exports in 1965 to less than 2 percent in 1987, while Liberia's stayed above 55 percent. So the relationship between oil and mineral exports and development performance seems inverse, at least in this case.

One might imagine a number of other explanations for these events. Take ethnic diversity, for example. Was it much harder to mobilize development in Liberia's linguistically and ethnically diverse population than in Korea's more homogeneous citizenry? In fact, Korea had one of the lowest scores on an important index of ethnic diversity (2) while Liberia had one of the highest (83).[4] This seems logical, but consider a counterexample. Cameroon had a higher score (89) than Liberia on the index of ethnic diversity. Although its per capita GNP in 1965 (US$431) was much lower than either Liberia's or Korea's, it turned out, along with Korea, to be one of the top thirty developing-country high performers during the 1965–1987 period.

Take another possible explanation—region, or more broadly, culture. Some experts argue that cultural factors make it more difficult to promote development in Africa than in Asia or Latin America.[5] While there are differences in development performance by region, there are, however, wide differences in performance within each continent as well. Mauritania, an African country with a per capita GNP (US$481) higher than that of Cameroon in 1965, had a much more homogeneous population than either Cameroon or Liberia (33 on the index of ethnic diversity). Yet it turned out to be one of the poorest economic and social performers between 1965 and 1987.

Such differences are evident in other continents as well. For example, in 1965 Costa Rica and Nicaragua were both middle-income developing countries with similar export products and markets and low levels of ethnic diversity (Nicaragua's diversity index score was 18 and Costa Rica's 7). Yet between 1965 and 1987 Costa Rica became a developing-country high performer while Nicaragua's performance was marginal.

Some people argue that Costa Rica's more recently arrived, largely European immigrant population was a key ingredient in its success. But Argentina provides a counterexample. Its population is similar to that of Costa Rica in its origins and ethnic mix, but it actually lost ground among the top thirty global economic and social performers between 1965 and 1987, the same period in which Costa Rica did so well. By 1987 Argentina's per capita gross domestic product (GDP) had dropped from twenty-sixth to thirty-sixth of the 120 nations for which the World Bank collects data—behind Korea, whose meteoric rise was astounding.

So simple explanations turn out to be too simple. Can we assess the relative importance of variables like ethnic diversity and region on development performance, other things being equal? In this chapter I plan to try. In fact, I will attempt to assess the relative importance of internal contextual factors, policies, and external influences in what I call "human development performance."

First we must unpack the idea of human development performance. What do I mean by developing-country high economic and social performance? Which countries were the high and low performers since 1965? Can we make any generalizations about salient characteristics of high versus low performers? Or is each nation so unique that there are no common threads? I will also look at the strengths and weaknesses of the use of large data sets for cross-national comparisons. This chapter addresses these issues.

Exploring the Labyrinth: Definitions of Human Development

The attempt to clarify the concept of human development has lasted for decades and, like the exploration of a labyrinth, has often resulted in frustrations and reversals. One cannot begin a discussion of human development performance in developing countries without referring to economic growth.[6] Of course, because of different rates of population growth, economic growth itself is not necessarily associated with increases in per capita income or improved income distribution, and none of these factors necessarily insures better quality of life. In fact, rapid economic growth may result in environmentally unsustainable development that risks the livelihood of future generations.[7] At the same time excessive attention to factors like income redistribution can stifle growth altogether. Thus, a well-rounded definition of high performance should take many factors into account.

Devising such a definition, however, is far from easy. First, there is little agreement about how to measure some aspects of high performance, like environmental sustainability or political and civil liberties, across nations. While environmental sustainability, for example, is crucial to world survival, it can sometimes become the subject of polemic discussion on the one hand or disappear entirely from the agenda on the other. Second, even where there is agreement on measurement instruments—for example, the use of Gini coefficients for comparison of income distribution across nations—few cross-national data may be available. Thus, economists often fall back on measures of economic growth, for which data are more readily available. Third, when cross-national data do exist, they often cover only recent periods. The World Bank data set, one of the most comprehensive available, gives data for 120 nations beginning in 1965.[8] This unfortunately limits detailed analysis of many important earlier periods of development. Fourth, even the best cross-national data sets exclude countries. For example, the World Bank provides little information on the more than forty countries with fewer than 1 million inhabitants. In fact, consistent data for the world's tiniest countries, as well as some of the poorest ones, are just beginning to be compiled. Thus, the nations with the most daunting development problems cannot be included.

If we agree to use per capita GNP as a surrogate for an individual's access to income, additional headaches turn up. For example, per capita GNP is the easiest measure to use given the availability of data from national income accounts. But it is not adjusted for real exchange rates and inflation and thus tells little about people's real purchasing power.

But even with more accurate economic and social measures, we can only begin to speculate about the relationships between them. If we try to use these economic and social indicators to construct a composite human development index, we enter the "occult realm of ethical metaphysics," in which we make judgments, for example, that a 1 percent increase in per capita GNP is more or less important than a 1 percent increase in a country's literacy rate.

In spite of the methodological problems of studying human development, it would be artificial to treat economic growth, per capita GNP, and social performance as independent of one another. They are in fact interrelated in people's lives. For example, without sufficient family income it is difficult to imagine nutritional levels adequate to allow people to live long and healthy lives.

The definition of human development used by the United Nations Development Programme (UNDP) is an initially attractive way of putting these concepts together. It describes human development as

> a process of enlarging people's choices. In principle these choices can be infinite and change over time. But at all levels of development, three essential ones are for people to lead a long and healthy life, to acquire knowledge and to have access to resources needed for a decent standard of living. If these essential choices are not available, many other opportunities remain inaccessible.[9]

Advances in social science are often incremental. New ideas are usually built upon the earlier work of others. The UNDP's definition of human development is no exception. It is based on earlier refinements of concepts and measurement of (1) access to economic resources, (2) social performance, and (3) the integrated treatment of both economic and social performance.

Access to economic resources

Measuring people's access to economic resources across nations is not an easy task. Ideally one would like to compare individuals' incomes and forms of wealth such as cash savings, land, and other assets and to disaggregate national data by region, race, tribe, and gender.

Since there have been no practical ways of obtaining these data cross-nationally, however, most students of the subject began with a concept of unadjusted per capita GNP. These data became available after World War II when comparable national income accounts began to be collected. This measure indicated, at least in theory, whether economic growth was rapid enough to keep ahead of population growth.[10]

But per capita GNP is not a very accurate measure of people's resources or purchasing power, since it is not adjusted for real exchange rates or inflation. For this reason the World Bank created a way of measuring per capita GNP, called the World Bank atlas method, that took into account differences in individual country population and economic data reporting procedures, made corrections in estimates, used a conversion factor to reflect real exchange rates, and accounted for the average annual rate of inflation.[11]

While the World Bank atlas method is a good one, it does not measure the relative domestic purchasing power of currencies or place them on an internationally comparable scale. An even better alternative, real per capita GDP adjusted for purchasing-power parity (PPP), was developed through the United Nations International Comparison Program (IPC), which began in the 1960s.[12] This measure, which uses purchasing-power parities instead of exchange rates as conversion factors, is the basis of one of the three indicators incorporated into the United Nations human development index.[13]

Those who worked on the IPC project over the years have done an excellent job of refining the per capita income concept. Many students of development, however, have been either unwilling or hesitant to broaden the discussion to include non-economic concepts or to mix them with economic ones in a composite index. They believe they have sound methodological reasons for not doing so.[14]

Social performance

The advances on social performance indicators therefore became the task of others. Probably the best-known work in this area was Morris Morris's physical quality of life index (PQLI).[15] This composite measure, with a maximum score of 100, gives equal weight to the life expectancy of a population, infant mortality (deaths of newborns up to one year of age per thousand live births), and literacy. The PQLI indirectly reflects the effects of investments in health services, water and sewage systems, quality of food and nutrition, housing, education, and changes in income distribution.

The PQLI helped redirect attention in the late 1970s away from growth and toward broader concepts of human development. It also helped show that some countries without strong economic growth actually made more substantial social gains than many high-growth countries. As a result of such efforts, development professionals at many of the large international development agencies gained new insights about how to target new programs to improve social performance.

But the PQLI was not without its problems as a human development measure. For example, literacy statistics are collected only sporadically, with different reporting procedures, and at uneven five- to ten-year intervals. They are notoriously poor for cross-national comparison. The PQLI appeared to give disproportionate attention to longevity, as well, since two of its three components have to do with length of life—infant mortality and life expectancy. Finally, Morris was uncomfortable combining economic and social measures in a composite index.[16] Instead he presented them side by side. While the case for keeping economic and social measures separate may be convincing, it unfortunately continued to dramatize an artificial dichotomy between economic and social development rather than encourage attention to their interrelationship.

Combining economic and social performance to monitor human development

In an effort to blend the two approaches, the United Nations *Human Development Report 1990* designed a human development index (HDI) based on the equal weighting of three factors: (1) PPP-adjusted real per capita GDP, (2) literacy, and (3) life expectancy.[17] The HDI measures a country's human development on a scale of 0 to 100, where the top score is the status attained by the best-performing industrial country in literacy and life expectancy and the poverty-line income level of an average of nine industrial countries. A nation's human development status is expressed as a percentage of the top industrial-country human development performance. For example, Togo's HDI score of 20 for 1965 indicates that its human development was one-fifth of the industrial-country standard.

The *Human Development Report 1991* broadened the concept of literacy to include educational attainment and gave more weight to industrial-country improvements in PPP-adjusted real GDP above the poverty line.[18]

The human development index has many strengths. For example, it focuses on three fundamental factors in people's well-being: access to economic resources, a long life, and educational opportunity. It uses the best conceptual formulations available, such as PPP-adjusted real per capita GDP and educational attainment. The data it uses are also relatively reliable. Furthermore, the HDI does not give disproportionate weight to longevity, as the PQLI did. Finally, the index draws attention to interrelated economic and social gains rather than to the tension between them.

Any new measure has its weaknesses. The HDI is no exception. For example, equally weighted interval scale treatment of all index components is artificial. Does it really make sense to say that a 1-point scale improvement generated from PPP-adjusted per capita GDP income gains of x dollars is really equal to a 1-point scale improvement due to y months of literacy gains? If interval scale assumptions are violated, how valid is the index?

The HDI is also a blunt measure. It is good at measuring long-term trends but insensitive to annual changes. For example, the 1987 HDI score for Nicaragua seriously overstates that country's human development status, because the United Nations used overly optimistic literacy and life expectancy survey statistics from the 1970s and early 1980s, when Nicaragua began its revolutionary literacy and health programs. There is broad agreement that these HDI gains were severely eroded by a combination of war, mass migration, and cuts in social spending in the last half of the 1980s. But Nicaragua's HDI score will continue to be overestimated until new literacy and life expectancy surveys are conducted.

Another example of the HDI's imprecision is that literacy and life expectancy data are not collected in the same year. Thus we cannot talk about annual gains for 120 countries, but rather gains from the mid-1960s to the late 1980s.

The Human Development Concepts Used in This Book

The concepts

The United Nations' concept of human development is as follows:

> the process of expanding people's choices through their access to economic resources, [and their] ability to acquire knowledge and to live a healthy and long life (as measured by ppp adjusted real GDP, educational attainment and life expectancy).[19]

In spite of its limitations, the concept is an appropriate one for this book. It gets to the heart of what many people in the world value for themselves and their children. It combines economic and social factors as people actually do when they think about their own lives.

A modified version of the 1990 HDI provides baseline data on human development for this study.[20] A country's HDI scores for 1965 and 1987 are derived from its performance on three equally weighted variables: (1) PPP-adjusted real per capita GDP, (2) literacy, and (3) life expectancy.

A country's improvement in human development between 1965 and 1987 is measured by computing its HDI disparity reduction rate (DRR).[21] The DRR, a measure developed by Morris, monitors the average annual rate at which the gap between a country's current and possible performance on a scale with a fixed upper limit is being reduced over time.[22] For example, Malaysia's HDI score in 1965 was 67. By 1987 its score was 90. Its DRR was 5.01. This DRR score indicates that during the twenty-two-year period between 1965 and 1987 Malaysia reduced the gap between its HDI status and that of the top industrial country by about 5 percent a year.

The countries and the analysis

This chapter reviews human development performance for the 120 nations for which the World Bank collected comprehensive data between 1965 and 1987, and in particular for the 90 developing countries, by income group, region, and country performance group.[23] Then it identifies important determinants of high human development performance through study of internal contextual factors, policies, and external influences.

Human Development Performance by Income Group, Region, and Performance Group

Human development performance by income group

The 120 countries in this study were home to 91 percent of the world's 3.2 billion people in 1965.[24] The countries had an average population of 15 million inhabitants (when India and China are excluded) and an average PPP-adjusted real per capita GDP of US$2,183.

Between 1965 and 1987 the quality of people's lives in these countries clearly improved (see Table 2.1 for detailed data). For example, in 1965 only half of the citizens of these countries could read, but by 1987 two-thirds were literate. During this same twenty-two-year period life

TABLE 2.1 Economic and Social Performance of Countries by Income Group, 1965–1987

Status of PPP-adjusted real per capita GDP, 1965	Number of countries, 1965	Average population, 1965[a] (millions)	PPP-adjusted real GDP per capita (US$)		Literacy rate (%)		Life expectancy (years)		Average HDI (%)		Average HDI DRR, 1965–87 (%)	Average GDP growth, 1965–87 (%)
			1965	1987	1965	1987	1965	1987	1965	1987		
Very low	30	13.1	383	724	19	36	42	50	20	38	1.24	2.76
Low												
Excluding India and China	28	12.1	746	1,876	34	50	49	58	36	55	1.90	4.44
Including India and China	30	51.2	740	1,857	34	50	49	58	37	56	1.93	4.52
Middle	30	11.8	1,784	4,385	57	76	58	66	60	79	3.62	5.47
High	30	23.8	5,221	10,328	87	92	68	73	88	93	4.00	3.31
Average												
Excluding India and China	118	15.2	2,213	4,318	52	64	54	62	55	67	2.87	4.04
Including India and China	120	25.0	2,183	4,272	52	63	54	62	55	67	2.86	4.07

a. Analysis of variance shows that the four groups (very low, low, middle, and high) have significantly different characteristics on all variables but population size. F tests were significant at the .0001 level. Since data for an entire population are presented, the F values are shown only to provide a rough indication of what the statistical significance might have been had there been an attempt to generalize from a sample to a population.

Source: World Bank, *World Development Report 1989* (New York: Oxford University Press, 1989); PPP-adjusted real per capita GDP data from Robert Summers and Alan Heston, "A New Set of International Comparisons of Real Product and Prices for 130 Countries, 1950–85," *The Review of Income and Wealth* (Series 34, no. 1), accompanying diskettes; HDI data are computed from U.N. statistics of health, literacy, and life expectancy using formulas adapted from *Human Development Report 1990*. See Appendix 1 of this book.

expectancy increased by eight years (from fifty-four to sixty-two years), and individual purchasing power doubled (from US$2,183 to US$4,272).

Even though these global improvements in human development were impressive, their pace slowed in the 1980s because of world recession, major political upheavals, and economic restructuring. For this reason World Bank data are divided into two distinct periods: (1) 1965–1980, a high-growth period when rises in GDP and PPP-adjusted real per capita GDP averaged more than 4.5 percent a year and (2) 1980–1987, a period of major economic and political instability when GDP growth slowed to 2.1 percent and PPP-adjusted real GDP growth plummeted to only 1.6 percent. The data on literacy and life expectancy were not collected frequently enough in the 1980s to show the accompanying HDI erosion. (Remember that the HDI is still a blunt, imprecise instrument.) But there is enough supporting data about, for example, the resurgence of deaths from waterborne diseases like cholera in Latin America in the 1980s and the reappearance of malaria and increased levels of malnutrition in Central America to speculate about the results of cutbacks in global social spending.

Another interesting finding is that a nation's per capita GDP and its levels of literacy and life expectancy are, in fact, closely related.[25]

Because countries' economic and social performance levels are so interrelated, grouping countries by income or human development level is a good way to represent a complex set of common country characteristics, problems, and policy options.[26] Countries within a very low-income cluster, like Chad and Haiti, appear to have more in common with each other than with Costa Rica and Malaysia. The major causes of death, for example, in these very low-income countries are more likely to be sanitation-related diseases like gastroenteritis than in the middle-income ones. By implication, development programs like primary health care expansion may be highly appropriate for countries in the very low-income group but may have already had their impact in middle-income countries like Costa Rica.

What else can be said about income groups and country performance? For better or worse, a country's per capita income and human development level in 1965 was an important determinant of its HDI performance between 1965 and 1987.[27] Apparently pre-1965 investments in human development paid off in stronger HDI performance through 1987. Even within each country income group, those countries that had attained higher levels of literacy and life expectancy by 1965 had significantly higher GDP growth and made more rapid HDI gains between 1965 and 1987 than countries in the same income groups that had not.[28] The implication is that early investments in human capital provide a foundation for later economic growth and human development achievement.

Human development performance by region

Location also influenced performance in the HDI race. Different geographic regions had significantly different initial baseline HDI levels and performance rates (see Table 2.2). For example, Africa and South Asia began the HDI race at the back of the pack in 1965 and were still there in 1987. Although the African countries doubled their literacy rates in that twenty-two-year period, the HDI gains in other regions were even greater.

Latin America and the Carribean began at the top of the developing-country pack in 1965 and made important gains by 1987. But their rate of improvement slowed, particularly in the 1980s, because of an unhealthy combination of debt, fiscal deficits, relatively closed economic policies, and world economic crisis. As a result the Latin American countries lost ground to the world's highest developing-country performers—the East and Southeast Asian nations.

By 1987 the Asian tigers and "kittens" had overtaken the Latin American "condors" and "quetzals" in real PPP-adjusted per capita GDP and had gained comparable levels of literacy and life expectancy. Their more open economic policies probably helped them ride out the world recessions of the 1980s with greater ease than the Latin Americans.

Finally, some regions like the Middle East started the human development race in the middle of the pack and stayed there. These countries made impressive gains in real per capita GDP but did not convert them into big improvements in either literacy or life expectancy.

Although the purpose of this book is not to look at industrial-country performance, a brief comparison of Eastern and Western European performance is enlightening. The picture of stagnant social conditions and deteriorating purchasing power in Eastern Europe provides a sobering message about why the seeds of discontent may have exploded in social revolution in the 1990s. Both Eastern and Western Europe began the mid-1960s with high HDI levels compared with their developing-country neighbors. During the next twenty-two years each made gains in real per capita GDP. But Eastern Europe's real PPP-adjusted GDP dropped from 56 to 36 percent of its Western cousin's real GDP. In the 1980s the East's real per capita GDP plummeted, while growth continued in the West. The East's social performance during the period was at best marginally improved, and at worst stagnant.

Human development performance by performance group

Grouping countries based on their actual HDI development performance from 1965 to 1987 sheds light on factors partially hidden by regional or income groupings.[29] (Tables 2.3 and 2.4 provide lists of the top, middle, and

TABLE 2.2 Economic and Social Performance of Countries by Region, 1965–1987

Region	Number of countries, 1965	Average population, 1965 (millions)	PPP-adjusted real per capita GDP		Literacy rate (%)		Life expectancy (years)		Average HDI (%)		Average HDI DRR, 1965–1987 (%)	Average GDP growth, 1965–1987 (%)
			1965	1987	1965	1987	1965	1987	1965	1987		
Sub-Saharan Africa	36	7.1	626	951	19	40	43	51	25	41	1.41	3.43
South Asia	7	24.7[a]	681	1,142	28	34	47	56	36	47	1.63	3.52
East and South-east Asia	12	27.1[b]	1,116	3,947	55	76	54	62	54	76	4.13	7.25
Caribbean	4	2.6	2,293	2,174	57	70	58	66	59	72	2.10	2.78
Latin America	17	13.4	2,150	3,289	65	79	57	66	63	79	2.96	3.93
Middle East and North Africa	18	8.2	2,079	4,328	36	52	51	63	47	65	2.38	5.55
Eastern Europe	4	20.0	2,917	4,500	93	96	68	71	85	92	2.31	4.70
Western Europe	19	32.5	5,217	12,560	95	98	71	76	91	97	5.11	3.52
Oceania	3	5.3	5,990	8,055	99	77	62	68	94	82	3.92	3.57
Average	120	15.0	2,183	4,272	52	63	54	62	55	67	2.86	4.07

a. Population figure excludes India. With India's population of 490.2 million added, the average is 91.2 million.
b. Population figure excludes China. With China's population of 709.2 million included, the average is 83.9 million.
SOURCE: World Bank, *World Development Report 1989* (New York: Oxford University Press, 1989); PPP-adjusted real per capita GDP data from Robert Summers and Alan Heston, "A New Set of International Comparisons of Real Product and Prices for 130 Countries, 1950–85," *The Review of Income and Wealth* (Series 34, no. 1), accompanying diskettes; HDI data are computed from U.N. statistics of health, literacy, and life expectancy using formulas adapted from *Human Development Report 1990.* See Appendix 1 of this book.

TABLE 2.3 Economic and Social Performance of Developing Countries by Human Development Performance Group, 1965–1987 (listed from lowest annual DRR to highest)

Human development performance group	Number of countries[a]	Average HDI DRR, 1965–1987 (%)	1965 raw data for the index				1987 raw data for the index				Average HDI	
			PPP-adjusted real per capita GDP (US$)	Log of PPP-adjusted real per capita GDP	Literacy rate (%)	Life expectancy (years)	PPP-adjusted real per capita GDP (US$)	Log of PPP-adjusted real per capita GDP	Literacy rate (%)	Life expectancy (years)	1965	1987
Lowest	24	0.87	577	2.73	18	42	758	2.84	31	51	24.1	37.2
Medium	24	2.07	1,507	3.03	40	52	2,274	3.24	62	61	45.4	64.9
Highest	23	3.95	1,437	3.08	54	56	4,099	3.49	79	66	54.6	79.9
Average	71	2.27	1,170	2.94	37	50	2,353	3.18	57	59	41.1	60.3

a. Within the group of 90 developing countries, 19 could not be assigned to a performance group because of insufficient data. The 71 countries with sufficient data were placed in equal-sized performance groups based on their DRR scores for 1965–1987.
SOURCE: Same source as Table 1.1 and author's calculations.

TABLE 2.4 Developing Country High, Medium, and Low Human Development Performers, 1965–1987 (listed from lowest annual DRR to highest)

Country	Average HDI DRR (%)	1965 raw data for the index				1987 raw data for the index				HDI	
		PPP-adjusted real per capita GDP (US$)	Log of PPP-adjusted real per capita GDP	Literacy rate (%)	Life expectancy (years)	PPP-adjusted real per capita GDP (US$)	Log of PPP-adjusted real per capita GDP	Literacy rate (%)	Life expectancy (years)	1965	1987
Low HDI performers (lowest 33%)											
Ghana	0.40	527	2.72	23	48	481	2.68	30	54	29.9	35.9
Chad	0.50	496	2.70	5	37	400	2.60	17	46	14.7	23.7
Sierra Leone	0.51	411	2.61	10	33	480	2.68	15	41	11.7	21.1
Senegal	0.58	800	2.90	6	41	1,068	3.03	10	48	23.0	32.3
Ethiopia	0.63	320	2.51	5	43	454	2.66	18	47	14.9	26.0
Sudan	0.63	729	2.86	13	40	750	2.88	20	50	23.7	33.8
Congo	0.66	841	2.92	35	50	756	2.88	63	49	39.7	47.9
Niger	0.67	340	2.53	3	37	452	2.66	13	45	10.4	22.8
Central African Rep.	0.67	463	2.67	15	41	591	2.77	20	50	20.4	31.5
Zambia	0.73	854	2.93	41	44	717	2.86	54	53	37.8	47.2
Nigeria	0.80	569	2.76	33	42	668	2.82	42	51	29.3	40.9
Zaire	0.84	305	2.48	25	44	220	2.34	55	52	22.0	35.4
Mauritania	0.93	527	2.72	3	37	840	2.92	17	46	15.0	30.9
Haiti	0.96	581	2.76	10	45	775	2.89	23	55	24.2	38.8
Liberia	0.97	557	2.75	10	44	696	2.84	25	54	29.4	37.7
Malawi	0.99	235	2.37	8	39	476	2.68	25	46	10.4	28.2
Uganda	1.03	333	2.52	25	45	511	2.71	52	48	24.0	39.6
Somalia	1.04	396	2.60	5	38	1,000	3.00	12	47	13.6	31.6
Cote d'Ivoire	1.07	889	2.95	20	42	1,123	3.05	35	52	29.2	44.3
Madagascar	1.10	614	2.79	35	43	634	2.80	53	54	31.5	46.4
Nepal	1.15	507	2.71	8	41	722	2.86	29	51	18.9	37.2
Pakistan	1.21	722	2.86	20	46	1,585	3.20	26	55	30.1	46.7
India	1.39	538	2.73	28	45	1,053	3.02	36	58	29.6	48.4
El Salvador	1.43	1,290	3.11	49	54	1,733	3.24	62	62	51.9	65.1
Average	0.87	577	2.73	18	42	758	2.84	31	51	24.4	37.2

Medium HDI performers (middle 33%)

Country										
Burma	1.51	399	2.60	60	48	752	2.88	66	60	39.6	56.9
Togo	1.53	550	2.74	8	42	670	2.83	45	53	20.4	43.5
Guatemala	1.59	1,365	3.14	38	49	1,957	3.29	48	62	45.0	61.5
Rwanda	1.61	152	2.18	8	49	571	2.76	47	49	13.5	39.7
Saudi Arabia	1.62	5,651	3.68	10	48	8,320	3.68	25	63	46.8	62.9
Honduras	1.62	824	2.92	45	50	1,119	3.05	56	64	42.9	60.3
Kenya	1.69	453	2.66	23	47	794	2.90	50	58	27.7	50.5
Egypt	1.75	644	2.81	30	49	1,357	3.13	44	61	34.6	55.8
Nicaragua	1.79	2,217	3.35	50	50	2,209	3.34	66	63	54.5	69.5
Morocco	1.83	826	2.92	13	50	1,761	3.25	34	61	31.9	54.9
Zimbabwe	1.87	651	2.81	20	48	1,184	3.07	50	58	30.6	54.4
Bolivia	2.14	1,022	3.01	32	44	1,380	3.14	75	53	36.5	60.8
Tanzania	2.15	256	2.41	18	43	405	2.61	75	53	17.2	48.9
Iran	2.16	2,216	3.35	23	52	3,300	3.52	48	63	46.7	67.2
Gabon	2.18	1,286	3.11	20	43	2,068	3.32	62	52	33.8	59.5
Dominican Rep.	2.28	992	3.00	65	56	1,750	3.24	78	66	56.0	73.6
Philippines	2.38	972	2.99	72	56	1,878	3.27	88	63	58.2	75.5
Peru	2.45	2,100	3.32	61	51	3,129	3.50	79	61	58.2	75.9
Uruguay	2.54	3,155	3.50	90	68	5,063	3.68	91	71	84.9	91.5
Paraguay	2.58	1,072	3.03	68	65	2,603	3.42	84	67	64.7	80.3
Tunisia	2.58	925	2.97	30	51	2,741	3.44	46	65	39.6	66.2
Iraq	2.59	3,173	3.50	20	52	2,400	3.38	67	64	48.8	71.4
Jamaica	2.61	1,807	3.26	74	65	2,506	3.40	82	74	71.8	84.3
Argentina	2.63	3,470	3.54	91	66	4,647	3.67	92	71	84.7	91.5
Average	2.07	1,507	3.03	40	52	2,274	3.24	62	61	45.4	64.9

High HDI performers (upper 33%)

Country										
Sri Lanka	2.75	971	2.99	75	64	2,053	3.31	87	70	65.1	81.2
Cameroon	2.79	556	2.75	10	46	1,381	3.14	65	56	24.1	59.5
Algeria	2.80	1,244	3.09	15	50	2,633	3.42	52	63	36.9	66.4
Lesotho	2.94	310	2.49	35	49	1,585	3.20	73	56	29.3	63.6
South Africa	2.97	3,142	3.50	35	51	4,981	3.68	70	60	53.5	76.2
Syria	2.99	1,552	3.19	35	53	3,250	3.51	60	66	47.8	73.4
China	3.06	812	2.91	50	57	2,124	3.33	70	69	50.0	74.9
Indonesia	3.12	461	2.66	43	44	1,660	3.22	72	60	32.6	66.6

(table continued on next page)

TABLE 2.4 *Continued*

Country	Average HDI DRR (%)	1965 raw data for the index				1987 raw data for the index				HDI	
		PPP-adjusted real per capita GDP (US$)	Log of PPP-adjusted real per capita GDP	Literacy rate (%)	Life expectancy (years)	PPP-adjusted real per capita GDP (US$)	Log of PPP-adjusted real per capita GDP	Literacy rate (%)	Life expectancy (years)	1965	1987
Turkey	3.29	1,407	3.15	46	54	3,781	3.58	70	64	51.3	76.8
Colombia	3.32	1,439	3.16	65	56	3,524	3.55	80	66	59.9	81.1
Brazil	3.38	1,391	3.14	61	57	4,307	3.63	76	65	59.0	80.9
Thailand	3.41	833	2.92	70	56	2,576	3.41	89	64	56.0	79.7
Ecuador	3.46	1,238	3.09	67	56	2,687	3.43	90	65	58.8	81.2
Botswana	3.76	530	2.72	20	48	2,496	3.40	71	59	28.6	69.5
Mauritius	4.00	1,153	3.06	60	61	2,617	3.42	94	67	59.7	83.7
Mexico	4.54	2,575	3.41	65	60	4,624	3.67	88	69	68.1	88.6
Panama	4.62	1,604	3.21	73	63	4,009	3.60	87	72	68.9	89.1
Costa Rica	4.93	1,930	3.29	84	65	3,760	3.58	93	74	75.5	92.0
Chile	4.98	3,347	3.52	84	59	4,862	3.68	92	72	76.8	92.6
Malaysia	5.01	1,309	3.12	43	58	3,849	3.59	80	70	52.6	84.9
Singapore	5.61	1,753	3.24	60	66	12,790	3.68	85	73	67.1	90.9
Korea	6.54	797	2.90	71	57	4,832	3.68	92	69	56.7	90.3
Hong Kong	6.56	2,704	3.43	71	68	13,906	3.68	90	76	76.5	94.8
Average	3.95	1,437	3.08	54	56	4,099	3.49	79	66	54.6	79.9

Developing countries with insufficient data to rank

Bhutan	n.a.	n.a.	n.a.	41	700	2.85	12	48	n.a.	28.9
Afghanistan	n.a.	669	2.83	8	n.a.	1,000	3.00	12	n.a.	n.a.
Guinea	n.a.	450	2.65	n.a.	35	500	2.70	48	42	n.a.	33.6
Yemen Arab Rep.	n.a.	n.a.	n.a.	n.a.	40	1,250	3.10	21	51	n.a.	39.8
Lebanon	n.a.	n.a.	n.a.	86	62	2,250	3.35	75	n.a.	n.a.
Yemen, PDR	n.a.	n.a.	n.a.	n.a.	40	1,000	3.00	39	51	n.a.	43.8
Lao PDR	n.a.	n.a.	n.a.	15	n.a.	1,000	3.00	41	48	n.a.	42.3
Burkina Faso	n.a.	n.a.	n.a.	n.a.	39	500	2.70	8	47	n.a.	23.5
Jordan	n.a.	1,459	3.16	35	50	3,161	3.50	n.a.	66	45.3	n.a.
Bangladesh	n.a.	n.a.	n.a.	n.a.	45	883	2.95	33	51	n.a.	40.5
United Arab Emir.	n.a.	n.a.	n.a.	n.a.	57	12,191	3.68	56	71	n.a.	79.4
Burundi	n.a.	n.a.	n.a.	n.a.	44	450	2.65	30	49	n.a.	31.5
Benin	n.a.	n.a.	n.a.	n.a.	42	665	2.82	27	47	n.a.	32.8
Papua New Guinea	n.a.	n.a.	n.a.	n.a.	44	1,843	3.27	32	54	n.a.	49.5
Oman	n.a.	n.a.	n.a.	n.a.	43	7,750	3.68	20	55	n.a.	55.3
Cambodia	n.a.	n.a.	n.a.	n.a.	45	1,000	3.00	48	n.a.	n.a.
Mozambique	n.a.	n.a.	n.a.	n.a.	38	500	2.70	14	48	n.a.	26.3
Mali	n.a.	327	2.51	5	n.a.	543	2.73	17	45	n.a.	26.0
Viet Nam	n.a.	n.a.	n.a.	55	43	1,000	3.00	94	66	n.a.	73.7

n.a. = not available.
SOURCE: Same source as Table 1.1 and author's calculations.

bottom third of HDI performers using the DRR). A quick look at Table 2.3 shows that between 1965 and 1987 the average developing country doubled its PPP-adjusted per capita income, raised its literacy rate from less than 40 to almost 60 percent of the population, and increased the life expectancy of its citizens by nine years to fifty-nine years of age. These gains can be compared with those of each of the three HDI performance groups.

One real benefit of dividing the developing countries into three equal-sized performance groups is that it allows us to look beyond the traditional well-known high and low performers. For example, although Hong Kong, Korea, and Singapore top the list of high performers, how did African nations like Botswana, Mauritius, and Cameroon make it into the top third? Why would the People's Republic of China be among the top twenty-four developing-country HDI performers?

A second benefit is that a country's performance can be compared with its group average. For example, Tables 2.3 and 2.4 show that Chad was one of the poorest performers in the low HDI group. Between 1965 and 1987 the average member of the low HDI group improved its status from 24 to 37 percent of the top industrial-country score. In contrast, Chad's improvement went from 14 to only 23 percent of the top score. In other words by 1987 Chad's HDI score was the same as that of the average low human development performer twenty-two years earlier. Chad's annual disparity reduction rate was about 0.5 percent a year, while the average for similar countries was almost double, or 0.87 percent. If Chad's HDI disparity reduction rate continued at this same slow pace until the year 2005, resulting in an HDI score of 30, its HDI status would be only about a third of the level attained by the top industrial country eighteen years earlier in 1987. Its performance in 2005 would still be well below the HDI status that the low performers attained in 1987. This grim picture indicates how important it is not to postpone major efforts to begin the process of human development and how long they take even when serious commitments are made.

A closer look at the list reinforces the initial assertion that region is an important predictor of subsequent development performance. For example, nineteen of the twenty-four poorest development performers are African nations. While the regions are better represented in the twenty-four top performers, there is still a bias toward the East and Southeast Asian nations.

Determinants of Human Development Performance

Until now I have presented statistics about human development performance by income group, region, and country performance group, but I have said very little about the determinants of human development performance. If, for example, we want to help Chad double its very slow rate of annual HDI disparity reduction, we need to know more about the internal, policy, and external influences that may affect its human development performance. Since this chapter presents no preexisting theory about the determinants of human development performance, its purpose is to use a set of ordinary least squares regressions to generate hypotheses about how human development improvements take place.

In this exploratory rather than confirmatory analysis, I will relax the normal rules of hypothesis testing. I will use stepwise regressions first to identify the variables that account for the largest proportion of variance explained. Then I will move from statistical to policy analysis to ask which independent variables might be most easily altered, for example, through policy changes, to get the largest and most cost-effective improvements in human development performance.

Internal contextual factors and human development

Internal contextual factors are characteristics within a national geographic boundary that are largely given. They remained relatively constant between 1965 and 1987. Some of them, like mineral wealth or natural resource base, come with the territory and as a result are difficult to change. Others, like population size, religion, language, or tribal mix, can in theory be altered by policy intervention, but changes usually take place slowly. Still others, such as institutional forms like political or economic systems, evolved over hundreds of years but can be altered slowly through policy choice. The dominant national institutional forms during the study period, however, were viewed as part of the internal context. Explicit attempts to change these institutional arrangements are considered in the section on policy intervention.

I will consider four categories of internal variables:

1. *Natural endowments.* Examples include mineral production as a percentage of exports, population size, and population density.

2. *Cultural and ethnic endowments.* Variables include ethnic, racial, and religious diversity and region—surrogates for both natural and cultural endowments.[30]

3. *Baseline human resource endowments.* These are conditions resulting from earlier social investments, such as initial levels of literacy, life expectancy, and infant mortality as measured by the PQLI and HDI in 1965.

4. *Political and economic institutional context and continuity.* This refers to the type of political regime and economic system. Long-term continuity is measured, for example, by the percentage of the time democratic regimes were in office and by measures of political instability like nonprogrammed changes of presidents or prime ministers as a percentage of total changes of such officials.[31]

The relation of these variables to developing-country HDI performance from 1965 to 1987 was assessed largely through a set of stepwise regressions.[32]

Which internal contextual factors mattered?   Internal contextual factors did influence the pace of nations' human development gains. In fact, five such variables accounted for two-thirds of the total variance in the regression of internal contextual variables on the speed of the HDI disparity reduction rate between 1965 and 1987. (The share of total variance that these five variables explained, known as their adjusted r squared, was 0.627; see Table 2.5 for the findings.)

A developing country's initial human resource base and its institutional context turned out to be far more important statistical determinants of the HDI disparity reduction rate than cultural, ethnic, or natural endowments. Of the contextual factors, the quality of the initial human resource base as measured by 1965 HDI status was most important (r squared of 0.511).

Political and economic institutional factors took second place. Together they had an incremental r squared of 0.074. Of these factors, long-term political stability turned out to be critical (0.066 of the 0.074 incremental r squared). Although the long-term presence of a market economy also contributed to high HDI performance, its overall impact on the incremental r squared was very small (0.008 of the 0.068 contributed by institutional factors).

Natural, ethnic, and linguistic factors mattered but proved to have the least impact on HDI performance. They contributed the final 0.042 incremental r squared. Among these factors, ethnic and linguistic homogeneity were the most important statistically (0.030 of the 0.042 incremental r squared). Regional location (that is, East and Southeast Asia compared with the rest of the world) explained the rest of the change.

Many internal contextual factors appeared to have little effect on the pace of human development improvement. For example, the presence or absence of oil and minerals and population size and density did not matter. Democracies and dictatorships were distributed fairly evenly among both high and low HDI performers. The specific high and

TABLE 2.5   The Effects of Internal Contextual Factors on Human
Development and GDP Growth, 1965–1987
(stepwise regressions)

			Effects on the human development index[a]			
Variable	Value	Standard error	Standard value	F to remove	Adjusted r squared	Incremental adjusted r squared
Intercept	−2.150					
1965 HDI status	0.728	0.115	0.611	40.237	0.511	0.511
Low political instability	−0.233	0.101	−0.211	5.342	0.577	0.066
Ethnic and linguistic homogeneity	−0.398	0.196	−0.193	4.118	0.607	0.030
Location in Asia	0.345	0.215	0.145	2.576	0.619	0.012
Capitalist economic system	0.167	0.116	0.126	2.059	0.627	0.008

			Effects on annual GDP growth rates[b]			
Variable	Value	Standard error	Standard value	F to remove	Adjusted r squared	Incremental adjusted r squared
Intercept	−3.376					
Low political instability	−0.204	0.125	−0.218	2.660	0.095	0.095
Location in Asia	0.507	0.274	0.244	3.418	0.131	0.036
Ethnic and linguistic homogeneity	−0.384	0.221	−0.217	3.621	0.164	0.033

a. The regression in the last step has an adjusted r squared of 0.627 and a standard error of 0.386. The degrees of freedom are 5 for the regression, 47 for the residual, and 52 total DF. The F test is 18.42, and the Durban Watson statistic is 1.93 (ns). An F score of 2 or more is significant at the .05 level. Variables with F scores of less than 2 were not entered in the regression.
b. The regression in the last step has an adjusted r squared of 0.164 and a standard error of 0.449. The degrees of freedom are 3 for the regression, 51 for the residual, and 54 total DF. The F test is 5.423, and the Durban Watson statistic is 1.65 (ns). An F score of 2 or more is significant at the .05 level. Variables with F scores of less than 2 were not entered in the regression.
SOURCE: Author's calculations.

low HDI country performance group profiles mirror the results of the broader analysis.[33]

Internal contextual factors and GDP growth   Although many of these same factors were also associated with more rapid GDP growth, internal contextual factors were a less important determinant of economic growth than of HDI improvement. In fact the effect of contextual factors on growth was minimal (0.164 of the adjusted r squared) compared with their impact on HDI performance (0.627 of the adjusted r squared). The major contextual factors that mattered in GDP growth were low political instability, region, and ethnic status (see Table 2.5).

Why might internal factors matter?   Data analysis at this level of aggregation sheds little light on why some internal contextual factors provided fertile soil for high rates of human development improvement. In the absence of a theory, here are some hypotheses about how these factors might have worked to stimulate the development process.

It might be argued that a healthier, better educated population provided a more receptive foundation for future development activity than a sick, largely illiterate one. This higher HDI base may be an outward manifestation of important cultural values that served as the fuel for past economic and social advancement and might do so in the future. If a nation's more solid initial HDI base was the result of successful earlier policies, then this experience might have provided policy makers with incentives to continue in the same direction.

How might a stable political context supportive of a market economy contribute to rapid HDI improvement? Political continuity may have provided clear, consistent long-term rules of the game for economic and political action. Stable, predictable rules might have helped build national confidence, attract investment, and keep talented citizens from becoming exiles or fatalities in wars or disturbances. Continuity might have allowed the necessary time for institutional capacity building and policy implementation. Linguistic and ethnic homogeneity might have provided fertile soil in which such capacity could be nourished. All of this might have combined to permit sufficient economic growth to keep PPP-adjusted per capita GDP increasing.

Policies and human development

If internal context was so important, what role did policies play in human development performance? Before we can begin to answer this question we need a definition of policies.

Policies can be thought of as levers or dials that the government can adjust to influence human development outcomes. Policies include guidelines, norms, laws, and procedures. While it would make sense to compare these features across countries, it is difficult and costly to get consistent data for long time periods. Thus, it is sometimes necessary to fall back either on indirect measures of policy commitment or on outcomes usually associated with particular policies. For example, the allocation of resources for large health expenditures as a percentage of GDP is an indirect measure of policy commitment to health compared with other priorities, while a high level of economic openness might indicate that export promotion policies are in place.

I will examine ten policy variables that can be divided into three groups:[34]

1. *Economic policies.* These are policies directly associated with an out-wardly oriented economic strategy, such as real exchange rates,

real interest rates, and low fiscal deficits, as well as less direct measures of particular economic policies, such as greater openness of the economy or greater product and market diversification.

2. *Social policies.* These are measured by the average annual expenditures for health, education, and defense as a percentage of GDP between 1965 and 1987.

3. *Political and civil rights policies.* These are measured by an average annual score on the Gastil indexes of political and civil rights.

Which policies mattered?   Of the ten policy variables studied, four accounted for about a third of the adjusted r squared in the stepwise regression of policy variables on human development performance between 1965 and 1987 (0.343 of the adjusted r squared; see Table 2.6).[35] Strong human development performers had higher levels of political rights (0.178 incremental r squared), higher expenditures for health and education as a percentage of GDP (0.080 incremental r squared), lower fiscal deficits (0.068 incremental r squared), and higher levels of export product diversification (0.017 incremental r squared). These results were similar when the regressions were performed to predict the lists of top thirty high performers. For the bottom thirty, however, only two variables were significant: low political liberties and low social expenditures.[36]

Policies and GDP growth   The policies studied here were more important determinants of GDP growth (0.394 of the r squared) between 1965 and 1987 than they were of human development improvement (0.343 of the r squared).[37] Outwardly oriented economic policies like openness and real exchange rates contributed about a quarter of the adjusted r squared.

In addition, countries with high GDP growth also maintained lower fiscal deficits than slower-growth countries. This additional economic policy variable contributed another quarter of the r squared. The higher growth countries also had higher military expenditures as a percentage of GDP and medium or high levels of political rights. These last two variables contributed the other half of the adjusted r squared.

While the importance of outwardly oriented economic policies for GDP growth in the past thirty years is well documented in other studies, the importance of military expenditures and political rights is not.[38] Military expenditures may have been used for pump-priming activity.

Why might these policies matter?   Although I offer no preexisting theory about the impact of policies on human development performance, some questions emerge that must be examined in more detail later.

TABLE 2.6   The Effects of Policies on Human Development and
GDP Growth, 1965–1987 (stepwise regressions)

| | | | Effects on the human development index[a] | | | |
Variable	Value	Standard error	Standard value	F to remove	Adjusted r squared	Incremental adjusted r squared
Intercept	−0.043					
High political liberties	0.648	0.141	0.476	21.100	0.178	0.178
High health and education spending	0.130	0.038	0.363	11.862	0.258	0.080
Low fiscal deficits	4.879	1.855	0.280	6.918	0.326	0.068
High export product diversification	0.004	0.003	0.164	2.587	0.343	0.017

| | | | Effects on annual GDP growth rates[b] | | | |
Variable	Value	Standard error	Standard value	F to remove	Adjusted r squared	Incremental adjusted r squared
Intercept	0.059					
Low fiscal deficits	0.234	0.056	0.411	17.298	0.119	0.119
High military spending	0.005	0.001	0.338	12.147	0.213	0.094
Real exchange rates	−0.027	0.010	−0.273	7.279	0.306	0.093
High political liberties	0.013	0.005	0.265	7.404	0.379	0.073
Open economy	9.643E-5	5.859E-5	0.161	2.079	0.394	0.015

a. The regression in the last step has an adjusted r squared of 0.343, and a standard error of 0.556. The degrees of freedom are 4 for the regression, 60 for the residual, and 64 total DF. The F test is 9.929, and the Durban Watson statistic is 1.791 (ns). An F score of 2 or more is significant at the .05 level. Other variables entered in the equation did not have significant F scores.
b. The regression in the last step has an adjusted r squared of 0.394, and a standard error of 0.019. The degrees of freedom are 5 for the regression, 62 for the residual, and 67 total DF. The F test is 9.729, and the Durban Watson statistic is 1.773 (ns). An F score of 2 or more is significant at the .05 level. Other variables entered in the equation did not have significant F scores.
SOURCE: Author's calculations.

First, why were economic policies (that is, high levels of export product diversification and low fiscal deficits) responsible for as large a proportion of the r squared in human development performance as social program expenditures in the regressions? One explanation is that export-led growth generates the per capita income increases that permit people to feed and clothe themselves and improve the quality of their lives directly rather than through government programs. Ranis and Fei's work on export-led growth in Taiwan supports this hypothesis and adds that income distribution improves dramatically because of the broad increases in general employment, permitting the social gains to be widespread.[39]

Second, one might have expected that governments with big HDI gains would have been more likely to run high fiscal deficits to pay for social programs, but the reverse was true. A possible explanation is that gains from a successful export strategy were contingent upon conservative fiscal policies as part of a package of more outwardly oriented economic policies. This package might have permitted greater overall GDP growth accompanied by less inflation.

Third, social expenditures matter but it is unclear why. At this level of aggregation it is impossible to discriminate among investments in particular kinds of programs, much less their cost-effectiveness. Such analysis can only be done with fewer countries and in more depth.

Fourth, education expenditures appeared to have a far more important effect on human development performance than health expenditures. Why? One plausible explanation is that education provides more than simply literacy. It increases awareness of how to protect individual and family health.

Finally, why did countries with medium and high levels of political rights appear to make greater human development gains between 1965 and 1987 than those with lower levels of rights? Here are some plausible hypotheses. First, a government's willingness to permit higher levels of political rights might also indicate its willingness to promote human development in other areas. Second, once citizens had minimal political rights, they may have had channels for pressuring their government to make investments in human development areas. Third, while medium levels of political rights were not associated with democratic elections of national leaders, they might have provided channels for more active citizen participation at local levels and with the bureaucracy, perhaps resulting in larger and more effective investments in social services.

External influences and human development

The analysis so far has shown that both a nation's internal context and its policies were important determinants of its ability to achieve human development gains for its citizens. What about the role of external influences? Did they serve as an impediment or stimulus to human development performance?

External influences are defined as forces generated outside a nation's borders or beyond its control that might affect its human development performance. For example, poor human development performers might have suffered from more natural disasters like droughts or floods, been pillaged more frequently during outside military interventions, or been victims of unfavorable terms of trade. The types of external influences considered were

1. *Natural disasters.* These are measured by the number of earthquakes, volcanic eruptions, droughts, and floods, for example.

2. *External military interventions.*

3. *External economic influences.* These are measured by changes in the terms of trade, and export product and market concentration at the start of the study period.

4. *Access to foreign resource flows.* This is measured by annual average total debt as a percentage of GDP, average debt service as a percentage of exports, and average aid as a percentage of GDP.

Which external influences mattered?   The data show that developing countries were not prisoners of most external forces between 1965 and 1987 (see Table 2.7). High and low human development performers were equally affected by changes in terms of trade, external economic shocks, military interventions, and natural disasters. External influences were less important than either policy or internal contextual variables. In fact they accounted for only 0.192 of the adjusted r squared in the regressions on human development performance.[40] The results were similar for country groups with both high and low HDI disparity reduction rates.[41]

TABLE 2.7   The Effects of External Influences on Human Development and GDP Growth, 1965–1987 (stepwise regressions)

		Effects on the human development index[a]				
Variable	Value	Standard error	Standard value	F to remove	Adjusted r squared	Incremental adjusted r squared
Intercept	0.478					
High debt service	2.406	0.660	0.423	13.231	0.121	0.121
Low total debt as % of GDP	−0.871	0.345	−0.294	6.389	0.192	0.071

		Effects on annual GDP growth rates[b]				
Variable	Value	Standard error	Standard value	F to remove	Adjusted r squared	Incremental adjusted r squared
Intercept	0.059					
High export product diversification	−2.14E-4	−1.154E-4	−2.30	3.443	0.045	0.045
High debt service	−0.015	0.001	−0.163	1.893	0.057	0.012

a. The regression in the last step has an adjusted r squared of 0.192 and a standard error of 0.650. The degrees of freedom are 2 for the regression, 60 for the residual, and 62 total DF. The F test is 8.369, and the Durban Watson statistic is 2.212 (ns). An F score of 2 or more is significant at the .05 level. The other six variables were not entered into the equation because of low F values.
b. The regression in the last step has an adjusted r squared of 0.057 and a standard error of 0.020. The degrees of freedom are 2 for the regression, 66 for the residual, and 68 total DF. The F test is 3.06, and the Durban Watson statistic is 2.333 (ns). An F score of 2 or more is significant at the .05 level. The other six variables were not entered into the equation because of low F values.
SOURCE: Author's calculations.

High performers, however, did have less total debt as a share of GDP and higher debt service as a share of exports than lower human development performers. These were the only two of the eight external influences studied with significant T values. Here are some plausible explanations. First, we have seen that high HDI performers had higher levels of GDP growth than low performers. Thus, while they might have continued to incur debt, their GDP growth rates might have insured that the debt-to-GDP ratio remained low. At the same time they may have been less likely to default on debt service and more able to carry a higher debt service load. Thus, debt service as a percentage of exports might have stayed higher. A second plausible explanation is that the high-performance countries might have needed fewer external resources for their development efforts.

External influences and GDP growth   External influences had a lower impact on GDP growth than policies or internal contextual factors, accounting for only 0.057 of the adjusted r squared.[42] Countries with higher GDP growth began the 1965–1987 period with a more diversified export product mix and had higher debt service as a percentage of exports during that period (see Table 2.7).

Common threads in human development performance

So far I have considered internal contextual factors, policies, and external influences separately. But such treatment is artificial since context and policies all interacted to produce an effect on human development during the past thirty years. Which factors proved to be most important when all significant variables were considered?[43]

Six common factors tie the high human development performers together (see Table 2.8). First, these countries began the development race in 1965 with a relatively high-quality initial human resource base. Second, they were more likely to be in East and Southeast Asia. Third, they were less linguistically and ethnically diverse than their neighbors. Fourth, they had a highly stable internal political context during the next twenty-two years. Fifth, they pursued more outwardly oriented economic policies. And sixth, they had higher levels of investment in education and health programs. These threads accounted for 0.657 of the adjusted r squared of human development performance.

The same six variables were important when used to predict the list of high- and low-performing countries, with one exception.[44] The top-performing countries were more frequently Asian, while the bottom performers were African.

TABLE 2.8   The Effects of Internal Contextual Factors, Policies, and External Influences on Human Development and GDP Growth, 1965–1987 (stepwise regressions)

						Effects on the human development index[a]
Variable	Value	Standard error	Standard value	F to remove	Adjusted r squared	Incremental adjusted r squared
Intercept	−1.737					
High 1965 HDI status	0.664	0.113	0.557	34.338	0.508	0.508
Low political instability	−0.275	0.106	−0.241	6.645	0.587	0.079
Real exchange rates	−0.325	0.220	−0.136	2.180	0.623	0.036
Ethnic and linguistic homogeneity	−0.352	0.200	−0.170	3.118	0.640	0.017
Location in Asia	0.360	0.213	0.152	2.874	0.652	0.012
High health and education spending	0.039	0.031	0.117	1.623	0.657	0.005

						Effects on average annual GDP growth[b]
Variable	Value	Standard error	Standard value	F to remove	Adjusted r squared	Incremental adjusted r squared
Intercept	−3.012					
Real exchange rates	−1.269	0.261	−0.611	23.631	0.227	0.227
High 1965 HDI status	0.336	0.145	0.294	5.395	0.288	0.061
Low fiscal deficits	3.743	1.878	0.246	3.951	0.317	0.029
High export product diversification	−0.006	0.003	−0.244	3.588	0.355	0.038

a. The regression in the last step has an adjusted r squared of 0.657 and a standard error of 0.380. The degrees of freedom are 6 for the regression, 43 for the residual, and 49 total DF. The F test is 16.068, and the Durban Watson statistic is 1.87 (ns). An F score of 2 or more is significant at the .05 level.
b. The regression in the last step has an adjusted r squared of 0.355 and a standard error of 0.465. The degrees of freedom are 4 for the regression, 43 for the residual, and 47 total DF. The F test is 4.745, and the Durban Watson statistic is 2.996 (ns). An F score of 2 or more is significant at the .05 level. Variables with an F score of less than 2 were not included.
SOURCE: Author's calculations.

Common threads in GDP growth

Four factors seem to combine to help predict about 0.355 of the adjusted r squared in high GDP growth between 1965 and 1987 (see Table 2.8). Countries with high GDP growth were characterized by real exchange rates, higher initial investments in human development, low fiscal deficits, and higher levels of export product diversification.

It appeared that policies mattered more than overall context in GDP growth in the 1965–1987 period. A combination of economic policies accounted for 92 percent of the shared r squared explained in the regression. Internal contextual factors such as initial human development status accounted for about 8 percent of the r squared.

Conclusions: The Fabric of Human Development Performance

Several conclusions emerge from the identification of these six common threads. Developing countries, it turns out, were not prisoners of contextual impediments to development, as is commonly assumed. Human development performance between 1965 and 1987 was not hindered by a nation's initial natural resource endowments, natural disasters, physical size, or population density. Some elements of the internal context as defined in this study, however, turned out to be very important. In fact, three of the less changeable internal contextual variables accounted for 80 percent of the r squared in the regressions on human development performance. They were high initial HDI status in 1965, region, and initial ethnic and linguistic diversity.

Factors that could be altered by policy measures between 1965 and 1987 accounted for only 20 percent of the r squared. These included exchange rates, expenditures on education and health, and political instability. But of the contextual factors studied here, only a country's initial geographic location (for example, Africa or Asia) was an immutable handicap or benefit to a nation, and region was responsible for only 2 percent of the total adjusted r squared. Contextual factors determined more directly by past or current policies were responsible for 91 percent of the r squared. For example, a nation's HDI status in 1965 was heavily influenced by past economic and social policies. Thus, policies played an important role not only in human development gains between 1965 and 1987 but also in shaping the initial national context in which change took place.

Optimism about the potential role of policy in improving people's lives must be tempered with the recognition that human development improvements do not take place rapidly. Any such improvements made by 1987 were heavily influenced by policy decisions made at least twenty and probably thirty to fifty years earlier. With this last conclusion comes a warning to policy makers not to lose track of the importance of sustained attention to investments in human development in their haste to overcome the economic imbalances of the 1980s. They risk the well-being of more than one generation of citizens.

Finally, there was no striking evidence that high human development performers embarked on rapid, revolutionary, simultaneous economic and political reform. Rather they had higher levels of long-term institutional continuity and lower levels of political instability than poor performers. This finding raises doubts about the potential for success of the shock-type economic reforms and democratic openings that are currently in vogue. (The next chapter will look at this issue in more depth.)

Interwoven elements: Statistical threads and policy threads

The threads I have identified are composed of two elements: one is their statistical importance in the explanation of human development performance, and the other is their policy importance as levers that can be moved to affect HDI status. While we now know which variables have a statistically more significant impact on human development performance, statistical importance should not be confused with policy impact. For example, region (where a country is geographically located) may explain a larger percentage of the r squared in human development performance than health and education expenditures. But policy makers can hardly move Chad from Africa to Asia in hopes that its performance will improve. They can, however, increase spending on health and education with the hope of improving people's lives. Sound exchange rate policy may play a smaller statistical role in explaining improvements in human development than linguistic homogeneity or political stability. But we know more about making exchange rate policy choices than we do about reducing political instability or promoting cultural harmony.

I will attempt to identify which variables might have more policy effects compared with statistical effects on human development performance. A good way to proceed is with an example of potential policy changes in one country—in this case, Chad. Chad turned out to be one of the poorest human development performers between 1965 and 1987. As noted earlier, in 1965 Chad's HDI status of 14.7 placed it well below the poor-country average of 24.1. Its disparity reduction rate was half a percent a year, while the poor country average was about 1 percent. By 1987 Chad's HDI status was 24.1, the average HDI level the poor performance group had achieved twenty-two years earlier.

What if we had been able to move any of the six threads that explain human development performance improvements (statistically) during the 1965–1987 period from Chad's very low level up to the average level for developing countries for that period? If we moved each thread, one at a time, while holding the others constant, which would give us the greatest annual rate of disparity reduction and overall improvement in Chad's HDI status by 1987? Table 2.9 provides the data.

Chad would have achieved the greatest gains if it had been able to raise its 1965 HDI score from 14.7 to the developing-country average of 37.0. This change alone would have allowed Chad to reach an HDI status

TABLE 2.9 Chad's 1987 Human Development Status Adjusted to Reflect Improvements up to the Poor-Country Average on Each Critical Variable

	HDI status in 1965	Political instability	Ethnic diversity in 1965	Exchange rate	Health and education spending as % of GNP, 1965–1987	Asia	Disparity reduction rate, 1965–1987	Unadjusted HDI status in 1987
Developing-country average	37.0	0.41	0.41	1.05	3.93		1.84	58.5
Poor-country average	24.1	0.52	0.67	1.14	3.01		0.87	37.2
Chad average	14.7	0.86	0.83	1.10	3.23		0.50	23.7
Chad's adjusted DRR rate[a]	1.19	0.79	0.75	0.65	0.66	0.93	0.50	
Chad's HDI in 1987 when variable is adjusted to the average for developing countries[b]	51.0	28.36	27.72	26.10	26.26	30.50		23.7

Blank cell indicates not applicable.
a. DRR adjusted by recomputing after bringing the key variable to the developing-country average.
b. Chad's HDI status in 1987 adjusted by recomputing after bringing the key variable to the developing-country average.
SOURCE: Author's calculations.

of 51.0 percent of the industrial country standard in 1987 instead of only 23.7 percent. If Chad had been located in Asia its HDI status would have improved to 30.5 by 1987. Chad might have made bigger human development gains between 1965 and 1987 if the ratio of coups to total changes of government had been reduced from eight out of ten to the developing-country average of four out of ten. In this case its HDI status in 1987 would have been 28.36. If Chad's overvalued exchange rate (1.10) had been devalued to a level similar to that of the other developing countries (1.05), it would have achieved a 1987 HDI score of 26.1. Finally, Chad would have gotten slightly more improvement by reducing its language diversity (a 1987 HDI score of 27.72) than by increasing its expenditures in education and health to the developing-country averages (a 1987 HDI score of 26.26). These HDI scores imply that Chad would have needed to reduce the probability that two randomly selected citizens would speak different languages from 83 percent to 40 percent over a twenty-two-year period, or it would have needed to increase expenditures on education and health from 3.2 percent of GNP to the developing-country average of 3.9 percent. Changing the level of education and health spending would have been the more realistic choice.

Paradoxically, the two factors that provide the biggest potential performance impact as well as the biggest combined statistical impact are least correctable with policy reform.[45] Policy makers cannot turn back the clock and make a set of human development investments in Chad between 1900 and 1965 to raise its 1965 HDI status. Nor can they put Chad on a boat and move it from Africa to Southeast Asia. They can and must, however, pay careful attention to human development policies in the present since they have almost a multiplier effect on the human capital base and future human development improvements. Postponing them sacrifices the quality of life of several generations.

In contrast, policy makers have more control over two other threads, the exchange rate and education and health expenditures. But changes in these economic and social policies have less impact on overall human development than reducing political instability or finding creative ways to manage language and cultural diversity. Unfortunately, we know less about reducing political instability than about increasing social expenditures or devaluing the currency. We know even less about reducing language diversity and managing complex cultural differences. But it would be easier to experiment with political institution building and innovative language and cultural policies than to move Chad out of Africa.

In summary, moving the threads that will have the largest effect on human development (HDI status in 1965 and region) is least feasible. Making the policy changes that are most feasible (exchange rates and social expenditures) will have the smallest effect on human development. In the middle are areas of political and cultural policy that have intermediate effects but about which we understand less.

Finally, even though the data show that changing exchange rate and social investment policies to reflect developing country averages for the 1965–1987 period had less impact on human development than lowering political instability or language diversity, it might have been realistic to alter these policies even more. For example, by adjusting the tax base, altering the public expenditure mix, and seeking additional donor grants, it might have been possible to move Chad's education and health expenditures from 3.2 percent of GNP to above the 3.9 percent developing-country average and get even more human development improvement by 1987.

What big data set analysis hides

While this analysis helped identify six common threads in human development performance and clarify which ones have more policy rather than statistical importance, there is much we still do not know. In fact cross-sectional and longitudinal analyses of big data sets like this one are more notable for what they do not tell us because of imprecise measures, the absence of accurate and timely data, and the trade-off of analytical breadth for depth. Yet it is precisely by investigating the questions that remain that we gain new insights into the secrets of development. Here are some puzzles worth thinking about further.

How was the initial human capital base formed?   First, although big data set analysis showed that the initial human capital base was one of the most important determinants of future human development performance, it told us nothing about the paths the strongest human development performers took to build this base. Nor do we know why, for example, outwardly oriented economic policies might have played a more important role in increasing HDI status between 1965 and 1987 than direct investments in education or health. Only a study of a smaller group of countries might tell us more about the paths to human capital formation. In Chapter 7 I will compare the social policies of Costa Rica and Guatemala to get a better sense of the differences.

What does region really mean?   This analysis confirmed that a nation's geographic location in Africa or East and Southeast Asia had an important influence on its future human development performance. But we learned little about what this influence really was. Region is probably a shorthand description of a complex set of cultural, linguistic, physical, and other determinants. Its importance lends strong support to the argument that regions and subregions should be studied separately.

Is political repression a necessary ingredient for human development gains? Low levels of political instability turned out to be fundamental in national human development gains between 1965 and 1987. But we learned little about the different paths through which this stability was achieved. Was it the result of high levels of repression that governments used to keep their citizens in line? The initial analysis indicates that this is not the case and that in fact the countries with the lowest levels of political rights made the slowest human development gains. But what was the relationship between political rights and political stability? Was there any relationship at all or were high levels of political stability achieved because successful economic strategies increased people's material well-being? Additional insight into these dynamics can be gained only by further study of a smaller group of countries.

Is regime type irrelevant for human development performance?   The big data set analysis showed that some highly successful human development performers used democratic forms to elect top leaders while others did not. We might be tempted to conclude that regime type was irrelevant in human development performance. But that conclusion might be premature since different regime types might have different governance styles that result in equally successful human development gains. Furthermore, the best human development performers had medium or high levels of political rights independent of regime type. This implies that they all relied on some forms of political participation even though this did not mean necessarily the popular election of national leaders. But what kinds of participation were involved, and what relationship did these have to human development performance? These are questions the blunt measures of big data set analysis cannot address.

Why were policies that promoted an outward economic orientation important to high human development performance?   Policies that promoted an outward economic orientation turned out to be important for high human development performance, but big data set analysis tells us little about why this might have been the case. Did they help increase per capita income for a broad segment of the population and thereby allow them to help themselves directly, as Ranis and Fei suggest? Were there major differences in the policy paths taken to promote export growth, or were they more or less uniform? Did some paths lead to more rapid human development gains than others? Was the general economic growth strategy really more important for human development gains than direct investments in education or health? Only deeper analysis with a smaller group of countries will help us understand these patterns.

What social investments really matter?   Finally, big data set analysis told us that investments in education and health were important factors in improving human development performance. But there were many unanswered questions. Were they as important as the direct gains made through economic strategies that increased per capita income? Were some kinds of investments more important than others? There was some indication that investments in education explained a greater proportion of the r squared for high human development performance than investments in health? Why?

A Final Word

So cross-sectional and longitudinal analysis of ninety developing countries between 1965 and 1987 helped to identify six threads that tied the past two decades of human development performance together. We also saw that if it were possible to pull some of the threads in particular directions— for example, to lower levels of political instability or increase social investments—it might be possible to speed the rate at which developing countries reduced their human development disparities with the industrial countries.

Much of this story, however, remained mysterious. We can ferret out additional clues about the mystery by looking more deeply into the development dynamics of a smaller set of countries with more similar characteristics. I will do this in the third part of this book.

But first I will take a broad look at the role of regime type, political rights, and political instability in development, one of the threads identified earlier. This is the task of the next chapter.

Regime Type and Economic Performance

At the end of the previous chapter we were left with some unanswered questions about the role of democracy in the economic and social performance of developing countries. To the dissatisfaction of ideologues of all persuasions, both democracies like Costa Rica and nondemocracies like the People's Republic of China were well represented among the ranks of top human development performers. In fact political regime type was a far less important determinant of developing country performance than low levels of political instability and more general political rights.

Yet there continues to be serious controversy about the role of democracy in fostering economic growth and turning ailing economies around. For national movements and newly formed governments contemplating massive economic reform, the answer is hardly an academic one. Its implications are enormous for the quality of life of its citizens, and perhaps the very survival of democracy.

Many continue to argue that authoritarian forms are far superior to democracies in bringing about economic stability in developing nations.[1] Thomas E. Skidmore's work on Latin America is representative of this viewpoint. He concludes that

> governments in competitive political systems find it extremely difficult to reduce inflation, once it has exceeded 20 percent, and they have paid very high political costs for their efforts; . . . no such government has proved able to pursue a successful anti-inflation effort; . . . all cases of successful

stabilization have been carried out by authoritarian (or one-party) governments; and . . . even authoritarian governments must have a high degree of internal consensus to carry through a successful stabilization.[2]

Critics respond that such findings are based on limited analyses of a few Latin American and Asian cases.[3] For example, Remmer finds that

democratic regimes have been no less likely to introduce stabilization programs than authoritarian ones, no more likely to break down in response to the political costs, and no less rigorous in their implementation of austerity measures. If anything, the evidence suggested that the edge with respect to program implementation was with the democracies.[4]

This chapter moves beyond the normal elements of the controversy about democracy and economic management.[5] Its purpose is to look more deeply at the role of regime type and economic performance, particularly after controlling for external factors like economic shocks and the initial level of gross domestic product (GDP). I was unable to do this in Chapter 2 because of insufficient data for the 1965–1987 period, but I can do it for the shorter 1973–1987 period.[6] A second purpose is to discover whether democracies were as willing as nondemocracies to embark on economic reform in the 1980s, particularly structural adjustment as opposed to stabilization. Finally, I hope to evaluate the performance of countries that embarked on "double-shock policies" in the 1980s—simultaneous economic reform and democratic opening. The specific questions I will try to answer are:

1. Did the developing world become more democratic between 1960 and 1990?

2. Did democratic nations perform as well economically as their nondemocratic counterparts?

3. Were democratic nations as likely as nondemocratic ones to initiate and successfully implement economic adjustment programs, particularly in the 1980s?

4. How did countries implementing double shock policies— simultaneous economic and political reform—perform?

The Growth of Democracy in the Developing World

Since 1960 not only have developing countries made increasing use of democratic forms, such as competitive elections, but they have also expanded civil and political liberties.[7] For example, between 1973 and 1989 the proportion of developing countries holding competitive democratic elections for top officials increased from 19 percent (of ninety-three countries) to 41 percent (see Table 3.1). At the same time the number of countries scoring medium or high on Gastil's index of political and civil liberties increased from 57 to 68 percent.

The use of democratic forms was significantly related to democratic substance—that is, countries having democratic elections scored significantly higher on the political and civil liberties index than those that did not. Yet this correlation was not perfect. In fact, in 1989 only 50 percent of newly democratic nations and 61 percent of the more established democracies had high rankings on Gastil's index.[8]

Furthermore, while the world became more democratic, this change did not take place uniformly across the globe. The most dramatic changes occurred in Asia and Latin America, where the proportion of democratic regimes grew from one-third in 1973 to more than two-thirds by 1989. (In Latin America the most dramatic shift took place between 1980 and 1989, when the number of democratic regimes virtually doubled from 39 to 70 percent.) In Asia, the changes occurred more evenly across 1973–1980 and 1980–1989. Yet there was virtually no change in sub-Saharan African nations and only moderate change in the Middle East and North Africa. Changes in these latter did not really begin until the early 1990s.

The regional differences were not important in 1973 but became significant by 1989 after radical changes came to Latin America and Asia. (See the results of the chi square measures reported in Table 3.1.)

Although the overall number of democratic regimes increased from 1973 to 1989, there was no evidence to support the politicians' contentions that democracy had won the day.[9] For example, in the 1980s 18 percent of all authoritarian regimes collapsed—a figure only slightly higher than the 13 percent collapse rate for democratic regimes.[10] In the global figures, the demise of democratic regimes in Africa helped cancel out the statistically significant collapses of authoritarian regimes in Latin America and Asia.

Economic Performance of Democratic and Nondemocratic Nations

Regime type and economic performance

Of the years under consideration, the period of greatest world economic crisis was 1982–1988. In this period democratic regimes grew more rapidly and redressed their external imbalances more effectively than did their

TABLE 3.1 Political Regime Type and Region, 1973, 1980, and 1989 (number of countries)

Region[a]	1973		1980[b]		1989[c]	
	Democracies	Nondemocracies	Democracies	Nondemocracies	Democracies	Nondemocracies
Latin America	6	15	9	14	16	7
Africa	3	35	7	31	5	33
Middle East	3	9	4	8	5	7
Asia	5	9	8	8	10	6
Europe	0	4	2	2	2	2
Total	17	72	30	63	38	55
Percentage	19	81	33	67	41	59

NOTE: A regime was coded as democratic if it came to power through competitive elections without accusations of fraud.

a. No region was significantly more democratic than any other in 1973 (chi square 10.83 p. 26) or 1980 (chi square 8.48 p. 31). There were significant differences in 1989 (chi square 24.83 p. 001).

b. By 1980 22 percent of the countries scored high on Gastil's index of political and civil liberties, and 35 percent scored medium, for a total of 57 percent.

c. By 1989 24 percent of the countries scored high on Gastil's index of political and civil liberties, and 44 percent scored medium, for a total of 68 percent.

SOURCE: Author's data coded based on Arthur Banks, Thomas Muller, Sean Phelar, and Elaine Talman, *Political Handbook of the World* (Binghamton, N.Y.: CSA Publications, State University of New York).

authoritarian counterparts. As shown in Table 3.2, they performed significantly better on three of four measures of economic performance and one of two measures of external balance, suggesting that they were more resilient in adapting their economic strategies to the problems of the 1980s than much of the literature indicates.

To be sure, a comparison of averages, or even nonparametric tests for systematic patterns in two-way tables, does not tell us whether initial factors other than regime type were responsible for the differential performance of these two groups. For instance, they do not control for differences in initial levels of GDP or other factors such as external economic shocks that might have affected the regimes' GDP growth rates differently. I was not able to control for these effects in Chapter 2 because of a lack of data for the longer 1965–1987 time series.

To study the impact of these factors, I will turn to two sets of least-squares regressions that cover the 1973–1988 period. In the first, I estimate a variant of a fixed-effects model of GDP growth and regime type to determine whether there is any systematic difference in either the level or the growth rate of GDP between democratic and nondemocratic regimes.[11] Table 3.3 shows that while there is no significant difference in GDP levels, there is a gap in growth rates: democratic regimes grew seven-tenths of a percent faster than their nondemocratic counterparts between 1973 and 1988.

The fixed-effects model does not allow for the possibility that these two groups of countries may have undergone different external shocks, which may, in turn, have affected their performance. I will turn, therefore, to a control group approach, comparing the relative performance of the two groups of countries between two subperiods, 1973–1982 and 1983–1988. My aim is to answer the question, Was the change in democratic regimes' performance between the two periods superior to that of nondemocratic ones, taking into account the change in the shocks between these two periods?[12]

Performance here is defined by four variables: GDP growth, investment-to-GDP ratio, inflation, and the current account-to-GDP ratio. The results show that the only variable in which democratic regimes performed significantly better was GDP growth (see Table 3.4). This result takes into account differences in the external shocks faced by the two sets of countries. Furthermore, investment and current account variables—which were significantly different in the nonparametric analysis above—are no longer significant. The reason is that democratic regimes experienced different shocks from those experienced by their authoritarian counterparts. When these shocks are taken into account, their performance in investment and current account reduction was not significantly different from that of nondemocratic regimes.

TABLE 3.2   Regime Type and Economic Performance for 93 Developing Countries, 1973–1981 and 1982–1988

Indicator	1973–1981		1982–1988	
	Nondemocracies	Democracies	Nondemocracies	Democracies
Number of countries[a]	69	23	59	33
Growth				
Average GDP growth (%)	4.6	5.2	2.5	5.7*
Exports as % of GDP	25.7	36.6[b]	25.6	36.5**
Investments as % of GDP	24.0	26.2	21.4	21.2
Average export growth (%)	5.5	5.8	4.2	10.7*
External balance				
Real exchange rate	1.049	0.968[b]	1.174	1.005
Current account deficit as % of GDP	-5.4	-4.4	-6.3	-3.7**
Internal balance				
Fiscal deficit as % of GDP	-4.3	-6.1	-5.5	-8.1
Inflation (%)	24.1	14.8	55.2	88.7
Debt burden				
Debt as % of GDP	27.8	19.2[b]	61.9	48.7
Debt service as % of exports	14.9	11.3	21.9	22.1

a. A country appeared in the democratic column if its government had competitive elections without accusations of fraud for more than 50 percent of the period. The same statistics were calculated using the number of democratic regimes at the midpoints of the periods and the same measures were statistically significant.

NOTE: A result was considered strongly significant (**) if the probability of its occurrence was less than .05 percent and weakly significant (*) between .06 and .09 percent. For 1973–1981 significant F test scores were for exports as % of GDP (6.924), real exchange rate (3.793), and debt as % of GDP (4.22). For 1982–1988 significant F test scores were for GDP growth (2.768), exports as % of GDP (5.432), average export growth (2.959), and current account deficit as % of GDP (4.326).

SOURCE: Data set from Ricardo Faini, Jaime de Melo, Abdel Senhadji-Semlali, and Julie Stanton, "Macro Performance under Adjustment Lending," Policy, Planning, and Research Working Paper 190 (Washington, D.C.: World Bank, 1989); author's regime coding completed with the assistance of Veronica Marseillan and Diemar Smith.

TABLE 3.3   Differences in GDP Growth Rates of Democracies and Nondemocracies, 1973–1988 (using a fixed-effects model)

Coefficient	Estimate	T value
B0	24.46	57.70[a]
B1	−0.50	−0.69
B2	0.0077	3.90[a]

NOTE: The coefficient B1 represents the difference in the levels of GDP between democratic and nondemocratic regimes. B2 represents differences in the rate of growth.
a. Significantly different from 0 at 99 percent confidence level. Note that while the estimate for B2 is small, .0077, the *t* value of 3.90 is significantly different from 0.
SOURCE: Author's calculations.

TABLE 3.4   Economic Performance of Democracies and Nondemocracies Controlling for the Effects of External Economic Shocks, 1973–1989 (using an error components framework)

Indicator	Previous period's value				Dummy variable for democracies	Shock variable
	GDP growth	Investment-to-GDP ratio (I/Y) −1	Inflation	Current account-to-GDP ratio		
GDP growth	−0.047[a]	−0.005	0.005	0.007	0.010[a]	−0.004
Investment-to-GDP ratio	0.411[a]	−0.309[a]	−0.041	0.164	0.004	0.970
Inflation	−0.577	−0.074	−0.322[a]	−0.280	0.009	−0.120
Current account-to-GDP ratio	0.072	0.044	0.008	−0.708[a]	−0.007	0.037

a. Significant at the 95 percent confidence level. The results are significant only for GDP growth.
SOURCE: Author's calculations.

New and old democracies and economic performance

Until now I have ignored the distinction between new and old democracies. Do new democracies, particularly those in transition during the 1980s, show weaker economic performance than the ones that entered this period with the experience of more than ten years of competitive democratic rule? The data say yes (see Table 3.5).

In fact old democracies outperformed both new democracies and nondemocracies. Their economic performance was significantly stronger on seven of the ten economic measures used in this study.

The performance of new democracies was similar to, and at times slightly weaker than, that of authoritarian regimes. For example, new democracies showed significantly less investment as a percentage of GDP, higher inflation, and higher debt service as a percentage of exports than authoritarian governments.

Regime type, rights, and economic performance

Although regime type is a useful analytical variable for studying differences in national economic performance in the 1980s, a closer look at the economic, civil, and political rights associated with political regimes provides a deeper understanding of which rights might be most important (see Table 3.6).

Although the number of countries in each group is too small to permit reliable statistical testing, there is some indication that countries with market economies and more economic rights had the highest levels of GDP growth. Older, more established democracies with market economies and high levels of economic rights outperformed all other nations.

Initiation of Economic Adjustment Programs in 1982–1988

Regime type, SAL initiation, and regime collapse

In the 1980s, democratic regimes were as likely as authoritarian ones to take strong economic medicine, such as participation in World Bank– and IMF-backed adjustment programs (see Table 3.7).[13] Once adjustment programs were started, democratic regimes were as likely to maintain themselves in power as were authoritarian ones.

Participating in a structural adjustment loan (SAL) program, however, appeared to be a little like open-heart surgery: it was significantly more risky for regime stability than doing nothing. Yet it was no riskier for democratic participants than for authoritarian ones (see Table 3.7). For

TABLE 3.5   Economic Performance in New and Old Democracies, 1982–1988

Indicator	New democracies	Old democracies	Nondemocracies	F test	Statistical significance
Number of countries	13	23	53		
Growth					
Average annual GDP growth (%)	2.0	7.3	2.6	2.781	.067[a]
Exports as % of GDP	21.0	43.4	25.6	7.143	.001[a]
Investment as % of GDP	16.0	22.0	21.4	3.130	.048[a]
Average annual export growth (%)	3.8	14.1	4.2	2.305	.100[a]
External balance					
Real exchange rate	1.152	1.001	1.179	0.418	.659
Current account deficit as % of GDP	−3.9	−3.2	−6.5	3.111	.048[a]
Internal balance					
Fiscal deficit as % of GDP	−7.8	−6.8	−5.9	0.356	.700
Inflation (%)	210.9	17.1	52.1	2.422	.094[a]
Debt burden					
Debt as % of GDP	49.0	46.7	66.3	1.771	.176
Debt service as % of exports	28.6	19.1	21.4	3.029	.053[a]

NOTE: A country was coded as an old democracy if it had competitive elections without accusations of fraud between 1973 and 1988. New democracies had competitive elections without accusations of fraud less than 49 percent between 1973 and 1981 and more than 50 percent between 1982 and 1989. Other countries were called nondemocracies.

a. A result was considered strongly significant if the probability of its occurrence was less than .05 percent and weakly significant between .06 and .09 percent.

SOURCE: Data set from Ricardo Faini, Jaime de Melo, Abdel Senhadji-Semlali, and Julie Stanton, "Macro Performance under Adjustment Lending," Policy, Planning, and Research Working Paper 190 (Washington, D.C.: World Bank, 1989); author's regime coding completed with the assistance of Veronica Marseillan and Diemar Smith.

example, 27 percent (eight out of thirty) of political regimes that undertook SALs collapsed during implementation of the program, compared with only 9 percent of the regimes of non-SAL participants.[14]

Without detailed case-by-case analysis it is difficult to assess the extent to which SAL implementation weakened governments' ability to remain in power. It is plausible that those governments needing to initiate SAL programs had already been weakened by economic collapse; otherwise, they would not have been forced to take such measures in the first place. It is also likely, of course, that SAL policies further eroded their political base.

TABLE 3.6   GDP Growth Rates by Regime Type, Economic System Type, and Economic, Civil, and Political Liberties, 1982–1988

Economic and political rights indexes	New democracies	Old democracies	Non democracies	Total
Economic system type				
Capitalist				
Number of countries	7	11	16	34
Annual GDP growth (%)	2.8	11.6	3.1	5.8
Noncapitalist				
Number of countries	6	12	39	57
Annual GDP growth (%)	1.2	3.5	2.3	2.4
Economic rights index				
High				
Number of Countries	0	9	1	10
Annual GDP growth (%)	n.a.	11.9	7.4	11.4
Medium				
Number of countries	11	14	30	55
Annual GDP growth (%)	2.3	4.4	2.1	2.8
Low				
Number of countries	2	0	24	26
Annual GDP growth (%)	0.1	n.a.	2.8	2.6
Civil/political rights index				
High				
Number of countries	7	14	1	22
Annual GDP growth (%)	1.5	3.6	1.8	2.8
Medium				
Number of countries	6	9	25	40
Annual GDP growth (%)	2.5	11.2	2.6	5.0
Low				
Number of countries	0	0	29	29
Annual GDP growth (%)	n.a.	n.a.	2.5	2.5

n.a. = not available.
NOTE: Regimes were classified as old democracies when they had competitive elections between 1973 and 1987; new democracies when they had competitive elections without accusations of fraud for less than 50 percent between 1973 and 1981 and more than 50 percent between 1982 and 1989. Countries not meeting these criteria were called nondemocracies. Economic system classifications appear on pp. 70–71 of Gastil and economic freedom scores for 1982 on pp. 78–83 of the 1982 edition.
SOURCE: The index scores come from Gastil's ratings of political and civil liberties: *Freedom in the World* (New York: Freedom House, 1989) pp. 50–61. High = 14–11, medium = 10–6, and low = 5–1 on the index. Regime classifications coded by Veronica Marseillan and Diemar Smith.

TABLE 3.7   Political Regime Type, SAL Participation, and Regime Collapse, 1982–1988 (number of countries)

	Regime type in 1982			Regime collapse, 1982–1988		
	Nondemocracy	Democracy	Total[a]	Yes	No	Total[b]
SAL participation, 1982–1988						
Yes	24	6	30	8	22	30[c]
No	39	24	63	6	57	63[d]
Total	63	30	93	14	79	93

NOTE: Regimes were classified as democratic if they had competitive elections without accusations of fraud. A regime collapse was coded if regime type changed during the years noted.
a. Chi square value of 2.273 not significant at P.13.
b. Chi square value of 3.426 significant at P.06.
c. Democratic countries that participated in SALs were no more likely to collapse than nondemocratic ones (chi square .001 not significant P.91). Among SAL participants, 2 of 6 democratic countries and 6 of 24 nondemocratic countries collapsed.
d. Democratic countries that did not participate in SALs were no more likely to collapse than nondemocratic ones (chi square .482 not significant P.46) Among SAL nonparticipants, 1 of 24 democratic countries and 5 of 39 nondemocratic countries collapsed.
SOURCE: Regime type classifications were developed by the author with coding assistance by Veronica Marseillan and Diemar Smith based on use of country data from World Bank, *Political Handbook of the World: 1989* (Washington, D.C., 1989).

SAL participation and economic performance

Not surprisingly countries that chose to participate in World Bank– and IMF-sponsored adjustment programs had, as a group, suffered significantly weaker economic performance in the prior eight-year period than those that did not (see Table 3.8). In particular, they showed weaker export growth and GDP growth and larger current account deficits, fiscal deficits, and debt service as a percentage of exports in 1973–1981 than non-SAL participants.

The performance of SAL and non-SAL participants between 1982 and 1988 was generally comparable. Neither group recovered the GDP growth rates it had exhibited in the earlier period. Their investment as a percentage of GDP continued to deteriorate; fiscal deficits, inflation, and debt burdens continued to grow. But exports grew more rapidly than in the previous period, both absolutely and as a percentage of GDP.

An optimistic interpretation of these results is that adjustment lending in the 1982–1988 period helped stop the collapse of those countries that had been the worst off initially (see Table 3.7) and helped return them to a par with the uneven, but less seriously deteriorated, performance of the nonadjustment countries.

There were, however, a few noticeable differences in the performance of SAL and non-SAL participants. SAL participants' investments as a percentage of GDP dropped by more than that of nonparticipants, and

TABLE 3.8   SAL Participation and Economic Performance for 93 Developing Countries, 1973–1981 and 1982–1988

Indicator	Performance in 1973–1981, before SAL participation			Performance in 1982–1988, after SAL participation		
	No future SAL negotiated	Future SAL negotiated	Statistical significance	Nonparticipant	SAL participant	Statistical significance
Number of countries	63	30		63	30	
Growth						
Average GDP growth (%)	5.2	3.8	.04[a]	4.2	2.5	
Exports as % of GDP	29.9	26.1		31.3	26.2	
Investment as % of GDP	24.8	24.1		22.6	18.6	.02[a]
Average export growth (%)	6.7	3.7	.03[a]	7.4	5.0	
External balance						
Real exchange rate	1.006	1.067		1.021	1.346	.06[a]
Current account deficit as % of GDP	-4.5	-6.3		-5.6	-4.7	
Internal balance						
Fiscal deficit as % of GDP	-3.8	-6.4	.01[a]	-5.7	-7.6	
Inflation (%)	20.3	23.6		50.8	103.6	
Debt burden						
Debt as % of GDP	23.0	29.6		53.4	64.5	
Debt service as % of exports	11.2	19.1	.002[a]	20.2	25.5	.04[a]

a. A result was considered strongly significant if its probability was less than .05 percent and weakly significant between .06 and .09 percent. In 1973–1981 significant F scores were average GDP growth (4.320), average export growth (4.598), fiscal deficit (6.017), and debt service as % of exports (10.185). In 1982–1988 they were investment as % of GDP (5.229), real exchange rate (3.461), and debt service as % of exports (4.16).

SOURCE: Ricardo Faini, Jaime de Melo, Abdel Senhadji-Semlali, and Julie Stanton, "Macro Performance under Adjustment Lending," Policy, Planning, and Research Working Paper 190 (Washington, D.C.: World Bank, 1989). Regime coding by Veronica Marseillan and Diemar Smith.

the difference is significant. At the same time, SAL participants improved their current account balances much more than did non-SAL participants. A number of observers argue that SAL resources were simply substituted for domestic resources to generate growth in GDP and exports and to improve debt repayment capacity, instead of providing a basis for more sustained growth.[15] Alternatively, SAL participants may have been obliged to cut large investment projects—including some "white elephants"—while nonparticipants continued with such investments.

SAL participation, regime type, and economic performance

The analysis so far has shown that democratic regimes were as willing to initiate World Bank– and IMF-sponsored adjustment efforts as were their authoritarian counterparts. Although such programs posed risks for regime stability, both democratic and nondemocratic regimes survived equally well during the implementation process. Democracies also performed at least as well economically as did the authoritarian regimes (see Table 3.9).

In fact, the democratic regimes that undertook SALs improved their GDP, export growth, and external balance more than their nondemocratic counterparts, although these differences were statistically significant in only a few cases. Still their internal balance and debt burden deteriorated to levels similar to those of their authoritarian SAL counterparts.

The poorest performance in the 1982–1988 period was registered largely by the thirty-eight nondemocratic, non-SAL participants. They grew the least and had the largest current account deficits and levels of inflation of all developing countries. Their export performance was weaker and their current account deficits were higher than the democratic nonparticipants.

The twenty-four democratic non-SAL participants showed the strongest economic performance of all groups between 1982 and 1988. Their GDP growth and export performance were particularly impressive. They had the best record of recovery of external balance, and while their debt burden increased over the 1973–1981 period, it was still the smallest increase of all of the countries studied.

Simultaneous economic and political liberalization and economic performance

Although it was frequently recommended to leaders in the Soviet Union, Eastern Europe, and the developing world, simultaneous economic and political opening turned out to be quite difficult to manage. The eight countries involved in simultaneous SAL implementation and political

TABLE 3.9   Regime Type and Economic Performance for 93 Developing Countries, 1973–1981 and 1982–1988

| | 1973–1981 | | | |
| | Nondemocracies | | Democracies | |
Indicator	SAL 1982–1988	No SAL	SAL 1982–1988	No SAL
Number of countries[a]	24	39	6	24
Growth				
Average GDP growth (%)	4.0	5.0	2.7	5.5
Exports as % of GDP	3.0	7.0	3.9	6.2
Investment as % of GDP	24.3	23.9	23.4	26.4
Average export growth (%)	25.1	26.2	30.4	36.0
External balance				
Real exchange rate	1.080	1.030	1.000	0.960
Current account deficit as %				
of GDP	−6.0	−4.0	−6.0	−3.0
Internal balance				
Fiscal deficit as % of GDP	−7.0	−3.0	−3.0	−5.0**
Inflation (%)	24.0	23.0	20.0	15.0
Debt burden				
Debt as % of GDP	31.0	26.0	20.0	18.0
Debt service as % of exports	19.0	10.0	17.0	11.8**
	1982–1988			
Growth				
Average GDP growth (%)	2.3	2.1	3.3	6.9
Exports as % of GDP	4.0	4.0	7.3	13.1
Investment as % of GDP	18.8	22.4	18.0	23.0
Average export growth (%)	24.1	26.0	34.0	40.0**
External balance				
Real exchange rate	1.300	1.030	1.200	0.990
Current account deficit as %				
of GDP	−4.0	−7.0	−4.0	−3.0[a]*
Internal balance				
Fiscal deficit as % of GDP	−7.0	−5.0	−7.0	−6.0
Inflation (%)	120.0	1.5	19.0	24.0
Debt burden				
Debt as % of GDP	65.0	58.0	61.0	45.0
Debt service as % of exports	26.0	20.0	22.0	19.0

a. A country was coded as a democracy if its government had competitive elections without accusations of fraud for more than 50 percent of the period.
NOTE: A result was strongly significant (**) if the probability was less than .05 percent and weakly significant (*) between .06 and .09 percent.
SOURCE: Data set from Ricardo Faini, Jaime de Melo, Abdel Senhadji-Semlali, and Julie Stanton, "Macro Performance under Adjustment Lending," Policy, Planning, and Research Working Paper 190 (Washington, D.C.: World Bank, 1989); regime coding by Veronica Marseillan and Diemar Smith.

transition turned out to be poorer overall economic performers than either SAL participants with no regime transitions or non–SAL participants in general.

The double-transition countries grew less and had significantly lower levels of investment relative to GDP and somewhat lower export growth than other countries. Their budget deficits skyrocketed, and inflation levels and debt service as a percentage of exports were significantly higher than other countries.

These results should be treated with caution, however, because of the small number of cases involved and the short time period for judging post-SAL performance.[16] Furthermore, at this level of data aggregation, it is difficult to determine whether the poor economic performance of these double-transition countries is the result of prior economic deterioration that may have been reversed after a regime transition began or conditions that worsened after the transition was initiated. Longer time-series analysis and a review of individual cases might help sort these matters out further.

Conclusions

This analysis of the problem of democracy and economic reform offers cause for both hope and caution. Between 1960 and 1990 the developing world did become more democratic, both in the formal sense of democratic elections and in terms of essential economic, civil, and political rights. Yet this democratic ascendancy was somewhat localized until 1990, embracing Latin America and parts of Asia but largely excluding Africa and the Middle East.

The contention that a strong, authoritarian hand is needed to reverse economic chaos has not been borne out. As noted in Chapter 2, democracies in developing countries performed at least as well economically as their authoritarian counterparts. Chapter 3 demonstrates that democracies showed even stronger economic performance when the data are controlled for economic shocks and initial economic conditions.

But new democracies did not have an easy time compared with the older, more established democratic regimes. While new democracies performed at levels no worse than the existing nondemocratic regimes, neither performed as well as the older democracies in the developing world. Finally, overall economic performance in the 1980s did not come close to the performance of the 1960s and 1970s. The history of the 1980s is about who lost less.

In the struggle against eroding standards of living, democratic regimes defied popular wisdom. They were as likely to administer strong economic medicine—structural adjustment programs—as authoritarian regimes and were no more likely to be overthrown as a result of their efforts. Their economic recovery during adjustment was at least as strong as that of nondemocratic regimes implementing similar policies.

While democracies must contend with greater political vulnerability than more authoritarian forms of government, they may be bolstered by greater resilience, superior flexibility, and broader political base, which allow them to institute changes more readily.

What lessons can we learn from the short-run economic results of countries that engaged in simultaneous economic and political opening in the period under study? Those who are contemplating a similar initiative in their own countries should proceed with caution. There is still much to be discovered about the sequencing of political and economic reforms and their effects on economic performance.

But the discussion of the strengths of democratic regimes must be tempered with the broader findings discussed earlier. While regime type did make a difference for economic and human development performance, it played a far less important role than low levels of political instability, economic policies favoring exports, a high initial human capital base, and significant human development investments between 1965 and 1987. The positive news is that the more extensive analysis provided here supported my contention in Chapter 1 that democracy was not an impediment as advocates of authoritarian rule have argued and that in fact it played a constructive, but mysterious, role in helping some countries outperform their nondemocratic counterparts economically between 1965 and 1987. The mystery, however, remains, particularly at this level of aggregation.

Perhaps democracy is a rough surrogate for a complex set of economic, political, and civil rights that form part of the overall governance structure in which individual confidence, economic growth, and restructuring actually take place. It may be that regimes that were not formal democracies but that were high human development performers also had participative mechanisms that allowed them to adjust their policies based on useful feedback from key elements of the population. Only by understanding the more detailed dimensions of the governance structure might we unlock some of the deeper secrets of successful human development performance.[17]

4

Governance Structures and Human Development

Advocates of democracy, reading earlier chapters of this book, should have been pleased that countries using democratic forms, particularly mature democracies, grew more rapidly than nondemocracies between 1973 and 1987. They should have been equally satisfied that democracies were just as willing as nondemocracies to take strong economic medicine in the 1980s and that they administered it just as effectively.

But they probably felt some discomfort when I also concluded that democratic forms were minor threads in the institutional fabric of the societal governance structure in countries with strong human development performance records.

Defining Governance Structures

Societal governance structures can be defined as a combination of institutions and rules that manage the relationships within and among civil society, political society, and the state within a nation.[1] These structures determine, for example, on what basis individuals can organize themselves in civic life, how they will participate in selecting political leaders, and whether the public sector will be responsive to their wishes.

Before continuing the discussion, it is important to define some additional components of governance structures, such as civil society, political society, and the state. Alfred Stepan's conceptions of these elements are particularly useful.[2] Stepan views civil society as the arena where individuals organize to advance their social and civic interests. Private citizens interact there to do business or to worship. But they also form associations such as business chambers, labor unions, and civic groups to promote their interests. Political society is the arena where the right to govern is contested. The state can be thought of as the mediating mechanism between the other two arenas. It includes "the continuous administrative, legal, bureaucratic and coercive system that attempts not only to manage the state apparatus but to structure relations between civil and public power and . . . many crucial relations within civil and political society."[3] The conception of governance structure I will use in this chapter is the overall set of relationships that Stepan's "state" attempts to manage.

For the purposes of this discussion, I will distinguish among three types of hypothetical governance structures—democratic, authoritarian, and totalitarian—based on different roles and relationships within the three arenas (see Table 4.1)[4] Where democratic governance structures exist civil society, political society, and the state are highly developed and differentiated and have strong two-way communication channels. The population has clearly defined, legally guaranteed space to carry out civic activity. Political society has separate, well-developed institutions that function according to stable, well-known rules. Citizens are free to change their national leaders through agreed-upon representative mechanisms. The state not only implements its citizens' policies based on guidelines transmitted through their representatives, but is also responsive to citizen pressure.

In contrast, in totalitarian societies the state, political society, and civil society are fused. A single party directs political society and dominates the state and civil society. Civil and political rights are denied. The state monopolizes communication channels and asserts control by directing orders downward. Fear promotes compliance.

Authoritarian societies are hybrids in which political society and the state overlap but are not fused. A single party dominates. Minority alternatives are permitted as long as they do not threaten the ruling party. Civil space is permitted, particularly for business activity. The connection between civil and political society is still controlled to assure continued preeminence by the dominant group. But this group renounces its monopoly of communication to permit some highly managed two-way information flows. The channels serve as a pressure valve, which allows the regime to adjust its economic and political strategy without losing control. (See Figure 4.1 for a graphic representation of these structures.)

TABLE 4.1 Typology of Governance Structures

Characteristics	Totalitarian regime	Authoritarian regime	Democracy
Who, what, and how			
Who participates in selecting leaders	Small group	Small group	All sectors
Civil liberties	Highly constrained	Constrained	Broad based
Ideology in initial stage of development	Very important	Important	Important
Ideology after initial stage of development	Very important	Less important	Important
Mass mobilization after initial stage	Very important	Less important	Somewhat important
Relation of state and civil society	Fused	Blurred	Separate
Key institutions			
Competitive parties	Eliminated	Permitted but controlled	Encouraged
Opposition press	Eliminated	Permitted but controlled	Encouraged
Nongovernment interest groups	Eliminated	Permitted but controlled	Actively encouraged
Military	Subordinate to party	Often dominates	Subordinate to civilians
Police and security	High coercive	Coercive	Subordinate to civilians

SOURCE: Based on Alfred Stepan's categorizations in *Rethinking Military Politics* (Princeton: Princeton University Press, 1988).

FIGURE 4.1   Civil and Political Relationships in the Three
               Governance Structures

Democratic governance structure

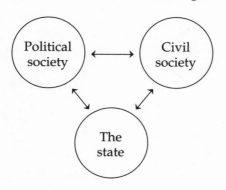

- Civil and political
  society and the state
  are fully differentiated.
- Full civil and political
  guarantees exist.
- Strong two-way channels
  of communication exist.

Authoritarian governance structure

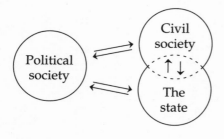

- Boundaries between
  state and civil society
  are blurred.
- Some civil space exists.
- Limited civil and
  political rights exist.
- Weak two-way channels
  of communication exist.

Democratic governance structure

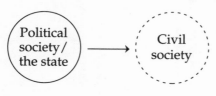

- State and political
  society are fused; civil
  society disappears.
- No civil or political
  rights exist.
- Communication is top-
  down, one-way.

SOURCE: Author, based on Alfred Stepan's typology in *Rethinking Military Politics* (Princeton: Princeton University Press, 1988).

These three hypothetical governance structures offer useful reference points for comparing elements of governance among the high, medium, and low human development performers.

Governance Structures and Human Development Performance

The governance structures of high human development performers

The governance structures of high, medium, and low human development performers are quite different (see Table 4.2).[5] The high human development performers had five enduring features that distinguished

TABLE 4.2   Developing Country Human Development Performance and Governance Structures, 1965–1987

	High HDI performers	Medium HDI performers	Low HDI performers
Number of countries	24	23	24
Political society			
Democratic regime type (%)	41	23	17
High or medium political rights (%)	65	54	29
Low political instability (%)	77	58	52
Civil society			
High or medium civil rights (%)	73	70	54
The state			
Regulator (0–20% of GNP) (%)	27	29	48
Promoter/provider (21–30% of GNP) (%)	54	29	26
Producer (above 30% of GNP) (%)	18	42	26
Average annual education and health expenditures as % of GNP	5	4	3
Economic policy			
Market economy (%)	60	29	41
Average total trade as % of GNP	48	32	36

SOURCE: Author.

them from other countries. First, there were virtually no totalitarian states in the high performance group. Almost all had relatively differentiated political, civic, and state arenas. For example, 73 percent maintained at least medium levels of civil rights with minimum guarantees of free speech, association, and press, and private property. Second, while fewer than half were democracies, two-thirds had some form of two-way communication channel between political and civil society that permitted corrective adjustments when there were problems. Some of the nondemocracies had, for example, open, nonpartisan municipal elections. Others permitted minority opposition parties even though they were kept in a disadvantaged position. Third, the state in these high human development performers was neither a weak and passive institution nor an immense, coercive, overly dominant producer state with an enormous public enterprise sector. Instead the majority of the high human development performers were active promoters of outwardly oriented, trade-based economic strategies that relied heavily on market-oriented economic institutions. Fourth, the state was not dormant in social policy either. It was a leader in basic education, technical education, and primary health delivery. These promoter states spent between 20 and 30 percent of gross national product (GNP) for all activity and about 5 percent for health and education. (None of this is meant to imply that all used their resources as efficiently as they might have.) Fifth, while levels of political and civil rights expanded during the period, this occurred with lower levels of political instability and regime turnover than in the medium and low performers.[6]

Why might this dynamic governance structure have served as a human development catalyst? The creation of civil space even within authoritarian regimes provided an arena from which a dynamic private sector could emerge. The long-term guarantee of at least some civil space under relatively stable economic and political rules encouraged confidence that permitted the private sector to expand. The presence of more than minimal political rights provided channels for dissent and policy correction even though it did not permit open competitive selection of national leaders. The economic leadership of these promoter states encouraged private initiative. The social investments built a human capital base, and the political channels allowed an increasingly educated population to pressure government for the maintenance of its social investments. Finally, the requirements of competing in a global economy reinforced the continued growth of differentiated, interactive civil, political, and state institutions. More specifically, competitive world-class enterprises needed a stable environment with open, fluid information, clear property rights, free association, and corrective mechanisms when government policy was not effective.

The governance structures of medium human development performers

The governance structures of the medium human development performers looked quite different from those of the high performers. Although medium-level human development performers had almost as large a civil space as the high level human development performers, the feedback channels between civil and political society were less developed (see Table 4.2). Not only did these nations make less use of democratic forms to elect national leaders (only 23 percent of the medium performers used democracy compared with 41 percent of the high performers), but they also permitted fewer general political liberties than the high performers. The long-term rules of the game were far more uncertain. More than 40 percent of the top executive officials were changed through coups in these countries between 1965 and 1987.

The medium-level performers also had a larger percentage of interventionist producer states (see Table 4.2) than the high performers. In 42 percent of these countries the state spent more than 30 percent of GNP. These nations had larger public enterprise sectors. They also pursued less outward-oriented, free market policies than their high-performing counterparts.

One might argue that medium human development performers did less well than the high performers because these states choked individual initiative, shielded their citizens from competitive pressures, and closed their ears to constructive policy criticism. Since their economic policies were more internally focused, these countries would have been less subject to international market forces. There may have been less incentive to expand information channels between civil and political society. By the time the 1980s arrived these countries were no longer capable of paying for a governance structure of this size and had serious problems developing a new economic model. Many had to adopt painful stabilization and structural adjustment programs.

The governance structures of low human development performers

The low human development performers had governance structures that hardly reached the large mass of their rural, subsistence agricultural populations. They maintained tight controls, however, on the groups they did reach. Within organized society governance took place through nondemocratic forms and with low levels of political and civil rights.

Although the governance structure of the low performers was repressive, the state was small in size and weak in its management of the economy and social policy compared with medium or high human development performers. These states might be thought of as regulators rather than promoters or producers. They spent a smaller percentage of GNP and invested less in social infrastructure than their counterparts.

Even though the leaders in these low-performing nations might have wanted to dominate and direct the entire economy, they lacked the resources or the talent base to do so. They did not have the dynamism to penetrate the subsistence sector and bring it into the market. Finally, the lack of two-way communication among civil society, the state, and politicians severely limited the state's ability to change its economic and political strategies to respond to pressing societal problems. This might explain why more than 50 percent of top national leaders were changed through coups.

The Roots of "Double Shock"

The analysis of the governance structures of high human development performers reveals that their market-oriented economic strategies were implemented within a relatively stable institutional and political context. The institutions developed slowly and incrementally and were built upon a human capital base that evolved even more slowly.

It seems strange then that "double shock"—rapid, simultaneous economic liberalization and democratization—became the treatment of choice for underdevelopment in the 1980s and 1990s, in spite of the evidence that no successful high human development performer in this study took such medicine while blazing its earlier path to high performance. Double-shock ideas also run counter to important recent studies by Samuel Huntington and Robert D. Putnam that conclude that the development of democratic institutions and civic culture takes decades, sometimes centuries.[7] Putnam argues that today's relatively effective democratic infrastructure in Northern Italy was built on a base of civic culture that evolved over centuries. He believes that a lack of similiar development in Southern Italy can be traced to the absence of this earlier civic base.

Why then did such a prescription emerge? It would be tempting to blame the international donors, particularly the World Bank and the International Monetary Fund (IMF), for the economic part of the recipe and the United States and European policy makers for the political formula. But the answer is a great deal more complicated.

The origins of the rapid economic and political changes that brought the twentieth century to a close ten years early can be found in the second oil shock in the late 1970s and the world recession in 1982. The international economic shocks touched every economy. They forced dynamic readjustment in healthy economies and virtually imploded those that already had imbalances exacerbated by heavy subsidies and large public sectors. They heightened popular discontent and put special pressure on all governments. Each continental transition had its own dynamics.

Latin American double shock

The first political transitions of the 1980s began in Latin America. In South America they were regime led—not externally imposed—and were probably triggered by a combination of external economic shocks and international events. Circumstances, rather than a single donor or foreign nation, led countries to self-administer double-shock medicine during the early Latin American transitions. The first countries to begin taking this medicine were Argentina, Brazil, and Uruguay. In Argentina, for example, the military elected to return to the barracks under extreme pressure from reform elements. Elections were held in October 1983, and Raúl Alfonsín became president. No outside nation or donor institution forced political reform on Argentina directly. The military opted for reform after its defeat in an unpopular war and its inability to solve the country's economic crisis. The economic side of the double-shock formula, Alfonsín's Plan Austral, emerged not because a donor imposed it, but rather because the nation was reeling from economic collapse and hyperinflation. The ideas of the World Bank and IMF influenced Argentina's policy makers, but these ideas were not imposed through conditionality, at least in early programs.

The second wave of Latin American political transitions, which took place in the mid-1980s in Bolivia, Honduras, Guatemala, and Panama, for example, was triggered by the same initial economic and political forces. By this time, however, international communications, donor pressure to conform to specific stabilization and economic adjustment guidelines, and political pressure for democratization played a more important role. By the mid-1980s the international media had informed most Latin Americans about the changes in the Southern Cone nations. The World Bank and the IMF had developed explicit conditions for the stabilization and structural adjustment loans that most nations needed. Bilateral donors like the United States had become advocates of democratization.

The story in Nicaragua and El Salvador in the 1980s was somewhat different than that in most of Latin America. While the same world economic shocks weakened authoritarian regimes in Nicaragua and El Salvador in the late 1970s, they contributed to societal rather than regime-led political transitions. Popular revolutions with international support helped overturn authoritarian governments. Furthermore, the economic polices of these new governments in the early 1980s were populist rather than liberal, and the political systems were either controlled or dominated by one party.

The dominant Latin American double-shock medicine reached Central America in the late 1980s. By this time the political side of double shock, democratization, emerged as an antidote for battlefield stalemates, the collapse of the former Soviet Union, United Nations and regional pressure for peace, and bilateral pressure from the United States. Stabilization and adjustment, the economic side of double shock, were the inevitable response to hyperinflation and the collapse of the populist economic models strained to the limits by war and instability. Even in these circumstances, the first Nicaraguan stabilization program was constructed by the Sandinistas rather than imposed by donors.

The Eastern European version of double shock

The transitions in the former Soviet Union and Eastern Europe were sparked and accelerated by the same worldwide recession that plagued Latin America in the early 1980s. There are a few initial parallels with the dynamics of the Latin American transition. In both regions economic reform was seen as a solution to a bankrupt economic model. In the Eastern European and Soviet case, the centrally planned economies exceeded their ability to generate economic growth successfully. In both regions the initial reforms were regime led. In the former Soviet Union glasnost and perestroika were President Gorbachev's initiatives to adapt his country's economic and political systems to the new global realities. In Eastern Europe embattled Communist parties negotiated transitions with strong domestic opposition groups, like Solidarity and the Catholic Church in Poland. Finally, neither donors nor outside nations imposed the political or economic formulas in either Latin America or Eastern Europe.

The similarities, however, stop there. While the new regimes in Eastern Europe and the former Soviet Union also took double-shock medicine as an antidote for economic collapse and political unrest, the results have been very different from those in Latin America. In former socialist states with few entrepreneurs and no capitalist institutions, the short-term economic transition is slow, painful, and uncertain in the eyes of the population. There is no blueprint for the construction of markets from the wreckage of a centrally planned economy.

The simultaneous political opening has permitted highly vocal discontent. Certainly there has been discontent in Latin America during the adjustment process. But the Eastern European and former Soviet variant is a special brew because of the combination of a real lack of sustained economic performance, the baggage of expectations from a previous welfare state, and the absence of a culture of initiative. The result is an environment of paralysis and suspicion that may make it difficult to keep the economic transition moving.

Asian rejection of double shock

The response of East and Southeast Asia to the economic downturns of the early 1980s has been to substitute double-shock with single-shock policies where possible. The more market-oriented Asian nations, such as Korea and Taiwan, have fine tuned their economic strategies while turning single shock into controlled political opening. The goal of such openings has been to open new channels for opposition while leaving the dominant political parties in power. For example, Taiwan began efforts at legalizing opposition political parties and guaranteeing broader civil liberties between 1986 and 1990. But the new rules make it difficult for the opposition to become more than a vocal minority.

The former centrally planned Asian nations, like China, Vietnam, and Laos, have adopted a second variant of single shock, using phased economic reform with little political opening. When these countries have considered political reform, it has been concentrated in the dominant party structure. The brief adventures with double shock were reversed quickly after experiences like Tiananmen Square in China.

African acquiescence to double shock

The African version of the double shock story began in the late 1980s, almost ten years after the first Latin American experiments. It is more a product of international ripple effects and external pressures than the story elsewhere in the world. This region began with single-shock stabilization policies in the early 1980s. After repeated false starts the impetus for double-shock policies grew because of donor discontent with African government performance. The second part of double shock in Africa—democratization—got a healthy boost from frustrated donors and powerful nations who felt that governments were ignoring economic targets and that corruption plagued the implementation process in many African nations. For example, donor working groups informed Kenya that resources for economic reform would not be forthcoming without changes in "governance," the code word for reducing corruption and pursuing democratization. Donors are now imposing double shock throughout Africa.

Double Shock: Performance Lessons from the 1980s

Although the debate about the judiciousness of rapid economic and political reform in the 1980s continues, there is enough evidence about country performance to begin to identify the initial effects of these reforms.

Positive effects

First and foremost, stabilization programs helped contain economic crisis by stopping hyperinflation in many countries. Hyperinflation is an ill that no country can afford. It destroys the average citizen's purchasing power, devastates people on fixed incomes, and undermines trust in a country's economic and political institutions. This is an important and positive contribution. Adjustment policies also helped reverse economic collapse in some nations.[8] Even though living standards eroded in the developing world in the 1980s, it is not difficult to imagine what might have happened had the economic collapse not been reversed. Another benefit was that most countries began to restructure the state to use their public resources more efficiently. This step reversed a long period in which the public sector had become bloated and inefficient and many of its public enterprises had become loss leaders. Furthermore, the pressure for competitiveness may have had an important psychological impact on the population and policy makers. People may have become more aware that there is no international "free lunch," and such awareness may have helped create a more receptive climate for new approaches to education, productivity in the workplace, and national policy. Finally, the overall crisis provided many nations with a chance to rethink their entire development strategy. In countries like Mexico, Chile, and Costa Rica, this may have resulted in a political and economic readjustment that will allow them to be competitive for several decades.

The political openings also had their benefits. The foundations for the two-way communication channels among citizens, politicians, and governments that proved essential in the high human development performers were constructed in many new settings. The evidence of these changes is documented by the overall improvements in civil and political liberty ratings in developing countries in the 1980s.

As this process continued, a new generation of citizens gained experience in shaping government policy and managing institutions. Greater citizen responsiveness also led to reforms in judicial systems, social service delivery, and the formation and professionalization of new political parties, legislatures, and civic organizations. There is at least the hope that these experiments will result in more service-oriented, responsive systems that will provide the foundation for lasting democratic political institutions.

Problems

While many important gains took place, the economic and political reforms of the 1980s also generated problems that have yet to be resolved. For example, while stabilization and adjustment might have been good recipes for stopping hyperinflation and reversing economic collapse, they generally did not stimulate the deep-rooted changes in economic and political institutions required to make the reforms sustainable. Furthermore, governments may have created unrealistic expectations by overselling the benefits of double-shock policies. As improvements in living standards have lagged, popular euphoria with democracy and market-oriented adjustments has turned sour. Such disillusionment can result in a return to military rule with popular support, as took place in Peru in 1992.

In addition, the indiscriminate attack on the state may have left the public sector in many developing countries too weak to promote human development at all. Table 4.2 shows that there were no tiny, regulator states among the ranks of the high human development performers in the past thirty years. By implication the poorest nations today may actually need the opposite medicine of that proposed in the 1980s—a slightly larger and clearly more dynamic state.

Furthermore, cutting investments in human capital to reduce fiscal deficits may have destroyed the life chances of at least a generation of citizens and weakened the very foundation on which high human development performance was based earlier. In addition, economic development based on resource-intensive production for the international market assumed that countries can pursue such a strategy without reaching global limits to environmental sustainability. What if this turns out to be a faulty assumption?

Finally, nations making a transition from totalitarian political systems and centrally planned economies presented special problems for which there are as yet no solutions. Introducing rapid market reforms in environments with a long history of central planning proved to be like pouring fertilizer on sand and expecting plants to grow. Neither citizens nor institutions responded rapidly or effectively to the market forces unleashed by macroeconomic reform. The short-term result was control of hyperinflation but with economic stagnation and high unemployment. The public backlash may turn out to be stronger than in most developing countries, since the citizenry has long been accustomed to being taken care of. One observer of the centrally planned economies argues that the early retirement age in those countries has produced an especially large group of pensioners who will vote to reverse reforms as their fixed incomes are destroyed.[9]

An Alternative View: Transforming Governance Structures to Promote High Human Development Performance

Given the performance of political and economic reform in the 1980s, policies must be adjusted in light of the lessons about the underlying conditions of high human development performance from earlier decades. Some general lessons from earlier decades are the following:

1. The high human development performers made early, active investments in social infrastructure that did not offer immediate benefits but provided a strong human capital base.

2. The public sector was an active promoter of outwardly oriented economic policies within the context of a market economy.

3. The state was neither too small and weak nor too dominant, production minded, and oppressive.

4. There was always room for more efficient public sector performance.

5. High human development performers were equally likely to use democratic as nondemocratic forms for the selection of national leaders but maintained medium to high levels of civil and political rights.

6. Regime type was not as important as the two-way feedback mechanisms between civil and political society that permitted dynamic adjustments in economic and social policy and in institutions.

7. Performance gains in high human development performers took place slowly and steadily during long periods of political stability, with fairly consistent and well-known rules of the game rather than abrupt, shock-type changes in leaders, institutions, and rules.

Policy makers should keep these lessons in mind, along with some special insights based on the experience with policy reform in the 1980s. For example,

1. Macroeconomic policy reform without simultaneous efforts at institutional capacity building may weaken the long-term sustainability of the reform. This lesson is particularly critical in systems moving away from totalitarian rule and central economic planning.

2. It is risky to mislead the population into thinking that the quality of their lives will improve dramatically in the short run from

stabilization and adjustment programs. It might be wiser to prepare them for losses first and then smaller gains during adjustment.

3. The government must continue to make investments in the human capital base of the society.

4. In an era of increasingly scarce resources, a focus on competitiveness and links between incentives and performance may be critical.

5. Promoting private initiative is vital, but slashing the state indiscriminately may destroy one of the key elements of the governance structure that played a critical role in achieving high human development performance elsewhere. An alternative approach might be public sector reform that takes each nation's special circumstances into account and that treats different elements of the public sector with different approaches.

The last point about a more tailored approach to the transformation of the public sector deserves special attention. For high performers like Chile, Mexico, and Costa Rica, the message may be to fine tune, restructure, and streamline the state in the 1990s. In contrast, in a country like Guatemala, where state expenditures for health and education have traditionally been among the smallest in Latin America, the message may be to collect more taxes and spend more to reduce illiteracy and improve health status. In addition, reform strategies must be tailored to the special state activities they address, such as (1) economic management (the activities of the ministries that make and implement economic policy); (2) public enterprises (electricity, water, and other activities); (3) social sector management (for example, education and health); (4) defense, security, and justice; and (5) decentralized activities of lower units of government and new civic and political organizations.

Here are some examples of what tailored approaches to transformation of the state in the 1990s might look like in high, medium, and low human development performers. They correspond to the typical profiles presented in Table 4.2 and are meant to be general examples. Specific strategies will have to be adapted to each country's individual circumstances.

Adapting the state in high human development performers

If countries like Costa Rica and Mexico, Botswana and Cameroon, and Korea and Thailand want to maintain their continued path of high human development performance, they must make their public sectors smaller, more dynamic in promoting private initiative, more client-oriented and efficient, capable of competing in quality service delivery, and effective in providing service to special groups others cannot reach successfully. The specific reform agenda might include changes in a number of areas.

Economic management   While high-performing developing countries have done a better job than others in economic management, they must still fine tune their policies, organizational structures, and processes. They might:

- Build a deeper institutional capacity for defining and implementing policies. Long-term and in-house training for key professionals and the development of stronger analytic staff units to support policy makers are essential.

- Cut red tape. Current regulations and the systems that produce them must be overhauled. A competitive environment with consistent rules must be promoted.

- Modernize economic management ministries. Ministries should update their methods of economic analysis.

- Improve revenue collection systems and implement tax reform.

- Bring public budgeting and control systems into the twentieth century.

- Encourage public debate of economic policy. Public officials should be comfortable meeting with representatives of business and labor to discuss economic policy. They should be capable of listening to suggestions and incorporating them into their own agendas. They need to be adept at negotiating and developing pacts with the community.

Public enterprises   Unlike the medium and low human development performers, the public enterprise sector has not been immense in the high human development performers. What is required is a combination of privatization in some critical areas and restructuring in others. These countries should:

- Withdraw from public production where private firms have been traditionally successful. The high human development performers have been less involved in direct production than other nations, but there are exceptions like the Costa Rican state cement enterprises and the Panamanian public sugar refineries.

- Privatize banking, insurance, and foreign trade. In many high human development performers, state monopolies in these areas have impeded the development of private agricultural and industrial enterprises that can compete on the international market.

- Restructure public utilities, transportation, and communications. The high performers could make major efficiency gains through full privatization of some enterprises, partial privatization of others, and restructuring of still others.

- Use performance contracts and introduce competition for improved performance where public enterprises must exist because of perceptions of national interest.

- Do not trade public for private monopolies. Insure that the newly privatized firms are subject to regulatory and market pressure to compete.

Social sector management The former high human development performers had more effective health and education delivery systems than their medium- and poor-performing counterparts. Budget deficits, however, make restructuring inevitable. These countries must:

- Reconsider universal coverage for elective health procedures, but make sure that high-quality basic services in health and education are maintained.

- Promote lower-cost alternatives in the delivery of education and health services. Experiment with cost-sharing and cost-recovery mechanisms.

- Improve the management of social security and pension funds. Provide private alternatives where possible.

- Reorient education systems to help citizens adapt to a more competitive global economy.

Defense, security, and justice These systems have lagged notoriously behind others in the former high human development performers. They have been slow, arbitrary, corrupt, and coercive. Major reforms are necessary. Policy makers should:

- Streamline slow, cumbersome police and judicial systems and procedures and make them more transparent.

- Promote an independent judiciary, with better-paid judges who are safe from intimidation.

- Experiment with model courts and judicial reform.

- Provide training and opportunities to reform police and security organizations. Make police more subject to citizen oversight.

- Institutionalize civilian oversight of the military and keep the military out of politics.

New civil and political actors and local governments   The continued capacity of high human development performers to adapt to economic and political change may depend upon the effective performance of new elements of civil and political society. Policy makers therefore must:

- Strengthen the new legislative staffs through training.

- Provide support services to improve management of new civic organizations and nongovernmental organizations.

- Encourage the professionalization of new political parties, labor unions, and business organizations.

- Promote dialogue among new civic groups and government.

- Decentralize funding, delivery, and control of key government services to more local governments where possible.

Transforming the state in medium human development performers

Public sector reform in the medium human development performers requires transformation rather than adaptation. The state must be converted from a heavy-handed, highly intrusive producer that spent far more than 30 percent of GNP to a smaller, more efficient promoter of economic and social activity. While the recommendations made for the former high human development performers also apply, some additional special comments are necessary.

Economic management   Economic management in the typical medium human development performers suffered from four serious problems. First, the state choked creative private initiative with regulations and procedures. Second, it created a culture of producer and consumer dependence through subsidies. Third, it monopolized policy analysis within the dominant party in government. Fourth, officials working in such systems often developed attitudes of arrogance, suspicion, distrust, and bureaucratic control. To break this vicious cycle, these countries must:

- Adjust macroeconomic policies to promote an outward orientation.

- Streamline procedures and regulations.

- Promote alternative sources of policy analysis within business chambers, labor unions, and political parties.

- Retrain economic policy makers and managers to be catalysts rather than bureaucratic controllers.

- Develop a professional second-level analytical staff in the ministries to provide continuity while political-level officials rotate.

Public enterprises   Unlike the high human development performers, the majority of medium human development performers had immense public enterprise sectors heavily involved in activities normally carried out by the private sector. Policy makers must:

- Prepare careful portfolio analyses of the public enterprises and decide which enterprises to close, restructure and keep, restructure and sell, and simply sell.

- Eliminate the soft budget constraint for public enterprises and impose efficiency criteria.

- Aggressively withdraw from public production of goods that can be produced efficiently by private sector enterprises.

Social sector management   In the social sectors medium human development performers have misdirected spending and delivered services inefficiently. For example, a disproportionate share of education expenditures in many of these countries went to support virtually free, poor-quality university education with weak admissions standards. The systems produced a mass of graduates, unaccustomed to performance standards, who could not be absorbed into the job market. In health, universal systems were promised. But budget constraints prohibited adequate staffing and provision of materials and supplies.

A revolution must take place in education and health that refocuses resources on the human capital base necessary for nations who must compete in a global economy. These countries must:

- Redirect educational expenditures to literacy, primary education, and technical education and to primary and preventive health.

- Refocus education on the development of problem-solving capacity, attitudes that promote performance and quality, and participation in a democratic society.

- Raise tax revenues for education and health, and cross-subsidize where necessary to build the human capital base.

- Pressure employers to provide more health and education opportunities for their workers.

Defense, security, and justice   Whereas in the high human development performers the goal is to make arbitrary systems conform to the letter and spirit of the laws, in the medium performers the task is to develop guarantees and transparent systems that did not exist previously. More serious adjustment of attitudes and longer-term institutional capacity building will also be necessary. These countries should:

- Study the problems in security, justice, and defense systems and design major reform plans.

- Promote dialogues and pacts that guarantee the time frames and conditions under which the military withdraws from politics and in which transitions can take place peacefully.

- Aggressively recruit and train new officials committed to a more open, participative society.

- Encourage the retirement of older officials who are less committed to societal change.

Civil society and decentralization   Probably the toughest task is expanding civil space and opening channels of political participation where they did not exist before. New initiatives should:

- Encourage special dialogues, pacts, negotiated settlements of disputes, and other mechanisms for reaching social agreement among groups unaccustomed to talking rather than fighting.

- Provide legal guarantees for new civil and political organizations.

- Support training and education to develop analytical and management capacity in new groups.

- Focus international media attention on government relations with new organizations to help provide some protection from repression.

Building basic public capacity in poor human development performers

Low human development performers have proved incapable of sparking human development at all. Officials are poorly trained, and services are inefficient. Citizens, unprotected by political and civil guarantees, can hardly be expected to pressure the state to be responsive. Furthermore, because of a lack of resources and overall weak capacity, the public sector has hardly touched the lives of the majority of the population, many of whom survive through subsistence agriculture. Although the state could not or did not reach these people, it served some other small but dominant groups far too well and repressed others under its control.

If human development is to take place in these small, regulator states, they must build basic capacity rather than dismantle it. This task requires a different approach than the adaptations and transformations described earlier. Three major reorientations must take place. First, the conditions must be created that will transform the state's allegiance from service to a small group to service to the nation. This will not be easy. It requires either sufficient civil and political pluralism to keep countervailing pressure on the bureaucracy or a well-indoctrinated elite of civil servants who will serve the public even in the absence of pressure to do so. In a world where monopolies have not proved to be responsive, it is hard to imagine that government by disinterested mandarins will work. So creating countervailing forces is essential. Second, a series of actions must help change the public sector from a regulator or rent seeker to a catalyst for development. This requires complicated institutional capacity building.

It will take time. Third, scarce resources must be used efficiently to begin to build the human capital base. Ironically all of these tasks may require spending more public funds in education and health, for example, rather than cutting back as the global recipe requires.

When resources are scarce, strong focus is required. Of the three reorientations, we probably know most about how to deliver health and education services to build human capital and how to build capacity for economic policy making. Perhaps initial efforts should begin here, based on best demonstrated practices in these areas.

Economic management   Basic economic management capacity must be created where it did not exist before. This requires investments in people and key institutions. These countries should:

- Develop a small cadre of macroeconomic policy professionals who will promote dynamic market-oriented initiatives and provide paraprofessionals to support them.

- Encourage the design of macroeconomic policies that send general signals rather than those that require lots of staff and complicated procedures to implement.

- Build small, efficient, professional institutions to perform the vital functions of economic management.

- Promote private enterprise support networks through small business extension programs and education and training programs.

- Encourage pacts among diverse political groups that will allow minimum consensus for continuity in economic policy and the development of a cadre of professional economic managers who can serve all government.

Public enterprises   The greatest opportunity in the low human development performers that have not developed large public enterprise sectors is the opportunity not to develop them in the areas of goods production. Where public enterprises have been developed, the earlier recommendations for privatizing, streamlining, and restructuring apply. Public enterprises in water, electricity, and social infrastructure, however, may be necessary and important.

- Stimulate the development of private systems to provide water, electricity, and sewage treatment where possible. Where private alternatives cannot be used, develop small-scale, efficient public or mixed enterprises.

Social sector management   Basic investments in health and education are necessary to begin to develop the human capital base. Accordingly, these countries should:

- Refocus educational resources on programs in literacy, basic education, and technical education rather than elite education.

- Target health resources for primary health care, health education, and sanitation (water systems) programs that have been shown to have the greatest impact on health status.

- Make cost-effective education and health investments based on best demonstrated practices in other parts of the world.

- Encourage as many community-based private services as is feasible. Provide seed money for these organizations to improve their delivery.

- Complement public services with donor programs and international voluntary programs.

Defense, justice, and security   These services have been among the worst delivered. They have often been coercive, arbitrary, and corrupt. Long-term capacity-building efforts must be undertaken to develop basic systems, train people, and make organizations responsive. Countries must:

- Reduce military spending and develop pacts with timetables to get the military out of government.

- Develop basic laws for civil and political guarantees.

- Follow the prescriptions discussed earlier to build responsive, fair institutions.

- Keep these systems in the spotlight of the international media and publicize abuses.

Political and civil society   The tasks in these areas are also massive and long term. Low performers should:

- Provide legal recognition to new civic organizations and political parties.

- Promote organizational development through training and education.

- Complement national efforts to strengthen local civic groups with efforts assisted by donors and international voluntary organizations.

- Publicize successes in civic organizations.

A special comment on Eastern Europe and the former Soviet Union

For the former totalitarian societies with centrally planned economies, there are special problems in the development of new structures of governance. There is a long-term task of building institutions that respond to market signals and empowering people to solve problems in organizations. Macroeconomic policy reform without long-term institutional development is doomed to fail.

Part II of this book has shown what can be concluded about high human development performers from the study of a big data set over a twenty-two-year period. In Part III I will ask some of the same questions with a smaller group of countries and look at the dynamics in more detail.

PART III

HUMAN DEVELOPMENT IN CENTRAL AMERICA

Context, Policies, and Human Development in Central America

Part II of this book identified six features of developing-country high human development performers between 1965 and 1987. They entered the mid-1960s with a higher-quality human resource base and were not likely to be in sub-Saharan Africa. They were highly stable politically and pursued outwardly oriented economic policies. Their economies grew more rapidly and their governments invested more in health and education than the poorer-performing nations.

But the cross-sectional and longitudinal analysis of large data sets presented in earlier chapters had two weaknesses. First, it showed little about how policies and context interacted to stimulate or impede human development at the country level. Second, human development performance was sufficiently varied by geographic region to make global comparisons of limited use.

To overcome these problems I will consider the same basic questions discussed earlier, but this time in more depth in one subregion, Central America. This chapter places Central American human development performance in the context of the global story presented earlier. It pays particular attention to the role of context and its interaction with economic and social policies.[1]

Why Central America?

Six Central American countries (Costa Rica, El Salvador, Guatemala, Honduras, Nicaragua, and Panama) have sufficient similarities to make them an ideal subregion for the study of human development performance.[2] Together they form a land bridge that links Mexico with South America, populated by 25 million citizens of a similar colonial, cultural, and racial heritage. The overwhelming bulk of the population is Catholic and shares both cultural and political institutions heavily influenced by Spanish colonial rule and a more recent North American overlay.

Certainly there are ethnic and racial differences within Central America. Fifty percent of the population is Ladino, a mixture of Spanish and Indian ancestry, while more than 20 percent are Indians whose primary language is not Spanish. Finally, there is a small English-speaking black population along the region's Atlantic coast. Differences in ethnic diversity among the Central American countries, however, are not nearly as great as those found in other regions of the world.[3]

Furthermore, the economic structure of these nations is remarkably similar. All have been exporters of primary products like coffee, cotton, cattle, sugar, and bananas. They have pursued similar economic policies to promote these exports over time. In addition, they are mostly small nations with between 3 and 5 million inhabitants in 1991 (with the exception of Guatemala, with 9 million).

In spite of their similarities these nations differ from one another in an important way. They include two high human development performers (Costa Rica and Panama), three medium performers (Honduras, Guatemala, and Nicaragua), and one low performer (El Salvador). This diversity mirrors the human development performance spread found in the global analysis in Chapters 2, 3, and 4. Part of the purpose of this chapter is to discuss how nations with so much in common could end up with such widely different human development performance records.

Central America in a global context

Central America is a good surrogate for world human development trends. The region's baseline characteristics in 1965 were similar to world averages. For example, although the Central American nations had smaller populations than the average nation (see Table 5.1), their initial human development index (HDI) score in 1965 was 56 and the world average was 55. Between 1965 and 1987 their human development and per capita income gains were close to world averages. For example, Central America's annual HDI disparity reduction rate averaged about 2.6 percent

TABLE 5.1 Central American Human Development Performance and Global Trends, 1965–1987

Region or country	Population, 1965 (millions)	1965 PPP-adjusted per capita GDP (US$)	1965 Literacy (%)	1965 Life expectancy (years)	1987 PPP-adjusted per capita GDP (US$)	1987 Literacy (%)	1987 Life expectancy (years)	HDI score (%) 1965	HDI score (%) 1987	Disparity reduction rate (%)	Average annual GDP growth (%)
Central America											
Costa Rica	1.5	1,930	84	65	3,760	93	74	76	92	4.93	5.1
El Salvador	3.0	1,290	49	54	1,733	62	62	52	65	1.43	3.1
Guatemala	4.5	1,365	38	49	1,957	48	62	45	61	1.59	4.2
Honduras	2.3	824	45	50	1,119	56	64	43	60	1.62	4.1
Nicaragua	1.8	2,217	50	50	2,209	66	63	55	70	1.79	1.8
Panama	1.3	1,604	73	63	4,009	87	72	69	89	4.62	4.7
Average	2.4	1,538	56	55	2,464	68	66	56	73	2.66	3.8
World average	15.0	2,183	52	54	4,274	63	62	55	67	2.86	4.1
Developing-country HD performance group average											
Lowest	8.6	577	18	42	758	31	51	24	37	0.87	2.5
Medium	12.0	1,507	40	52	2,274	62	61	45	64	2.07	4.9
Highest	17.2	1,437	54	56	4,099	79	66	55	80	3.95	6.0
Developing country average	12.6	1,174	37	50	2,377	57	59	41	60	2.30	4.5

SOURCE: Author's data set.

a year while the world averaged 2.8 percent. The region's economy grew at 3.8 percent while the global economy expanded at 4 percent a year.

Central America's human development performance was above average for the ninety developing countries included in this study (see Table 5.1). In 1965 Central Americans enjoyed a level of human development higher than that of citizens of Africa, South Asia, and the Middle East; lower than that of citizens of the rest of Latin America and the Caribbean; and about equal to that of citizens of Southeast Asia (see Table 2.2). The Central American countries reduced their human development index disparities more than their African, South Asian, Middle Eastern, Caribbean, and Eastern European neighbors.

Individual Central American countries were generally better off than the average developing country in their specific human development performance group (see Table 5.1). No Central American country was as poor as the average African or South Asian country. For example, Costa Rica and Panama were above the average for the global top human development performers' group. El Salvador, in the low human development group, performed far above the group average. The three nations in the medium group, Guatemala, Honduras, and Nicaragua, were fairly representative of that group.

Central America and global high human development performers

Central American's two high human development performers, Costa Rica and Panama, had many of the same characteristics that distinguished other high human development performers (see Table 5.2). For example, they entered the mid-1960s with a much stronger human capital base than their neighbors. Costa Rica, in particular, had substantially lower levels of political instability than other nations in the region. Both nations had more open economies and greater annual gross domestic product (GDP) and export growth. Finally, they invested substantially more in social expenditures and spent far less on defense than their medium- and low-performing Central American neighbors.

Conflicting Views on the Role of Context and Policies in Central American Economic Performance

The pessimists: Central America as a prisoner of world economic cycles

Although Part II of this book showed that external factors were not a great impediment to high human development performance, pessimists might

TABLE 5.2   Key Economic, Political, and Social Characteristics of Central American Countries

	Costa Rica	El Salvador	Guatemala	Honduras	Nicaragua	Panama	Central American average
Index of ethnic diversity	0.07	0.18	0.64	0.16	0.18	0.28	0.25
HDI score, 1965	75.53	51.91	45.00	42.90	54.54	68.86	56.46
% of nonprogrammed changes in presidents	0	54	71	64	62	57	51
% of democratic regimes, 1965–1987	100	18	22	57	0	22	37
Economic openness	0.69	0.64	0.42	0.68	0.62	0.84	0.65
Annual export growth	7.0	2.4	4.8	3.1	2.3	5.8	4.2
Annual GDP growth	5.1	3.1	4.2	4.1	1.8	4.7	3.8
Education spending as % of GNP	5.20	2.86	1.60	3.19	1.43	3.30	2.93
Health spending as % of GNP	3.10	1.31	0.83	1.28	1.13	3.14	1.80
Defense spending as % of GNP	0.61	1.56	1.13	2.02	2.15	0.13	1.27
Defense spending as % of education and health spending	7.30	37.50	46.70	45.20	83.60	2.00	37.05
Annual disparity reduction rate (%)	4.93	1.43	1.59	1.62	1.79	4.62	2.66

SOURCE: Author's data set.

predict that the Central American nations would be more sensitive to these forces than the norm because of their small size and greater economic openness.[4] The preliminary evidence provides support for the pessimists' arguments. Figures 5.1 and 5.2 describe the relatively greater influence of external shocks on the small, highly open Central American economies compared with their large Latin American neighbors. Figure 5.1 shows that the Central American recessions coincide closely with global recessions. (Total trade was used as a measure of economic activity from 1930 to 1982 since GDP data for the region exist only after 1950.)[5]

In contrast, the business cycles of the six largest Latin American economies exhibit a greater degree of independence from fluctuations in the global economy (see Figure 5.2). While the large economies of Latin America were heavily affected by global recessions, particularly in 1975 and 1982–1983, there were other downturns in 1952, 1956, 1964, and 1972 that were not related to world economic recession.

Many factors coincide to make small nations much more sensitive to world business cycles than their large neighbors, and the Central American countries are no exception.[6] First, dependence upon a small number of export products that have a disproportionately large impact on overall economic activity make the Central American economies highly vulnerable. For example, in 1984 exports comprised almost one-third of Central America's economic activity but only 14 percent in the large Latin American countries (see Table 5.3). At the same time the top ten export products in Central America accounted for almost 50 percent of their total exports. In contrast the top ten exports of the six largest Latin American countries accounted for less than 30 of their total exports. Thus, Central Americans feel the effects of price fluctuations and changes in overall world demand much more acutely than their neighbors.

Second, this problem is exacerbated by the kinds of products that Central America exports: coffee, sugar, bananas, beef, and cotton. The barriers to entry for production of these products are few, and as a result world overproduction is great. At the same time substitutes for many of these products, for example, high-fructose corn syrup as a replacement for sugar, are becoming more abundant.

Third, in spite of the success of Central America's regional common market, its small size and the even smaller size of each country's internal market left the region with little to fall back on when there were problems in the world economy. The average population of the Central American countries in 1965 was only 2.5 million people and its common market of 25 million people compared unfavorably with the average population size of the six largest Latin American countries of 49 million inhabitants. It has been much easier for Mexico and Brazil to turn inward in their import substitution phase than for El Salvador or Costa Rica. In addition,

FIGURE 5.1   GDP Growth for the United States and the United
Kingdom and Growth Rates of Total Trade for Central
America, 1930–1985

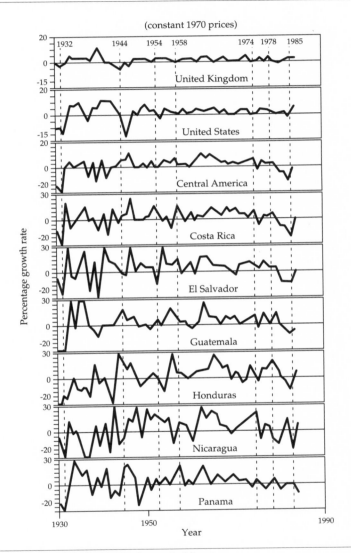

(constant 1970 prices)

NOTE: Recessions are marked with a broken vertical line.
SOURCE: Prepared by Antonio Colindres and Rodrigo Valverde, Central American Institute of Business
Administration (INCAE), 1986. Data for the Central American countries use central bank and customs
data 1930–1985; data for the United Kingdom and United States are from The Economist, *World Business
Cycles* (London, 1982).

FIGURE 5.2   GDP Growth for the World and the Six Largest Latin American Countries, 1950–1984

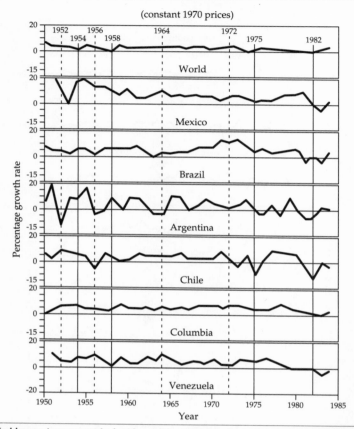

NOTE: World recessions are marked with a solid vertical line. Latin American recessions that do not coincide with world recessions are marked with a broken vertical line.
SOURCE: Central American Institute of Business Administration (INCAE), 1986. Prepared with data from The Economist, *World Business Cycles* (London, 1982).

problems in implementing common tariff legislation and establishing regional integration industries made the common market less effective than had been hoped.

Other problems that normally inhibit the performance of small economies are the limited human resource base, the lack of ability to generate technology, difficulty in developing products with international brand-name recognition, lack of resources to establish

TABLE 5.3   Structural Comparison of Six Largest Latin American Countries with Central America

Country	Population, 1984 (millions)	Exports as % of GDP, 1984	Contribution of 10 main products to total exports, 1978-1984 (%)	Agricultural sector as % of GDP, 1981-1984	Industrial sector as % of GDP, 1981-1984
Central America					
Costa Rica	2.4	39	60	20	21
El Salvador	4.7	21	66	26	17
Guatemala	7.7	15	47	25	15
Honduras	4.2	28	34	30	15
Nicaragua	3.1	18	60	23	24
Panama	2.1	41	32	10	9
Total[a]	24.2	27	49	23	16
Six largest Latin American countries					
Argentina	30.0	14	16	15	23
Brazil	131.1	11	31	9	27
Chile	11.8	24	47	9	20
Colombia	28.4	13	54	22	21
Mexico	77.0	13	4	9	24
Venezuela	16.8	11	n.a.	6	18
Total[a]	295.1	14	30	12	22

n.a. = not available.
a. Unweighted numerical averages.
SOURCE: Inter-American Development Bank, *Economic and Social Progress in Latin America: 1985* (Washington, D.C., 1986).

marketing channels, and the inability to develop strong local banking and insurance sectors.[7]

If the arguments of the pessimists are convincing, one would expect Central American business cycles to closely mirror world cycles. Furthermore, other external factors such as negative terms of trade and downturns in specific commodity prices should affect the region a great deal. The most extreme forms of the argument advanced by dependency theorists in the past concluded that Central America was a prisoner to world economic forces and that its domestic economic policy could do little to change the situation.

The optimists: economic policies matter

Despite the arguments of the pessimists, if the global findings presented earlier about the importance of policies in overcoming external constraints to human development apply to Central America, we would expect the high performers to have found effective strategies to reduce the risk of economic downturn due to external shocks.

There are at least four potential strategies for lowering the risk of poor performance because of such shocks. First, countries could increase agricultural acreage, productivity, and quality, to maintain returns even with deteriorating world prices. Second, they could diversify agricultural products and expand into non–Central American markets. Third, they could form regional common markets. And fourth, sectors like industry or services might provide new sources of growth. A combination of all four options might provide an economic strategy that would lower the risk of being dependent on the world economy.

These strategies can be illustrated through the use of a payoff matrix (see Figure 5.3). The y-axis has a continuum of low to high GDP growth and the x-axis shows the level of risk due to external economic shocks. The economic options with high payoff potential (high GDP growth) and low risk due to fluctuations in the world economy appear in the upper left-hand box of the matrix (labeled A). The options with low payoff potential and low risk appear in the lower left-hand box of the matrix (labeled B). High-payoff, high-risk strategies are in the upper right-hand box of the matrix (labeled C), and high-risk, low-payoff strategies are in the lower right-hand box (labeled D).

Export monoculture is a high-risk, variable-payoff strategy. It would appear in box C during world commodity price booms and in box D during bust periods. Strategies based on highly diversified products and markets might appear in boxes A and B. These strategies might never produce the phenomenal returns of export monoculture during commodity price

FIGURE 5.3   Classification of Economic Strategies by Risk and Payoff

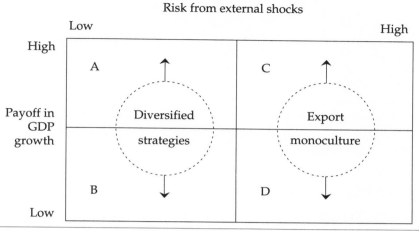

SOURCE: Author.

booms. They would, however, never be subject to the total collapse that is a result of dependence on a single product.

Few optimists would argue that world economic cycles, commodity prices, and terms of trade do not matter. But if policies indeed make a difference, one might expect a region like Central America to outperform the world economy when its strategies are based on diverse products and markets.

Now I would like to use the region as a laboratory to study the interaction of external factors like world economic cycles, commodity price fluctuations, and changes in terms of trade, with policy responses like getting greater productivity out of single products, diversifying products and external markets, forming regional common markets, and adding dynamic growth strategies in additional sectors like industry or services. This can be done by identifying periods in the development of the world economy and observing what happened simultaneously in Central America. Four types of economic periods are distinguished: (1) major crisis (which includes a strong contraction and the first two years of immediate recovery), (2) minor crisis (which includes a weak contraction and the first two years of immediate recovery), (3) weak sustained growth, and (4) strong sustained growth.[8] I shall review the trend periods first and then discuss the interaction of context and policies.

A Review of Central American Economic Cycles since 1930

Table 5.4 identifies eight trend periods in the world economy since 1930: two major crises (1930–1934 and 1944–1949); three minor crises (1954–1961, 1974–1977, and 1978–1985); and three periods of strong sustained growth (1935–1943, 1950–1953, and 1962–1973).[9] In six of the eight periods, the region's expansions and contractions move in the same direction as the world economy. In two of the eight periods, 1935–1943 and 1944–1949, Central American economic cycles moved in the opposite direction of the world trend, for reasons that will be explained shortly. I shall review the specific history of each period briefly before returning to the discussion of the role of context versus policies.

1930–1934: Major world crisis

Between 1930 and 1934 the world economy suffered the most serious three-year contraction that it would experience for the next sixty years. The combined rate of GDP growth of the United States and the United Kingdom was −1.7 percent. Economic decline reached its trough in 1932, and world recovery began with moderate average growth for 1933–1934 of 3.2 percent.

In Central America the rate of economic decline was sharper than that of the world economy. World prices for the region's key products, coffee and bananas, plummeted, ending a product expansion phase that began in 1900 (see Table 5.4). World coffee commodity stocks increased and terms of trade moved against Central America. The 1930s signaled a decline of the banana industry, which would continue until well into the late 1940s (see Table 5.5). This decline had a particularly severe impact on Honduras and Panama, since bananas were their principal export product.

1935–1943: Strong sustained world growth and contraction in Central America

Preparation for the series of wars between 1935 and 1943 helped stimulate a healthy 7 percent annual GDP growth rate for the United States and the United Kingdom. The combination of the Sino-Japanese War in Manchuria, the Spanish Civil War, and finally World War II reversed the decline in commodity prices, brought down inventory stocks, and helped reverse terms of trade in Central America. The region's growth for the period was negative, however, because trade was reoriented away from Europe, shipping was interrupted, and its principal wartime market, the

TABLE 5.4 Performance Data for Key World and Central America Economic Trend Periods, 1930–1985

Performance data classification	Major crisis 1930–1934	Strong sustained growth 1935–1943	Major crisis 1944–1949	Strong sustained growth 1950–1953	Minor crisis 1954–1961	Strong sustained growth 1962–1973	Minor crisis 1974–1977	Minor crisis 1978–1985
Average annual world GDP growth[a] (%)	−1.74	7.0	−1.9	4.56	4.12	5.06	3.29	2.5
Average annual Central America GDP growth[b] (%)	−11.65	−0.55	8.10	5.08	4.13	5.97	4.80	0.9
Central American outperformance or underperformance of world GDP	Under-performance	Under-performance	Out-performance	Out-performance	Equal performance	Out-performance	Out-performance	Under-performance
Central American terms of trade[c]	90–69	50–62	66–90	114–117	144–90	92–95	84–117	103–66
Central American export price index[d]	292–198	131–33	37–74	87–108	126–85	86–121	151–271	254–237
Export product diversification index (100 − % share first 2 export products)[e]	14–20	19–29	32–26	20–22	20–29	32–43	46–41	40–44

(table continued on next page)

TABLE 5.4 Continued

Performance data classification	Major crisis 1930-1934	Strong sustained growth 1935-1943	Major crisis 1944-1949	Strong sustained growth 1950-1953	Minor crisis 1954-1961	Strong sustained growth 1962-1973	Minor crisis 1974-1977	Minor crisis 1978-1985
Export market diversification index (100 – % market share of primary market)[f]	35-43	42-24	22-25	26-33	35-44	50-65	65-66	65-61
Annual growth of agricultural sector[g] (%)	n.a.	n.a.	n.a.	n.a.	n.a.	5.3	2.8	2.1
Annual growth of industrial sector[h] (%)	n.a.	n.a.	n.a.	n.a.	n.a.	8.5	5.1	-1.3
Total exports sold in Central America[i] (%)	1.5	1.8	4.5	5.8	4	16.5	18.3	14

n.a. = not available.

a. Between 1930 and 1949, the world GDP growth rate used in the unweighted average of U.S. and U.K. annual GDP growth is based on data from The Economist, *World Business Cycles* (London, 1982). After 1950, it is world GDP growth from the same source.

b. Between 1930 and 1949, the surrogate for Central American GDP growth is the average annual rate of growth of total trade (imports and exports) at constant prices that appears in Antonio Colindres, Marc Lindenberg, and Rodrigo Valverde, "Economic Trends in Central America and Panama since 1900" (INCAE technical note, San José, 1986). After 1950 Central American annual GDP growth is the unweighted average of country GDP data from *World Business Cycles*.

c. Central American terms of trade were computed by INCAE from an index which appears in Colindres, Lindenberg, and Valverde, "Economic Trends in Central America." Data are given for the first and last year for each period.

d. Ibid.

e. Ibid.

f. Ibid.

g. Inter-American Development Bank, *Economic and Social Progress in Latin America: 1985* (Washington, D.C., 1986).

h. Ibid.

i. Colindres, Lindenberg, and Valverde, "Economic Trends in Central America."

TABLE 5.5   Output and Productivity Measures for Banana Production in Costa Rica, Honduras, Guatemala, and Panama, 1900–1985

Period	Volume of exports (thousands of 40-lb. boxes)	Hectares planted (thousands)	Productivity index (boxes per hectare)	Value of exports (thousands of US$)
1900–1930	8.2–43.3[a]	n.a.	n.a.	n.a.
1930–1933	43.3–24.6[a]	n.a.	n.a.	n.a.
1934–1943	24.6–27.1[a]	n.a.	n.a.	n.a.
1944–1949	63.7–58.8	65.9–66.3	966–877	94,815–103,800
1950–1953	55.8–54.2	62.7–70.3	888–771	107,440–116,030
1954–1961	49.5–53.8	62.9–55.9	779–962	106,248–96,118
1962–1973	47.6–143.9	52.9–65.9	901–2,183	97,368–275,882
1974–1977	124.5–129.2	63.7–59.7	1,953–2,163	258,462–354,302
1978–1985	n.a.	n.a.	n.a.	n.a.

n.a. = not available.

NOTE: Data are given for the first and last year for each period.

a. Before 1944 banana exports were measured in thousands of bunches; after 1944 they were measured in 40-pound boxes.

SOURCE: Frank Ellis, *Transnacionales del Banano en Centro América* (San José: Editorial Universitario Centroamericano (EDUCA), 1983); Richard Allen La Barge, "A Study of United Fruit Company Operations in Isthmian America" (Ph.D. dissertation, Duke University, 1960).

United States, whose share of export trade from the region increased to above 75 percent, imposed price controls (see Table 5.6).

The world economy's expansion from 1935 to 1943 actually includes two trend periods in Central America. From 1935 to 1937 terms of trade and export prices recovered, and the coffee-producing countries in the region showed substantial recovery. From 1938 to 1943, however, wartime dislocations brought the region's growth to a standstill. Costa Rica and Guatemala suffered most from the problem of trade reorientation, since 50 and 40 percent of their exports went to Germany and England. Although the region tried to compensate with new products like rubber, lumber, gold, silver, and cacao and with some increases in the use of the Central American market, real recovery did not take place until the next trend period.

1944–1949: World economic contraction and sustained economic growth in Central America

While the post–World War II period signaled a contraction in the industrial economies, Central America's annual growth was 8 percent. The region benefited from the lifting of price controls in the United States, the heavy pent-up demand for commodities, and the slow reopening of European markets. Coffee prices, for example, climbed more than 300 percent in the period. Inventory stocks began to drop, and terms of trade moved strongly in favor of commodity producers.

Although the region's efforts at product diversification actually slowed down owing to excellent prices for traditional commodities, favorable cotton prices in the late 1940s provided the incentive for product experimentation in El Salvador. Cotton would prove to be a remarkable new catalyst for both the Salvadoran and Nicaraguan economies in the next two trend periods.

1950–1953: The Korean War boom and strong Central American performance

While the Korean War is sometimes described as the turning point when terms of trade and commodity prices began to shift against the nonindustrial developing countries, Central America fared rather well. The expanded world demand created by the war resulted in annual world GDP growth of 4.5 percent. The region grew even more rapidly. Central America's export price index jumped 36 points, and terms of trade remained moderately favorable (see Table 5.4). Export market diversification efforts continued but still did not recover their pre–World War II levels.

TABLE 5.6 Central American Product and Market Diversification Indexes, 1930–1983

Type of period	1930-1934	1935-1943	1944-1949	1950-1953	1954-1961	1962-1973	1974-1977	1978-1983
	Major crisis	Strong sustained growth	Major crisis	Strong sustained growth	Minor crisis	Strong sustained growth	Minor crisis	Minor crisis
Average annual world GDP growth	1.74	7.0	-1.9	4.56	4.12	5.06	3.29	2.50
Average annual Central American GDP growth	-11.65	-0.55	8.10	5.08	4.13	5.97	4.80	0.90
Export product diversification index[a]								
Costa Rica	10-13	20-19	24-31	15-14	17-23	19-47	50-44	44-48
El Salvador	13-14	11-22	16-11	7-8	6-23	22-10	26-27	15-36
Guatemala	9-5	7-24	22-13	18-9	10-31	29-56	58-42	43-59
Honduras	8-9	11-45	46-26	17-24	25-33	39-45	59-43	42-47
Nicaragua	28-25	24-28	27-50	27-45	34-49	49-62	52-45	47-30
Panama	16-50	40-35	56-28	32-32	26-11	33-35	34-41	47-46
Central America	16-20	19-29	32-26	20-22	20-29	32-43	46-41	40-44
Export market diversification index[b]								
Costa Rica	40-53	64-26	26-21	23-35	41-45	46-67	69-71	69-66
El Salvador	45-52	60-33	32-28	33-39	43-61	64-81	69-70	69-67
Guatemala	41-48	59-40	40-27	31-35	36-53	52-69	69-70	73-69
Honduras	26-29	18-21	15-24	24-24	26-43	42-46	54-52	44-46
Nicaragua	50-50	44-12	9-36	30-56	55-55	62-67	81-77	77-79
Panama	8-29	6-12	15-12	14-8	7-8	33-38	50-57	58-41
Central America	35-43	42-24	22-25	26-33	35-44	50-65	65-66	65-61

NOTE: Data are given for the first and last year for each period.

a. Product diversification index = 100 − percentage of total exports share held by top two products.

b. Market diversification index = 100 − percentage of total export market share held by top market.

SOURCE: Antonio Colindres, Marc Lindenberg, and Rodrigo Valverde, "Economic Trends in Central America and Panama since 1900" (San José: Central American Institute of Business Administration (INCAE), 1986) for product and market diversification data and Central America GDP in 1930-1949. The Economist, World Business Cycles (London, 1982) for world and Central American GDP data.

Between 1950 and 1953 a shift took place in the product life cycles of bananas and cotton in Central America. While the banana industry reached a low point in productivity and acreage, cotton production took hold in both Nicaragua and El Salvador. In Nicaragua, for example, cotton acreage jumped from 24,000 to 60,000 manzanas, and the number of bales per manzana rose from 0.93 to 1.6 (see Table 5.7).[10]

1954–1961: Mini recessions in the world economy and transition in Central America

The period from 1954 to 1961 marked a turning point in both the world and the regional economy. At the world level two recessions punctuated the shakedown period between the end of the Korean War and a remarkable fifteen-year period of sustained global economic growth. In Central America a transition took place between the last phases of a product and market diversification strategy and a new, more dynamic mixed strategy involving the industrial sector and the regional common market.

An interesting paradox emerged in Central America between 1954 and 1961. In spite of sharply declining export prices and terms of trade, the region kept pace with world economic growth because of a mix of acreage expansion in existing products, traditional product diversification, productivity gains, and market diversification. For example, coffee finally reached its maximum acreage in Central America with its emergence as an important export product in Honduras. The banana industry recovered thanks to new productivity gains. Cotton production and productivity increased substantially in Nicaragua and El Salvador and began to take on importance in Guatemala. Sugar emerged as a new product in Nicaragua. Finally, the region's export market diversification surpassed

TABLE 5.7	Output and Productivity Measures for Cotton Production in Nicaragua, 1950–1985		
Period	Area planted (thousands of manzanas)	Bales harvested	Bales per per manzana
1950–1953	23.9–60.6	22.3–101.0	0.93–1.6
1954–1961	123.6–107.3	203.4–245.2	1.6–2.2
1962–1973	134.1–259.3	319.2–657.8	2.3–2.5
1974–1977	254.3–310.8	535.4–540.0	2.1–1.7
1978–1985	248.1–160.6	498.9–309.4	2.0–1.9

NOTE: A manzana is 0.81 hectares. A standard bale weighs 480 pounds. Data are given for the first and last year for each period.
SOURCE: Enrique Bolaños, Nicaraguan Cotton Grower's Association, 1986.

the previous high point reached in 1934 owing to the reincorporation of European markets and entrance into the Japanese market.

1962–1973: Strong sustained world and Central American economic growth

Between 1962 and 1973 Central America outperformed world annual GDP growth by almost 1 percent. The world economy grew at an impressive 5 percent per year, while the region grew at 5.9 percent. Central America's strong performance was the result of stable terms of trade, highly improved export prices, and a new mixed economic strategy, which included continued traditional product and market diversification, industrial import substitution, and a regional common market. Among traditional products, sugar appeared as an important export not only in Nicaragua, but also in Guatemala, El Salvador, and Costa Rica. Beef exports became important in Honduras, Guatemala, Nicaragua, and Costa Rica. Cotton and bananas continued their acreage expansion and registered their highest productivity gains. Coffee held its own. In addition, the industrial sector grew at over 8 percent per year. Exports to the Central American common market as a percentage of total exports grew from 4 to more than 16 percent by 1973. Finally, foreign aid and capital transfers as a result of the Alliance for Progress program increased overall investment in the region.

1974–1977: The first oil shock, world contraction, and recovery

The first oil shock caused a decline in world average GDP growth of 0.5 percent for the 1974–1975 period, followed by a recovery of 5 percent annually for 1976–1977. The drop and recovery hid a massive process of adjustment that would turn the terms of trade against Central America, raise the costs of industrial goods, and help set off a severe contraction between 1978 and 1983 at the global level and in the region.

Central America rode an astronomical acceleration in export prices that hid a series of structural problems with its mixed strategy. The region grew annually at almost 5 percent, more than 1 percent faster than the world economy. Terms of trade continued to favor Central America. Market diversification stagnated, however, industrial and agricultural growth began to slow down, and the percentage share of exports sold within the common market stabilized. There was some evidence that industrial import substitution was reaching its limits. At the same time the indexes of product diversification actually decreased. Cotton acreage and productivity continued to improve but at a slightly declining rate, and banana production leveled off along with productivity.

1978–1985: Crisis and contraction

The second round of oil price hikes brought an end to the stability of the economic relationships that began to take shape after the Korean War. The world experienced four consecutive years of declining growth and did not begin to recover until 1983. Average growth of world GDP was below the level of world population growth for the first time since 1944. Although Central America had grown faster than the world on an annual basis since 1944, this trend reversed itself in 1978. World recession coincided with declining terms of trade, poor export prices resulting in the end of the product life cycle for three of five main export products (bananas, sugar, and cotton), the end of the easy phase of industrial import substitution, and the breakdown of the regional common market.

Each of the traditional agricultural export products encountered special problems. The transnational banana producers withdrew from Costa Rica, Panama, and Nicaragua after labor and cost difficulties. Banana production in Honduras continued but was threatened by more efficient operations in Ecuador. Sugar prices plummeted, the victim of overproduction and new product substitutes. Cotton prices increased because of reduced demand for oil-based synthetic fibers. Revolution and a reorganization of the productive process in Nicaragua as well as guerrilla activity in El Salvador reduced overall acreage to less tnan half of 1977 levels. The industrial sector began to operate at less than 50 percent capacity. Without foreign exchange to cover currency imbalances in intraregional trade, the common market broke down.

Central America's economic decline bottomed out with −2 percent growth in 1982 and began a slow process of recovery in 1983 and 1984 with 0.6 and 1.4 percent growth annually. The recovery has been slower than the world recovery in general.

The Dynamic Interactions between Context and Economic Strategy

This brief review of economic trend periods since 1930 suggests that although the Central American economies are highly sensitive to fluctuations in the world economy, they are not prisoners whose future is totally determined by that economy. Policies do matter in their GDP growth and human development performance, as they do for countries in the larger data set from Part II. In fect, the Central American countries demonstrated considerable resilience in the alteration of their economic strategies to respond to changes in world economic conditions. These changes normally began to take place during economic crisis periods when experimentation with product, market, and sectoral diversification was initiated. Table 5.8 groups the data from earlier tables into periods of Central American outperformance and underperformance of the world economy. The number of trend periods is too small for adequate statistical analysis (four periods of outperformance, three periods of under-performance, and one period of equal performance), but the discussion that follows supports the thesis that the region is not a passive prisoner of international forces.

Terms of trade and export prices

The impact of external factors on the Central American economies is undeniable. Between 1930 and 1985 Central America's terms of trade and export price indexes improved in all four periods of outperformance and deteriorated in two of the three underperformance periods (see Table 5.4). Average improvement in terms of trade was sixteen points per outperformance period, and average deterioration in periods of

TABLE 5.8	Differences in Central American Key Economic Variables in Periods of Underperformance and Outperformance of the World Economy, 1930–1984	
Variable	Periods of underperformance	Periods of outperformance
Number of periods	3	4
Terms of trade (average change per period)	−15	+16
Export prices (average change in index per period)	−36	+53
Export product diversification index (average per period)	27	35
Export market diversification index (average per period)	43	45
Export participation in Central American common market (%)	4	11
Industrial growth (average % per period)	−1.3	7
Agricultural growth (average % per period)	2.1	4
Cotton productivity (average bales per manzana per period)	1.9	1.7
Banana productivity (average boxes per hectare per period)	1,503	1,498

SOURCE: Prepared by INCAE from Exhibits 5, 6, and 9 of Marc Lindenberg, *Central America: Crisis and Economic Strategy 1930–85, Lessons from History* (San José: Central American Institute of Business Administration (INCAE), 1986).

underperformance was fifteen points. Average improvement in the export price index was fifty-three points per outperformance period, and average deterioration was thirty-six points in underperformance periods.

The dangers of the high-risk, high-payoff strategy of export monoculture (few products and few markets) in Central America are highlighted by its sensitivity to fluctuations in export prices and terms of trade. On the one hand, even while the world economy was in contraction owing to the post–World War II slump, the region grew at 8 percent between 1944 and 1949 thanks to the pent-up demand for commodities, the sudden access to shipping, and the lifting of price controls. This growth occurred even though its only major export products were coffee and bananas, almost 75 percent of which went to the United States. On the other hand, falling prices and negative terms of trade with the same monoculture strategy contributed to severe Central American underperformance of the world economy during the Great Depression (1930–1939) and World War II (1939–1945), even though the industrial economies were growing rapidly during the latter period.

Product and market diversification

It appears that product and market diversification should have provided small, open export economies with protection against fluctuations in the world economy. As Part II of this book showed, product diversification mattered in Central America between 1930 and 1984, but market diversification did not. The export product diversification index averaged 35 in outperformance periods and 27 during periods of underperformance. In 1954–1961 product diversification through the introduction of cotton and sugar helped counteract poor export prices and deteriorating terms of trade. From 1962 to 1978 additional product diversification, with the inclusion of beef, cotton, and sugar, helped keep the region growing much more rapidly than the world economy.

Market diversification did not seem to have any relationship to Central America's out- or underperformance of the world economy. The market diversification index averaged 43 and 45 for periods of under- and outperformance. Changes in the market diversification index seemed to result more from the onset and aftermath of World War II than from any other factor. For example, in 1930 the index was at 35. It dropped to 22 during the war and then rose continuously between 1944 and 1978.

Productivity, product life cycle, and outperformance

While we might have expected productivity levels for Central America's export products to be higher when the region outperformed the world economy than when it underperformed, this was not the case; individual product life cycles did not coincide with overall economic trends. For example, of the three new traditional agricultural export products introduced between 1930 and 1984, cotton, beef, and sugar, two took hold during a period of Central American outperformance of the world economy, 1950–1953, and one in a period with two world recessions, 1954–1961. In spite of the apparent lack of a general relationship between productivity of export production and the region's economic outperformance of the world economy, when productivity gains coincided with market and product diversification and good terms of trade and prices, as they did in 1962–1978, they contributed to the region's outperformance of the world economy.

Mixed strategies

The keys to a mixed strategy were to diversify products and markets and to seek additional sources of growth and employment. In Central America these sources were industrial import substitution and the regional common market.

Since agriculture, industry, and the common market were to be key internal catalysts for growth, it would be logical to expect higher growth rates in outperformance periods than in underperformance periods. This is in fact the case. Industry averaged 8 and 5 percent growth in 1962–1973 and 1974–1978, respectively, and agriculture averaged 5.3 and 2.8 percent.

Finally, the average percentage of total exports to the Central American common market was higher in periods of outperformance than in periods of underperformance. There appear to have been three trends in the behavior of intraregional trade since 1930. First, between 1930 and 1943 exports to the regional market were less than 2 percent of total exports. Second, from 1944 to 1961 the percentage of exports to the regional market increased to around 5 percent, probably because of the need to seek new markets during and after World War II. Third, between 1961 and 1985 exports to the newly formed common market grew to 19 percent of total exports.

A Review of Central American Economic Strategies

External shocks, then, were a key threat to sustained economic growth and employment in small, open, export economies like those in Central America. The fundamental policy challenge for the region was to find economic strategies that reduced the threat and provided more stable payoffs at lower levels of risk.

Since 1930 Central America has tried three economic strategies: (1) monoculture export agriculture, (2) product and market diversification, and (3) the mixed strategy. Each strategy had a different risk level and payoff potential (see Figure 5.4 for a classification of strategies and time periods by risk and payoff potential). In the matrix the arrows that connect the strategies to each other show the order in which each was tried historically.

Export monoculture

The first strategy, export monoculture (1930–1933, 1934–1943, and 1944–1949), was a high-risk strategy with an extremely variable payoff. When it went well owing to favorable world prices and terms of trade such as in 1944–1949, growth rates were phenomenal and the region outperformed the world economy. When international export prices were poor, however, and terms of trade moved against the region, as during 1930–1934 and 1935–1943 (particularly from 1939 to 1943), the region suffered severe recessions and underperformed the world economy.

Traditional agricultural product and market diversification

The second strategy, traditional agricultural product and market diversification (1950–1953 and 1954–1961), helped to reduce the risk due to external factors at the cost of slightly lower payoffs in GDP growth. The addition of new traditional products like beef, cotton, and sugar and the opening of European and Asian markets helped to diversify risk levels and reduce variability. In the 1954–1961 period the product and market diversification strategy helped to counterbalance sharply deteriorating export prices and terms of trade.

The mixed strategy: Product, market, and sectoral diversification

The third strategy, the mixed strategy (1961–1973 and 1974–1978), provided maximum diversification and solid payoffs with relatively low risk. The Central American countries continued to diversify their products and markets in the area of traditional agricultural exports and identified new strategies for the internal and regional market such as industrial import substitution. The mixed strategy provided the most protection to the region and the most consistent positive rates of growth of any period since the Great Depression.

FIGURE 5.4 Classification of Central American Economic Strategies by Risk and Payoff, 1930–1990

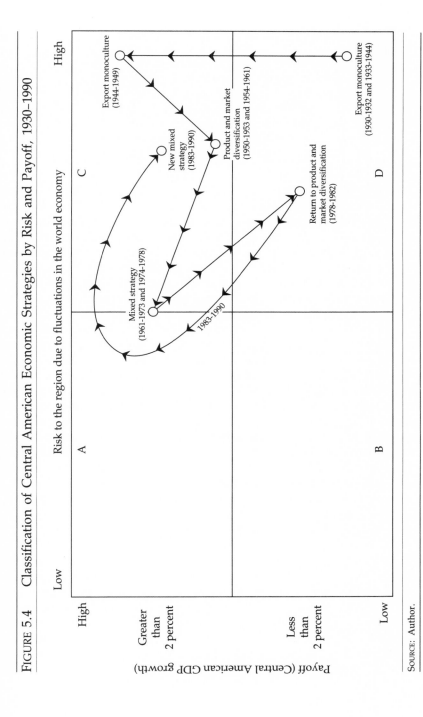

SOURCE: Author.

113

*The crisis of 1979–1982: Return to a few
traditional agricultural products*

Beginning in 1979 the region resumed its reliance on a few traditional agricultural products because of problems with world oversupply of sugar, difficulties in the banana and cotton industries, and the collapse of industrial import substitution and the regional common market. It must now find a way to readjust to new conditions in the world economy.

Conclusion

Central America's economic performance was more strongly influenced by external constraints than we might have predicted based on the global analysis in Part II of this book. Yet this tiny region was not as trapped by the constraints imposed by world economic cycles as the early dependency theorists might have suggested. Certainly external factors likes terms of trade and prices for traditional export products helped shape the parameters within which the Central American economies performed. But within these parameters national policy makers and producers experimented with different economic strategies to mitigate the worst effects of external shocks. The most successful strategy, a mixed strategy (1961–1987), relied on highly diverse products, markets, and sectors.

Viewing one region in greater depth provided a clearer picture of the complex interactions between context and policies that were invisible at the level of aggregation used in Part II. The region's economic performance data, however, left some additional paradoxes. For example, while all the Central American nations grew at above the developing-country average between 1965 and 1987 and did so using similar economic strategies, there were substantial differences in their human development performance. To help explain this paradox, I will look more closely at how political instability, regime type, and governance structures affected human development performance in Central America.

Regime Type, Political Instability, and Human Development in Central America

High political instability and low levels of political and civil rights turned out to be important signposts along the road to low human development performance in the global analysis presented earlier.

If the global conclusions about the negative impact of political instability on human development are valid for regions, then the Central American nations should be poor human development performers. Since 1930 more than half of the region's 126 presidents have been removed from office through coups. The average length of a presidential term of office has been less than 2.6 years. Central Americans who turned sixty in 1990 have lived through at least two extremely violent revolutionary periods, 1930–1934 (Nicaragua and El Salvador) and 1978–1985 (Nicaragua, El Salvador, and Guatemala). They have been witnesses to small wars with their neighbors, like the soccer war between Honduras and El Salvador in 1969, countless border disputes, invasions, and foreign interventions. They have spent 20 percent of their lives under state of emergency legislation that suspended basic civil rights and 40 percent of the time under military rule.

Yet in spite of high levels of political instability, the region has two high human development performers, Costa Rica and Panama; three medium performers, Guatemala, Honduras, and Nicaragua; and just one poor performer, El Salvador. Ironically, the two high performers have the lowest (Costa Rica) as well as the highest (Panama) levels of nonprogrammed changes of presidents in the region. Does this mean that other economic and social policies may be sufficiently strong to overcome contextual problems like political instability?

This chapter will look more closely at the role of context and policies in accelerating or inhibiting waves of political instability. It will also document how political instability affected Central American governance structures as well as their human development policies and performance. Finally, it will subject the global conclusions to more focused scrutiny in one region.

The Underpinnings of Central American Political Instability

In the previous chapter I referred to the extensive literature about the impact of international forces on economic performance in the developing world.[1] Some observers have focused on the effects of these same forces on developing countries' internal political dynamics. On the one hand, theorists of neo-imperialism argue that international capital imposes externally rooted class structures on developing countries to maintain social control of the population and extract surplus.[2] They contend that this dependent relationship not only inhibits local capital formation, but also heightens political instability as an increasingly impoverished population challenges the dominance of local elites subservient to foreign interests. In contrast, modernization theorists argue that political instability in developing countries is not the result of economic dependence, but rather the consequence of the modernization process itself.[3] They assert that development triggers instability as the population's demands grow more rapidly than the capacity of political and economic institutions to meet them.

Latin American scholars have provided substantial contributions to this debate.[4] For example, the early works of Paul Baran and Andre Gunder Frank established the foundations of Latin American dependency theory with their discussion of "metropolis-satellite" relationships.[5] Fernando Henrique Cardoso and Enzo Faletto, as well as Bill Warren, reformulated the dependency argument in the 1970s to make it more consistent with a Latin America where domestic investment, industrial output, and national income actually increased.[6] They argued that in spite of growth and capital accumulation, the Latin American nations were still dependent because they had to import technology and capital goods and that local political instability was still triggered by contradictions in the international economy that pitted local elites aligned with foreigners against other elements of the local class structure.

Even though many prominent students of Latin America did not subscribe to dependency theory, they still assigned an important role to international forces in triggering political instability.[7] For example, Guillermo O'Donnell argued that the end of the stage of easy import substitution helped produce economic stagnation, a breakdown of alliances between governments and populist groups, increased social discontent, and political instability.[8] New alliances among the military, technocrats, and a transnationalized bourgeoisie, created to maintain social control, resulted in the emergence of the "bureaucratic authoritarian state." The work of David Becker, Jeff Frieden, Sayre Schatz, and Richard Sklar on post imperialism rejected dependency theory but focused on the vital role of multinational capital in the formation of Latin American class structure.[9]

Paradoxically, the small Central American countries, relegated to the footnotes of most theoretical discussions, provide the most fertile testing ground for such theories.[10] By the normal measures presented in the last chapter, they should be among the most dependent in Latin America and the developing world. They were small, highly open, and susceptible to external shocks, and although they made strategic adjustments to such forces, these adjustments were accompanied by short-term political instability.

The key role of external economic shocks

By juxtaposing elements from the existing Marxist and non-Marxist literature with empirical analysis, I will extend the analysis of the thesis introduced in Chapter 5 that because the Central American economies are so small and highly open, a world economic downturn helps to trigger a cycle of internal destabilizing forces.[11] These internal forces, always latent, but ever present owing to continued population growth, high unemployment, and social inequities, would accelerate during periods of economic crisis. During such periods the region's levels of living would deteriorate further. Discontent would grow.[12] Governments would lose the political resources to maintain control, and political instability would increase.[13] Military governments would appear and disappear through coups and countercoups until a stable military coalition would intervene, usually with repressive measures to gain control.[14]

One might have expected that such a stable military coalition would have emerged during the last phases of the economic crisis of the 1930s and the beginnings of world and Central American economic recovery. It would have presided over a reordering of the Central American economic strategy and reestablishment of the same dominant social coalitions although different individuals would govern. These periods of relatively stable military rule would continue until the next world economic crisis set off a new spiral of political collapse.[15]

Other determinants of political instability

Although we might expect the classic crisis and military rule cycles to take place in the way just described, a number of factors might make political crisis more or less intense. For example, political instability might be less acute in crisis periods when the Central American economy was outperforming the world economy, or when there was more product, market, or sectoral diversification. Second, the influence of external political actors might either moderate or accentuate cycles of political instability. For example, it might be argued that in the World War II period the U.S. administration found supporting loyal military governments in Central America against Germany and Japan more important than the undemocratic inclinations of those governments.[16] If this were true it would have been easier for military rulers in the region to consolidate their power in spite of the economic downturns of the late 1930s. Third, Nicaragua, El Salvador, and Guatemala have generally experienced more violence and severe political instability in times of crisis than their neighbors Costa Rica, Honduras, and Panama. It is possible that the countries whose populations are denser or more ethnically diverse had higher levels of instability in times of crisis than those countries with less density or ethnic diversity.[17] It may be that in countries with higher population density, like El Salvador and Guatemala, people have less chance to go back to subsistence agriculture when there is a world economic downturn. They must rely more heavily on their wages from coffee, sugar, and exports. With family survival more threatened by world economic cycles and without the option of subsistence agriculture, their discontent levels might be higher than in countries like Honduras, where there is more access to land for subsistence. Another possibility is that ethnic tensions explode more readily when there is a crisis.[18] If this were true, then crisis would be more violent in Guatemala, Panama, and El Salvador than, for example, in Costa Rica or Honduras. Fourth, it is possible that differences in colonial settlement patterns might have determined the level of equity in some countries (higher in Costa Rica and lower in Guatemala and El Salvador), as well as the type of regime (authoritarian or democratic) that emerged by 1930. Some students of the region believe that the differences in initial colonial settlement patterns explain more about differences in levels of political instability than many other factors.[19] Finally, differences in income distribution and landholding patterns might be important as well.[20] One might expect more social discontent in countries with more unequal income distribution or landholding patterns.

The analysis that follows covers three areas. First, it develops definitions and describes how data were collected. Second, it reports the findings. Finally, it initiates the discussion of the effects of political instability on governance structures and human development performance that will continue in the following chapter.

Definitions and Data Collection Methods

To examine the dynamics of economic crisis and political instability in Central America, I will use the information about world and Central American economic cycles provided in Chapter 5, along with new data about (1) Central American leadership instability, (2) regime instability, (3) repression, (4) social discontent, (5) political instability, (6) population density, (7) ethnic populations, and (8) urbanization.

Leadership instability is defined as the president's inability to maintain him- or herself in office for the duration of the pre-established term.[21] Leadership instability was measured by examining the official records in each country to determine the percentage of nonprogrammed changes of presidents per year (for example, coups, resignations, and assassinations) out of total changes per year and average number of changes of presidents per year. Leadership instability was distinguished from government and regime instability.

Political repression is defined as a process in which a government limits its people's rights of life, free expression, and association through the use of legal as well as extralegal procedures. The two measures of repression used in this study are the number of days in which constitutional guarantees were suspended per country per year and an index of the number of repressive measures per year that appeared in the official government publications called *Gazettas*.[22]

Social discontent is defined as the overt manifestation of disagreement by different population sectors with the actions and policies of the government. Examples of such disagreement might be strikes, demonstrations, protest marches, written manifestos, skirmishes, combat incidents, and assassinations. Unfortunately, there are no systematic records of social discontent in Central America since 1930. For this reason, I used content analysis of a sample from the major daily newspaper in each country between 1930 and 1987 to determine the frequency, intensity, and origin of discontent in different time periods.[23] The sample was drawn in the following way. First, a major newspaper in each country whose records were available for the study period was identified. Second, for each country researchers did content analysis of that newspaper for two randomly selected days of every week from 1930 through 1985, based on the procedures described in note 23.

Economic periods accompanied by Central American political instability were defined as those with higher than average levels of social discontent, repression, and leadership instability. High levels of leadership instability might certainly contribute to overall political instability owing to the lack of policy continuity in a government whose president might be changed as frequently as once every eleven months.[24]

This chapter uses data already collected by official sources in each country on population density (inhabitants per square kilometer), the ratio of ethnic group population to total population, and the ratio of urban to total population.[25]

Economic Cycles and Political Instability

World economic cycles and Central American leadership instability

The data support the hypothesis that a world economic crisis helps set off cycles of leadership instability in Central America. Periods of world economic crisis are accompanied by higher levels of leadership instability in Central America than periods of economic growth (see Table 6.1). Under normal circumstances, with six countries and a scheduled presidential election every four years, one could expect about 1.5 presidential elections per year in Central America. The average number of changes of presidents per year in the region during the five world economic crisis periods is 2.6, and for the four periods of world economic growth it is 1.6. The average share of nonprogrammed changes due to coups and resignations during world economic crisis periods is 57.3 percent, and for periods of world economic growth it is 36.3 percent. Presidents with a military background ruled regardless of whether there was an economic crisis (39 percent) or economic growth (40.9 percent).

Although in 1986–1988 the region experienced its first period of democratic opening since 1930, it is useful to separate the three periods of economic growth with military rule from the 1986–1988 period of democratic rule. While the average number of changes of presidents per year is not much different between democratic rule (1.3) and military rule (1.6), there are substantial differences in the percentage of nonprogrammed changes during democratic rule (25 percent) and military rule (37.5 percent). Finally, although military officers could have run for president in the 1986–1988 period, as they have in other periods, they did not do so, and as a result the percentage of military presidents during the brief period of democratic rule is 0, whereas it is 45 percent during periods of military rule.

There are even greater differences when I make three divisions in the data: economic crisis, economic growth with military rule, and economic growth with democratic rule. Crisis periods have the most

TABLE 6.1   World Economic Cycles and Central American Political Instability, 1930–1988

Period	Number of years in period	Average number of changes of presidents per year[a]	Share of nonprogrammed changes of presidents in total changes[b] (%)	Share of military presidents in total presidents[c] (%)
World economic crisis[d]				
1930–1934	5	3.2	31.3	43.8
1944–1949	6	3.0	66.7	33.3
1954–1961	8	2.6	66.7	42.9
1974–1977	4	1.5	33.3	83.3
1978–1985	8	2.8	63.6	27.3
Summary	6.7	2.6	57.3	39.0
World economic growth with military rule in Central America[d]				
1935–1943	9	1.3	41.7	33.3
1950–1953	4	1.5	16.7	66.7
1962–1973	12	1.8	40.9	45.5
Summary	8.3	1.6	37.5	45.0
World economic growth with democratic rule in Central America[d]				
1986–1988	3	1.3	25.0	0.0
Summary	3	1.3	25.0	0.0
Total periods of world economic growth[d] (military and democratic rule)				
Summary	7	1.6	36.3	40.9

a. Derived by analysis of the official country records of the length of term of each Central American president between 1930 and 1988 and the changes of presidents during each economic period.
b. Nonprogrammed changes are changes that took place for reasons other than a scheduled election, such as a coup.
c. Based on the official listing of the professional background of each president.
d. Economic periods are defined based on Marc Lindenberg, "Central America: Crisis and Economic Strategy 1930–85, Lessons from History," *Journal of Developing Areas* 22, no. 2 (January 1988).
SOURCE: Author.

changes in presidents per year, the highest percentage of nonprogrammed changes, but an intermediate number of military presidents. Growth periods with military rule have an intermediate percentage of changes of presidents per year and nonprogrammed changes but the highest percentage of military presidents. The democratic period clearly offers the most political stability, with the smallest number of changes of presidents per year, the smallest share of nonprogrammed changes, and no military presidents.

Central American economic cycles and leadership instability

The data on Central American economic cycles also support the thesis that once economic crisis periods begin within the region they are accompanied by higher levels of leadership instability than are periods of economic growth (see Table 6.2). In the four periods of local economic crisis the average number of changes of presidents in the region per year

TABLE 6.2   Central American Economic Cycles and Political Instability, 1930–1988

Period	Number of years in period	Average number of changes of presidents per year[a]	Share of nonprogrammed changes of presidents in total changes[b] (%)	Share of military presidents in total presidents[c] (%)
Economic crisis[d]				
1930–1934	5	3.2	31.3	43.7
1935–1943	9	1.3	41.7	33.3
1954–1961	8	2.6	66.7	42.9
1978–1985	8	2.8	63.6	27.3
Summary	7.5	2.4	53.5	36.0
Economic growth with military rule[d]				
1944–1949	6	3.0	72.2	33.3
1950–1953	4	1.5	16.7	66.7
1962–1973	12	1.8	40.9	45.5
1974–1977	4	1.5	33.3	83.3
Summary	6.5	2.0	48.1	48.1
Economic growth with democratic rule[d]				
1986–1988	3	1.3	25.0	0.0
Summary	3	1.3	25.0	0.0
Total periods of Central American economic growth[d] (military and democratic rule)				
Summary	5.8	1.9	45.4	43.6

a. Derived by analysis of the official country record of the length of term of each Central American president between 1930 and 1988 and the changes of presidents during each economic period.
b. Nonprogrammed changes were changes that took place for reasons other than a scheduled election, such as a coup.
c. Based on the official listing of the professional background of each president.
d. Economic periods are defined based on Marc Lindenberg, "Central America: Crisis and Economic Strategy 1930–85, Lessons from History," *Journal of Developing Areas* 22, no. 2 (January 1988).
SOURCE: Author.

is 2.4, the share of nonprogrammed changes is 53.5 percent, and the share of military presidents is 36 percent. In contrast, in the five periods of Central American economic growth, the average number of changes of presidents in the region per year is 1.9, the share of nonprogrammed changes is 45.4 percent, and the share of military presidents is 43.6 percent.

Different types of regimes also correspond with substantial differences in leadership stability. Instability was generally lowest in periods of Central American economic growth with democratic rule, higher in periods of growth with military rule, and highest in economic crisis periods.[26]

Social discontent

Although the number of periods is too small for accurate statistical testing, economic crisis periods appear to be accompanied by more violent expressions of social discontent than noncrisis periods (see Table 6.3).[27] The

TABLE 6.3   Central American Economic Cycles, Social Discontent, and Repression, 1930–1986

Period	Violent incidents as a % of total reported incidents[a]	Rural incidents as a % of total reported incidents[b]	Days of suspended guarantees per year per country[c]	Number of repressive measures per year per country[d]
Economic crisis[e]				
1930–1934	29	40.6	114	0.9
1935–1943	18	39.3	88	0.6
1954–1961	29	32.7	49	0.8
1978–1985	65	51.9	124	1.5
Average	35.2	41.2	93.7	0.95
Economic growth with military rule[e]				
1944–1949	23	34.0	130	1.3
1950–1953	15	34.3	3	0.6
1962–1973	32	35.1	12	0.4
1974–1977	33	35.9	57	0.6
Average	25.7	34.8	50.5	0.72

NOTE: Data on types and origins of incidents of social discontent come from a 28 percent sample of Central American newspapers from 1930 to 1986. The newspapers are *El Cronista*, *La Epoca*, *Diario Comercial*, *El Dia*, *El Pueblo*, and *La Prensa* in Honduras; *El Dia*, *La Prensa Gráfica*, and *El Diario de Hoy* in El Salvador; *El Imparcial* and *La Prensa Libre* in Guatemala; *El Diario* and *La Nación* in Costa Rica; *El Centroamericano*, *La Prensa*, *La Noticia*, and *El Nuevo Diario* in Nicaragua.

Days of suspended civil guarantees were computed through analysis of each country's official government gazette from 1930 to 1985 by finding the date of the initiation of legislation to begin as well as end a period of suspension of guarantees.
a. Violent reported incidents were articles that reported acts of terrorism or armed confrontations. Nonviolent incidents were strikes and demonstrations.
b. Incidents were classified as rural, urban, or national in origin.
c. Days of suspension were recorded by using the starting and ending day and year of emergency decrees.
d. Examples of repressive measures were censorship, laws outlawing groups, confiscations, and jailings of political prisoners.
e. Economic periods are defined based on Marc Lindenberg, "Central America: Crisis and Economic Strategy 1930–85, Lessons from History," *Journal of Developing Areas* 22, no. 2 (January 1988).
SOURCE: Author.

average number of violent expressions of discontent in relation to total reported incidents of social discontent was 35.2 percent in crisis periods and 25.7 percent in noncrisis periods. Rural violence tended to rise in crisis periods as well. It averaged 41.2 percent of reported incidents in crisis periods, as opposed to 34.8 percent in noncrisis periods. Rural violence usually had its origins in conflicts in the banana plantations, disputes over land, or armed confrontations between the government and guerrillas.

Repression

Central American governments have resorted to repressive measures more frequently during economic crisis periods than during periods of economic growth and expansion. Table 6.3 also shows that the average number of days in which civil guarantees were suspended per country per year during crisis periods was almost double (93.7 days) that of periods of economic expansion (50.5 days). One possible explanation is that once a new military regime consolidated itself and new economic expansion took place, social discontent was reduced, making repression less necessary for regime maintenance. In contrast, during times of economic collapse, social discontent and political instability might have been accentuated until some new faction of the military stepped in and began a process of restoring order that included suspension of guarantees and repression.

Cycles of economic crisis, discontent, and repression

Table 6.4 sheds light on the way cycles of economic crisis, social discontent, and repression function. It appears that even though less violent discontent and repression generally took place in periods of economic growth than in crisis periods, both violent social discontent and repressive measures did occur in growth periods but were more frequent in the second half of those periods. One explanation is that toward the end of a cycle of stable economic growth, violent expressions of social discontent begin to build, forcing the government to resort to repression to maintain itself, until it is finally toppled.

At the beginning of the crisis periods, instability became even greater as manifested by continued high levels of violent social discontent (see Table 6.4). While repressive measures were used widely in crisis periods, they were in fact used less strongly in the first half of crisis periods than in the second half. A possible explanation might be that in the first part of the crisis period high levels of leadership rotation do not leave governments in power long enough to implement their control measures successfully.

Violent expressions of discontent appeared to drop in the second half of crisis periods, while repressive measures appeared to rise (see Table 6.4). This increase in repression appears to coincide with government consolidation, which helps set the base for the new economic growth cycle with a new strategy, a more stable coalition, and less need to suspend guarantees, at least during the first half of the next growth cycle.

A detailed example of how cycles worked

To get a clearer picture of how the cycles of discontent and repression worked, let us look at each of the economic periods identified.

1930–1934   Between 1930 and 1934, a period of world and Central American economic crisis, social discontent was quite violent and more

TABLE 6.4   Central American Cycles of Political Instability, Social Discontent, and Repression, 1930–1986

			Discontent		Repression	
Period	Average changes of presidents per year[a]	% nonprogrammed to total changes	First half of period	Second half of period	First half of period	Second half of period
Economic crisis[e]						
1930–1934	3.2	31.3	High	Low	Low	High
1935–1943	1.3	41.7	High	Low	Low	High
1954–1961	2.6	66.7	High	Low	High	Low
1978–1985	2.8	63.6	High	Low	Low	High
Average	2.4	53.5	High	Low	Low	High
Economic growth with military rule[e]						
1944–1949	3.0	72.2	Low	High	Equal	Equal
1950–1953	1.5	16.7	Low	High	Low	High
1962–1973	1.8	40.9	Low	High	Equal	Equal
1974–1977	1.5	33.3	Low	High	Low	High
Average	2.0	48.1	Low	High	Low/equal	High/equal

NOTE: Data on types and origins of incidents of social discontent come from a 28 percent sample of Central American newspapers from 1930 to 1986. The newspapers are *El Cronista, La Epoca, Diario Comercial, El Dia, El Pueblo,* and *La Prensa* in Honduras; *El Dia, La Prensa Gráfica,* and *El Diario de Hoy* in El Salvador; *El Imparcial* and *La Prensa Libre* in Guatemala; *El Diario* and *La Nación* in Costa Rica; *El Centroamericano, La Prensa, La Noticia,* and *El Nuevo Diario* in Nicaragua.

Days of suspended civil guarantees were computed through analysis of each country's official government gazette from 1930 to 1985 by finding the date of the initiation of legislation to begin as well as end a period of suspension of guarantees.

a. Derived from official country records of the length of term of each Central American president between 1930 and 1985 and the changes of presidents during each economic period.

b. Nonprogrammed changes were changes that took place for reasons other than a scheduled election, such as a coup, death in office, or resignation.

c. Each period was divided into two subperiods of equal length and the number of reported violent incidents from the 28 percent content analysis survey of Central American newspapers was regrouped by the subperiods. The subperiod with more incidents was marked high and the other low. In some cases the number was equal.

d. Each period was divided into two subperiods of equal length and number of days of suspended guarantees from the review of official government gazettes between 1930 and 1985 was regrouped by the subperiods. The subperiod with more incidents was marked high and the other low. In some cases the number was equal.

e. Economic periods are defined based on Marc Lindenberg, "Central America: Crisis and Economic Strategy 1930–85, Lessons from History," *Journal of Developing Areas* 22, no. 2 (January 1988).

SOURCE: Author.

rural in its origins than in most other periods (see Tables 6.3 and 6.4). Violent discontent was particularly high at the beginning of the period. For example, in Nicaragua the government and the U.S. Marines battled Augusto Cesar Sandino, who refused to give up his arms after a peace agreement was negotiated between warring Liberals and Conservatives. In Honduras advocates of the National and Liberal parties fought for the presidency, and strikes took place in the banana plantation areas. In El Salvador in 1932 the troops of General Maximiliano Hernández Martínez are reported to have killed more than 10,000 Salvadoran peasants after an uprising led by Farabundo Martí.

Many governments suspended all civil guarantees, particularly in the second half of this period, as part of their struggle against rural-based insurgencies and their attempts to cleanse the national universities of what were perceived to be radical elements. For example, El Salvador lived under martial law for almost four of the five years of the period (see Table 6.5). In 1930 meetings of "communist-inspired groups" were banned entirely.[28] The government fought to purge communist influence from the university, which it saw as a focal point for sympathy as well as the base for leadership of the peasant uprisings. In 1932 it dissolved the university governance statutes and appointed a subsecretary of public instruction to ensure public order in the university. Possession of communist literature became a crime. A nationwide system of mandatory identity cards for citizens was established, and the police were reorganized.[29]

Nicaragua relied on the simple suspension of civil guarantees in its various departments, and occasionally on a national level, rather than on press censorship or other measures.[30] A state of siege was declared in parts of Honduras for almost half of this period in Jaaro, Colón, Cortés, and Atlántida.[31] In December 1932 a special decree prohibited communication and passage to the Port of Amapala where an uprising took place. By the end of 1934, three military dictators emerged: Generals Hernández Martínez in El Salvador, Ubico in Guatemala, and Carias Andino in Honduras. Joined in 1936 by General Anastasio Somoza García of Nicaragua, these military officers would rule their countries until the end of World War II.

1935–1944   By the beginning of the next period, 1935–1944, the new military regimes had consolidated themselves and contained the region's revolutionary impulses. The level of violent expressions of social discontent dropped from 29 percent in the previous period to 18 percent (see Table 6.3). Overt levels of repression dropped substantially until 1940 when all of the countries reinstated state of siege legislation in response to World War II. Typical of this period were declarations of war against Germany, Japan, and Italy;[32] prohibition of the sale and

TABLE 6.5   Central American Political Instability by Country, 1930–1985

| Country | Total years of suspended guarantees | | Average length of presidential term[b] | % of nonprogrammed changes of presidents[b] | % of violent social discontent[c] |
	Years[a]	%			
Panama	n.a.	n.a.	2.11	64	n.a.
El Salvador	20.1	36	2.57	57	48
Nicaragua	16.8	30	3.11	53	31
Guatemala	7.7	14	2.81	57	39
Honduras	7.6	13	3.11	47	27
Costa Rica	1.5	3	3.69	6	16
Central American average	10.7	19	2.81	50	33

n.a. = not available.
a. Days of suspended guarantees were computed through analysis of each country's official government gazette from 1930 to 1985 by finding the date of the initiation of legislation to begin as well as end the period.
b. Length of presidential terms and programmed and nonprogrammed changes come from official country records.
c. Percentage of violent social discontent data come from the 28 percent sample of the region's newspapers in 1930–1985 by Marc Lindenberg and María Joaquina Larraz de Quant.
SOURCE: Author.

possession of arms by private individuals;[33] the confiscation of property of German, Japanese, and Italian citizens;[34] and the seizure of communications systems.[35]

1944–1949   Between 1944 and 1949 social discontent held in check by wartime measures reemerged strongly as new, urban-based groups struggled for wage and salary increases not possible during the war. They also fought to bring down three of the region's military strongmen. U.S. foreign policy favored this brief democratic opening in the euphoria of anticolonial spirit that emerged at the end of World War II. As state of siege measures were lifted, urban-based groups began to exercise their right to organize. Urban discontent rose to 67 percent of all reported incidents and did not drop substantially again until 1978. In Guatemala urban groups like teachers and new unions were particularly active.

Measures of repression were high for the period. Wartime restrictions dominated the early years. Repression remained high in the latter part of the 1940s, however, as new military and civilian factions struggled first to wrest control from Ubico, Hernández, and Carias Andino and then quarreled among themselves. The Costa Rican revolution of 1948 was one of the few times when that country had emergency legislation and suspended civil guarantees. Typical measures during the 1944–1949 period included seizure of the properties and dismissal of public employees connected with previous dictatorial regimes;[36] nationalization of public utilities, banks, and insurance companies;[37] and temporary suspension of radio station licenses.[38]

The 1944–1949 period represents the beginning of the only attempt at democratic opening until 1986. In Guatemala Juan José Arevalo successfully completed his six-year term as a civilian president and passed the presidency to General Jacobo Arbenz through what was generally judged to be an election without fraud. In Panama longtime candidate Anulfo Arias took the presidency after the death in office of the incumbent, and in Costa Rica the revolutionary junta sponsored an electoral process that resulted in a return to civilian rule under Utillio Ulate. By 1949, however, new military leaders emerged in El Salvador (Osorio) and Honduras (Galvez), while in Nicaragua General Anastasio Somoza maintained his control through a carefully "managed" electoral process.

1950–1953   The 1950–1953 period was one of economic growth for both Central America and the world, and it was a quiet one by Central American political standards. The four military leaders and two civilians who emerged from the previous crisis period attempted to consolidate their governments. Violent expressions of social discontent were at an all-time low for the region (15 percent). Only one president, Anulfo Arias of Panama, was removed through a coup d'état. The only country with a state of siege briefly in place was El Salvador. Toward the end of the period, however, both discontent and repressive measures began to rise (see Table 6.5). For example, in Guatemala both landowners and the U.S.-based United Fruit Company became increasingly preoccupied with what they perceived to be "socialist" policies of President Jacobo Arbenz.

1954–1961   The period from 1954 to 1961 was one of both world and Central American economic crisis and high levels of Central American political instability. Incidents of violent discontent rose from 15 percent in 1950–1953 to 29 percent in this period. The region averaged 2.6 presidential changes per year, and 66 percent were by coup d'état. The Central American economic strategy collapsed with the depressed banana and coffee industries, and by 1961 there was discussion of a new strategy based on product and market diversification and a regional common market.

The Cuban Revolution, which took place in 1959, had a profound impact on the region and on U.S. foreign policy. The United States initiated the Alliance for Progress in an effort to stimulate Latin American economies and to provide a non-Marxist option. In Central America the period was accompanied by the installation of new military governments. The most prominent reversal took place in Guatemala where a coup supported by the U.S. Central Intelligence Agency (CIA) forced President Jacobo Arbenz from power. At the same time leadership changed hands through coups almost every other year in Honduras and El Salvador. Costa Rica repelled an invasion of the Calderonistas launched from Nicaragua. Worker discontent in the Costa Rican, Honduran, and Guatemalan banana plantations was high, and urban discontent grew as well. The country with the most days of civil guarantees suspended was Honduras. Typical legislation included outlawing the Communist party,[39] strengthening the military,[40] and controlling strikers in the banana plantations.[41] In Guatemala the new military government reversed the slide to the left that had taken place during the Arbenz period.[42] For example, legislation abolished workers' and farmers' organizations, returned land to those who had lost it during land reform, closed progressive newspapers, and prohibited trade with socialist countries.[43] The period ended with the beginning world and Central American economic recovery and the consolidation of largely new military leaders.

1962–1973   The years 1962–1973 were characterized by the most rapid economic growth and greatest political stability of the sixty-year period of this study. The world economy boomed. The Central American regional common market flourished and the region's economies reached their peak in product and market diversification. Although military leaders predominated, presidents in each country changed on the average of every three to four years, through elections rather than through coups.[44] The region averaged very low levels of suspension of civil guarantees and repressive measures (see Tables 6.2, 6.4, and 6.5). Where such measures were used, they included censorship of Marxist magazines, deregistration of political parties with "Marxist leanings," and the closing and restructuring of universities.[45] Social discontent did not begin to revive until the end of the period.

1974–1977   Between 1974 and 1977 both world and Central American growth slackened. The region continued its period of stable military rule, with few nonprogrammed changes of presidents but with increasing tension that culminated in the next period with revolutions in Nicaragua and El Salvador and instability in Guatemala. With the exception of Nicaragua, where armed struggle against General Somoza accelerated from 1975 on, governments did not find it necessary to suspend civil guarantees. Although Costa Rica did not declare national emergencies, it established special emergency zones in both Golfito and Limón because of strikes in the banana plantations, land seizures, and tensions between the Atlantic Coast population and outsiders.[46]

1978–1985   Between 1978 and 1985 a world and Central American economic collapse combined to produce one of the most serious periods of political instability and realignment since the Great Depression and the post–World War II period. Armed insurrections resulted in the overthrow of General Anastasio Somoza Debayle in Nicaragua and General Carlos Romero in El Salvador. Coups and countercoups took place in Honduras and Guatemala. More than 65 percent of the reported incidents of discontent in the media concerned terrorist actions, skirmishes, or battles. Rural discontent increased from 36 to 52 percent of reported incidents.

Civil guarantees were suspended not only by regimes trying to maintain themselves during revolutions but also by new revolutionary juntas seeking to establish control. Typical legislation used by those trying to maintain themselves against the revolutionaries included censorship, denial of rights of assembly and organization, and martial law.[47] Guatemala, for example, created military zones and special military commands and units, abolished its political parties, started its own munitions factories when it had trouble importing arms, and established popular militias.[48] In Costa Rica, where social discontent was due to eroding living standards, the government declared emergencies in the banana areas in Golfito.[49] In 1983 and after, the governments of Costa Rica, Honduras, and Guatemala began a series of economic reforms aimed initially at stabilization and later at structural adjustment and the stimulation of nontraditional exports outside of the region.

The legislation of the postrevolutionary period in Nicaragua and El Salvador reflected increased state intervention and attempts to improve income inequality while keeping tight social control. State of emergency legislation was in place in Nicaragua and El Salvador for almost seven of the eight years of this period. Typical legislation included nationalization of the banking sector, mining, and foreign trade;[50] land reform;[51] confiscation of property of those connected with the old regimes;[52] confiscation of unused land and property due to absenteeism; creation of popular militias and people's tribunals; and suspension of the right to strike.[53] Later the governments were forced to begin economic stabilization programs owing to their own difficult economic situations.

1986–1992   The instability and consolidation of the 1980s laid the basis for a series of weak democratic openings between 1986 and 1988. This period has been one of weak economic growth and recovery in three countries—Costa Rica, Honduras, and Guatemala—and continued economic deterioration in Panama, El Salvador, and Nicaragua. It is, at the same time, the only period of predominantly civilian rule with only one nonprogrammed change of president (in Panama) and the lowest levels of changes of presidents per year in the history of the region. The period has one of the highest registered levels of social discontent, probably because the newly elected governments, first in Guatemala and Honduras and later in El Salvador and Nicaragua, lifted states of emergency and censorship and permitted freedom of assembly and expression by opposition groups. The political openings were accompanied by high violence levels as armed struggles continued between governments and guerrillas. In 1988 the Arias Peace Plan attempted to reduce violence and consolidate democratic processes in each country through commissions of reconciliation, amnesty, talks between a country's government and opposition groups, abolition of press censorship, recognition of rights to organize and participate in elections, and a series of other measures.[54] In 1989 tensions in the region began to ease, except in Panama.

The changes between 1990 and 1992 in the region were unprecedented in their importance. Internationally, the Soviet Union disintegrated, and with its demise support to guerrilla movements in the region was reduced to a trickle. More important, Central American leftist parties and guerrilla movements were faced with ideological crisis. Tensions were substantially eased in the three most conflict-ridden environments. Internationally monitored elections in Nicaragua resulted in the Sandinista government's being voted out of power. The elections established the basis for negotiated transition agreements between the Sandinistas and their opposition. In Panama a U.S. military intervention forced General Manuel Noriega out of power after two coup attempts failed to remove him. The intervention established the basis for a transition to democratic government. Finally, the government of El Salvador reached a negotiated agreement with the revolutionary group FMLN, and a transition to democratic government was begun there as well.

Other Factors and Political Instability

Global and regional economic instability were far more important determinants of political instability in Central America than any of the other factors considered, with the exception of one—a country's regime type (democratic or authoritarian) at the beginning of the study period.[55] The role of initial regime type leads to an extremely important finding. World and Central American economic crises were necessary but not sufficient forces to exacerbate cycles of higher leadership turnover and political instability in all countries.

Initial regime type

Although all of the countries in the region had higher levels of social discontent during periods of economic crisis than during periods of economic growth, Costa Rica's levels of leadership instability, repression, and political instability were much lower than the other countries (see Table 6.5). Since 1930 Costa Rica managed social discontent with less repression and fewer unprogrammed changes in leadership than the other countries.

It appears that once peaceful and routine procedures for the transfer of political power were established, they were sufficient to help one of the six countries weather economic chaos in a manner quite different from the other five authoritarian regimes.

Political instability, regime type, and human development performance

The global findings about regime type and human development performance are supported by the regional data. The four Central American medium and low human development performers used predominantly authoritarian governance structures. The two high human development performers showed no predominant regime type. Costa Rica maintained democratic institutions, while in Panama authoritarian regimes dominated for forty of the sixty years after 1930.

The discussion of political instability and human development performance left us with some unanswered questions. In five of the six Central American nations, there was a clear relationship between high political instability and low human development performance. Panama, however, one of the two high human development performers, suffered high political instability during the sixty-year period but still managed to make major human development gains.

The origins of these differences and their relationship to the governance structure, class structure, values, and human development performance will be discussed in the next chapter of this book.

Conclusions

Since the 1930s Central America has been highly sensitive to external economic shocks. There is general evidence to support the thesis that world economic crises have helped set off cycles of Central American economic crisis and political instability. While the effects of these shocks have been mitigated by changes in economic strategy, the shocks have been a more important determinant of political instability than any other factor like population density or ethic composition of the population with the exception of initial regime type.

The region's periods of instability triggered by economic shocks have been accompanied by high levels of leadership rotation, social discontent, and repression, which have added up to political instability in five of the six countries. Usually these conditions have ended after a new set of military rulers has taken control of the government. In the military periods that have followed, new economic strategies have generally helped the region adapt to the new cycle of world economic growth and have resulted in Central American economic growth. This growth, however, in virtually all countries but Costa Rica and Panama has not been accompanied with conscious attempts to improve income distribution or develop mechanisms for the peaceful transfer of power from one group of rulers to another. Thus, the seeds of discontent for the next crisis cycle have been planted during the period of stable military rule.

During the periods of economic growth with military rule, external manifestations of social discontent have diminished or been otherwise controlled. Eventually repressive measures have been lifted. These periods have usually lasted until the next world economic collapse helps to set off a new cycle of Central American economic and political instability.

How might such cycles be broken? First, if periods of economic growth in the region have coincided with less political instability, social discontent, and repression than periods of economic crisis, then figuring out how to make the Central American economies less sensitive to external shocks may be a useful first step. As we saw earlier, the region was more economically independent and at times actually outperformed the world economy when its markets and products were more diversified. It also outperformed the world economy when the prices offered for its products were high and when terms of trade for the region were increasing. The implication for policy is that sensitivity to external shocks can be reduced by diversifying the region's sources of inputs as well as the mix of its products, as noted in the last chapter. The region would gain as well from worldwide agreements to stabilize the prices of key products. It would benefit from reopening its common market as well as from an outward orientation to a variety of world markets. Central American countries would benefit from a concentration on both traditional and nontraditional exports as part of this process.

Economic performance alone, however, has not been enough to guarantee high levels of investment in human capital, lower levels of social discontent, and the absence of political instability. Violence levels, coups, and levels of repression stayed high even in periods of economic growth in most countries. They simply became even higher in crisis periods. Why some governments opted for social investments and peaceful participation mechanisms for managing citizen demands while others did not still remains a mystery. How and why two countries, Panama and Costa Rica, chose a path of high human development while the others did not is the topic of the next chapter.

Historical Roots of Human Development Performance in Central America

Although the countries of Central America all underwent strong external economic shocks and countered those shocks with similar economic policies, their human development performances were substantially different. Costa Rica and Panama were among the top thirty human development performers between 1965 and 1987; Nicaragua, Honduras, and Guatemala were middle-level human development performers; and El Salvador was one of the thirty poorest performers.

What accounts for these differences? Did the region's high human development performers somehow manage the double-shock transitions of the 1980s more effectively than their neighbors? To answer these questions, I will compare some of the underlying characteristics of the two highest Central American human development performers, Costa Rica and Panama, with those of the two lowest performers, Guatemala and El Salvador.[1]

What Accounts for the Human Development Performance Differences among Central American Nations?

Differences in human development performance can be viewed on three levels. First, the Central American nations made different policy choices. Second, these choices were the results of different underlying governance structures. Finally, the governance structures were founded on different prevailing policy values, political coalitions, and implementing institutions. Each of these levels is worth exploring.

Policy choices

The simplest reason the Central American nations had radically different human development performances is that they chose fundamentally different approaches to social policy. Costa Rica and Panama made important investments before 1965 that had helped build a much stronger human capital base by that year. Between 1965 and 1987 they continued this different pattern, in which their expenditures in health and education almost doubled those of their medium- and low-performing neighbors.

Tables 7.1, 7.2, and 7.3 help illustrate these differences. By 1930 both Panama and Costa Rica had made important investments in primary education that resulted in higher rates of literacy. In contrast, according to most sources their infant mortality rates in the 1930s, at more than 180 infant deaths per 1,000 live births, were not much different from those of Guatemala and El Salvador, probably because less was known at that time about how to make major reductions in mortality rates. But between 1930 and 1990 both Panama and Costa Rica pursued policies that led to major reductions in infant mortality and increases in life expectancy. By 1970 adult mortality had fallen substantially and urban health was greatly improved. Both nations made major advances in rural health and the reduction of infant mortality between 1970 and 1980. Such a reduction did not take place in either Guatemala or El Salvador.

Health policies, 1930–1990   A comparison of Costa Rican and Guatemalan health policy between 1930 and 1990 helps to highlight what each nation did (see Tables 7.2 and 7.3).[2] From the 1930s through 1960s, Costa Rica developed a legal framework for its public health outreach system and an institutional infrastructure to deliver critical services. It made major investments in urban water and sewage systems; antimalaria, vaccination, and inoculation campaigns with broad coverage; and health education programs. In its 1942 campaign against hookworm, the government distributed 250,000 pairs of shoes, reaching virtually all of the population under fifteen years of age.[3] The revolution of 1948 in Costa Rica resulted in a more concrete commitment to improved national health. Spinoffs included a social security system that covered 80 percent of the population by 1980. By the 1960s the country had virtually eliminated malaria and tuberculosis and eradicated most diseases that are controllable with vaccinations, like polio.

TABLE 7.1   Infant Mortality, Life Expectancy, and Literacy Levels for Central America, 1950–1990

| | Top two human development performers | | | | | |
| | Costa Rica | | | Panama | | |
Year	Infant mortality	Life expectancy	Literacy	Infant mortality	Life expectancy	Literacy
1950	95	56	79	93	58	70
1960	80	63	82	63	62	77
1965	72	64	84	51	64	73
1970	61	65	89	43	66	81
1980	21	73	90	25	71	85
1987	18	74	93	23	72	87
1990	15	75	93	21	73	88

| | Middle two human development performers | | | | | |
| | Honduras | | | Nicaragua | | |
Year	Infant mortality	Life expectancy	Literacy	Infant mortality	Life expectancy	Literacy
1950	195	42	35	167	42	38
1960	147	48	45	130	48	50
1965	123	50	n.a.	121	51	50
1970	100	54	57	100	55	59
1980	78	62	59	88	60	n.a.
1987	69	64	n.a.	62	63	66
1990	64	65	73	65	65	65

| | Bottom two human development performers | | | | | |
| | Guatemala | | | El Salvador | | |
Year	Infant mortality	Life expectancy	Literacy	Infant mortality	Life expectancy	Literacy
1950	140	42	29	151	45	38
1960	119	47	32	122	52	45
1965	107	49	38	110	56	49
1970	95	54	46	99	59	58
1980	70	59	48	77	57	62
1987	59	62	56	59	62	n.a.
1990	62	63	55	53	64	73

n.a. = not available.
NOTE: Infant mortality is given in number of deaths per thousand live births; life expectancy is given in years; and literacy is given as a percentage.
SOURCE: For Costa Rica data from 1950–1980 are from Leonardo Mata and Luis Rosero, *National Health and Social Development in Costa Rica* (Washington, D.C.: Pan American Health Organization, 1988), pp. 35 and 38; data from 1980–1987 are from World Bank, *World Development Report 1991* (New York: Oxford University Press, 1991). For the other countries data from 1950–1980 come from ECLA, *Statistical Yearbook for Latin America and the Caribbean* (New York: ECLA, 1989), pp. 13, 45, and 50; Data for 1965, 1987, and 1990 are from World Bank, *World Development Report 1991* (New York: Oxford University Press, 1991).

TABLE 7.2   Health Status and Health Policies in Costa Rica, 1920–1990

Variable	1920–1940	1940–1950	1950–1960	1960–1970	1970–1980	1980–1990
Health status						
Life expectancy (years)	42	46	55	62	65	72
Infant mortality[a]	156	130	87	76	61	22
Urban infant mortality[a]	120	89	56	49	36	19
Deaths from public health–related diseases (%)	60	58	46	35	30	7
Literacy (%)	67	73	79	82	89	93
Women completing primary school (%)	12	14	22	27	43	65
Health resources						
Social security coverage (%)	0	0	8	15	39	78
Piped water (%)	n.a.	25	53	65	75	84
Urban	n.a.	n.a.	n.a.	77	97	99
Rural	n.a.	n.a.	n.a.	36	60	80
Sewage (%)	n.a.	25	48	69	86	93
Rural population with health post (%)	0	0	2	10	60	70
Doctors per 10,000 people	2.5	2.7	3.1	2.8	5.6	7.8
Health expenditures/ GNP (%)	n.a.	n.a.	2.2	3.0	5.6	7.4 (1980)

Variable	1920–1940	1940–1950	1950–1960	1960–1970	1970–1980	1980–1990
Major diseases reduced	Malaria Tuberculosis	Malaria Tuberculosis Diseases reduced with immunizations Parasites	Malaria Tuberculosis Diseases reduced with immunizations Parasites	Modest reductions	Diarrheal diseases Respiratory illness	
Health policies	Health protection law passed, 1923 Health Ministry established, 1927 Compulsory municipal health budgets of 15% Hookworm campaign Antimalaria campaign Antituberculosis campaign Food and drug controls adopted	Social security institute established, 1942 Urban water and sewage systems built Shoes distributed to 250,000 children Vaccination campaign Antibiotics adopted New antimalaria spraying campaigns	WHO founded Social security expanded 1940s programs expanded Child nutrition centers started	Medical school founded, 1961 DPT vaccine campaign[b] Aqueduct Institute established, 1961 Family planning introduced	Major rural health service expansion Preventive rural health campaigns Universal social security Hospital transfer to social security Health Ministry pursues preventive health and rural outreach Campaign for community participation	Major budget cuts and reductions in health services Experiments in privatization

n.a. = not available.

a. Deaths per thousand live births.

b. DPT = diphtheria, pertussis, tetanus.

SOURCES: Luis Rosero and Caamano, "Tables de vida de Costa Rica, 1900–1980," in *Mortalidad y Fecundidad en Costa Rica* (San José: Asociación Demográfica).

TABLE 7.3   Health Status and Health Policies in Guatemala, 1920–1990

Variable	1920–1940	1940–1950	1950–1960	1960–1970	1970–1980	1980–1990
Health status						
Life expectancy (years)	n.a.	n.a.	42	47	54	59
Infant mortality[a]	n.a.	n.a.	140	119	95	70
Urban infant mortality[a]	n.a.	n.a.	n.a.	n.a.	n.a.	n.a.
Deaths from public health–related diseases (%)	n.a.	n.a.	n.a.	70	63	51
Literacy (%)	n.a.	n.a.	29	32	46	48
Women completing primary school (%)	n.a.	n.a.	n.a.	n.a.	n.a.	n.a.
Health resources						
Social security coverage	0	6	10	10	16	20
Piped water (%)	n.a.	n.a.	n.a.	n.a.	n.a	n.a.
Urban	n.a.	n.a.	35	42	86	88
Rural	n.a.	n.a.	4	8	11	20
Sewage (%)	n.a.	n.a.	29	38	45	50
Rural population with health post (%)	n.a.	n.a.	n.a.	n.a.	20	22
Doctors per 10,000 people	n.a.	n.a.	n.a.	1.8	2.0	2.4
Health expenditures/ GNP (%)	n.a.	n.a.	1	1.2	1.4	1.5

Variable	1920–1940	1940–1950	1950–1960	1960–1970	1970–1980	1980–1990
Major diseases reduced	Malaria and tuberculosis reduced but not eradicated	Some diseases reduced with immunizations		Modest reductions		
Health policies	Health code under Ubico administration, 1932 Antimalaria campaign in banana plantations funded by Rockefeller Foundation	Social security institute established, 1946 Urban water and sewage systems Ministry of Health founded	WHO founded Social security expanded 1940s programs expanded but primarily urban focus	Rural health technicians program introduced at San Carlos University	Some rural health service expansion Urban water and sewage systems improved	Major budget cuts and reductions in health services

n.a. = not available.

a. Deaths per thousand live births.

SOURCES: ECLA, *Statistical Yearbook for Latin America and the Caribbean* (New York: ECLA, 1989); Molina, "Políticas de Salud de Guatemala," *Revista Centroamericana de Administración Pública*, no. 15 (July/December 1988), pp. 5–19; José Rómulo Sánchez, "Consideraciones Generales de la Salud en Guatemala," *Revista Centroamericana de Ciencias de la Salud* (May/August 1976), pp. 37–121.

The situation in Guatemala was much different. In the period from 1930 to 1965 Guatemala developed the legal and institutional basis for urban health coverage but did not follow through with major health investments or key programs. The country established a social security institute in the 1940s and made an ideological commitment to improved national health during the Arevalo and Arbenz administrations. But the coup that overthrew Arbenz in 1954 signaled a policy reversal, and the new leadership failed to invest the resources necessary to turn the vision of improved national health into a reality. Investments in urban water and sewage systems yielded some benefits, but Guatemala's poor health performance between 1930 and 1965 reflects a policy largely of neglect.

In the 1970s Costa Rica shifted its focus from urban to rural health. It made major new investments to extend rural primary health services and water and sanitation systems. Costa Rica's health expenditures as a percentage of gross national product (GNP) doubled in the 1970s. These changes were accompanied by dramatic increases in the percentage of women completing primary school, resulting from reforms in the 1970s. Many Costa Rican health policy experts argue that the substantial increase in women's educational levels from 1970 to 1990 as well as general economic development during the bonanza of the 1970s ensured that the population would be receptive to the health practices promoted through the new rural health infrastructure. Oral rehydration programs, health education, and preventive health practices helped to reduce deaths from gastrointestinal diseases substantially. The results for Costa Rica were greatly reduced infant mortality and an impressive narrowing of the gap between urban and rural health between 1970 and 1990.

In Guatemala investments in rural health infrastructure and preventive health programs simply did not take place. As the country entered the 1980s, therefore, deaths from major public health–related diseases remained high (see Table 7.3).

In their analysis of the impact of policies on health performance in Costa Rica, Leonardo Mata and Luis Rosero argue that the most important factors in overall health improvement between 1930 and 1990 were general economic development, the increasing education of women, and the primary health care system, including programs of health education, vaccinations, rural water supply, and sewage treatment.[4] They attribute 41 percent of the reduction in infant mortality between 1970 and 1980 to primary health care, 32 percent to secondary health care, 22 percent to general socioeconomic progress, and 5 percent to a decline in fertility.[5]

Education policies, 1930–1990   The educational achievements of top performers and bottom performers also differed substantially (see Table 7.4).[6] By 1980 Guatemala still had not achieved the 60 percent

TABLE 7.4   Education Performance in Costa Rica and Guatemala, 1960–1987

Variable	1960	1965	1970	1980	1987
Costa Rica					
Literacy (%)	67	n.a.	88	92	99
Males	n.a.	n.a.	n.a.	92	n.a.
Females	n.a.	n.a.	n.a.	92	n.a.
% enrolled in					
primary school	96	106	106	108	100
Males	97	107	n.a.	109	101
Females	95	105	n.a.	106	99
% who completed					
primary school	n.a.	n.a.	n.a.	75	n.a.
Education spending					
as a % of GNP	n.a.	n.a.	4.5	4.5	n.a.
Guatemala					
Literacy (%)	32	n.a.	44	52	n.a.
Males	n.a.	n.a.	n.a.	60	n.a.
Females	n.a.	n.a.	n.a.	44	n.a.
% enrolled in					
primary school	45	50	52	69	77
Males	50	n.a.	n.a.	74	n.a.
Females	39	45	n.a.	63	70
% who completed					
primary school	n.a.	n.a.	n.a.	36	n.a.
Education spending					
as a % of GNP	n.a.	n.a.	1.4	1.8	n.a.

n.a. = not available.
SOURCES: World Bank, *World Development Report* (New York: Oxford University Press, 1981–1992); United Nations, *Human Development Report* (New York: United Nations Development Program, 1990–1992).

literacy goal attained by Costa Rica in 1930. As late as 1980 only half of Guatemala's adults could read, while more than 90 percent of the Costa Rican population was literate. In that year less than half of Guatemala's eligible primary school population attended school and two-thirds of those who attended did not graduate. In contrast, 80 percent of Costa Rica's eligible primary school population was enrolled and more than 75 percent completed school. Finally, in 1980 Costa Rica's men and women had equal levels of literacy. In Guatemala 60 percent of men could read while only 40 percent of women could do so.

Earlier chapters showed that high human development performers had already built a strong human capital base by 1965. In Costa Rica four out of five adults could read as early as 1965, while only one of two Guatemalans could do so. What policies and practices might have led to these differences?

While both nations had established free, universal, compulsory primary education in their constitutions by 1880, successive generations of Costa Ricans allocated resources to implement these programs while the Guatemalans did not (see Table 7.5). Between 1869 and 1882, Costa

TABLE 7.5   Education Policies in Costa Rica and Guatemala, 1965–1985

Costa Rican education policies

Before 1965	After 1965
1869: Free universal, compulsory primary education decreed	1970: Education reforms lead to:
1869–1882: Municipalities given responsibility for primary education	1. extension of rural primary education to remote areas
1882–1887: Reforms instituted by Mauro Fernández included:	2. better links between rural primary and secondary education
1. national coordination	3. better secondary education
2. improved primary education	1970–1985: More private universities open and more technical education available
3. closing of the university	
1915: Ideas of the French active school movement adopted	
1940: University reopened	
1948–1965: New plans lead to:	
1. more rural coverage	
2. curriculum revision	
3. better secondary education	
4. technical education	

Guatemalan education policies

Before 1965	After 1965
1869: Free, universal, compulsory education decreed; little extension of rural primary education	1972–1978: National education plan lead to:
1944–1954: Education reforms promoted by Presidents Arevalo and Arbenz	1. expanded coverage for primary education
1. rural primary education	2. first cycle of middle school made compulsory
2. compulsory schools in rural enterprises with more than 100 employees	3. teacher training
	4. curriculum revision
3. teacher training	5. EBR rural adult education
1954: Reforms end with coup against President Arbenz	6. PENEM middle school improvement
	7. PMEP primary education improvement
1965: Little progress to this date	1976: Earthquake forces change of focus away from plan
	1980s: Few resources available to continue with plan

SOURCES: See note 6 for this chapter for sources on education policy.

Rica gave responsibility for primary education to the municipalities, with a mandated portion of local budgets allocated for this function.[7] State religious education was replaced with more practical, empirically based topics. Between 1882 and 1887 President Mauro Fernández directed a major educational reform.[8] The central government assumed responsibility for coordinating national primary education. Fernández and others believed that Costa Rica should not devote resources to secondary or university education until it had high-quality, universal primary education. As a result Fernández closed Costa Rica's only university (the University of San Tomas) and advocated spending more resources on primary education. From the 1880s to the 1920s education based on positivism and empiricism was strengthened, the quality and geographic coverage of primary education improved, and teacher training was expanded. In 1915 currents in French education were incorporated into the Costa Rican school system through the ''active school movement,'' which attempted to make education relevant to national economic development.[9] In 1940 the university was reopened.

After Costa Rica's revolution of 1948 the government drew up a new plan to improve the quality and coverage of the education system and to make the curriculum relevant to the revolutionary goals of economic development and economic and social justice. The new plan emphasized further rural coverage for primary education, curriculum revision in and improvement of secondary education, and the beginnings of special technical education at the university level. Between 1960 and 1985 Costa Ricans spent more than 4 percent of their GNP annually on education.

The education and skills of Costa Ricans improved further with education reforms in the 1970s. The goals in that decade were to

> raise the education level of the population, especially in poor and neglected areas, to achieve nationwide integration and ensure for all citizens better living conditions, and thus to contribute to the socioeconomic development of the country, to modernize the system, and to maintain its current budget share without harm to the quality and quantity of education.[10]

Among the practical results of the new policy were strengthened links between primary and secondary education in rural areas. As a result many more rural students had a chance to complete secondary education and to continue to the university. In the 1970s and 1980s private universities and primary and secondary schools proliferated. The Costa Rican education system improved until the early 1980s, when the nation's economic collapse forced budget reductions. Today another education reform is in the making to help students adapt to the increasingly competitive world economy, but fewer resources are available for education.

Guatemalan policies between 1840 and 1990 provide a stark contrast. Although Guatemala introduced liberal reform plans similar to those of Costa Rica, it allocated insufficient resources to put them into practice on a large scale, particularly for the majority rural, non-Spanish-speaking communities. Furthermore, in Guatemala the reform periods alternated with even longer periods of reversal by the conservatives, who resisted change and upheld traditional values.

The Guatemalan education system was established during the colonial period primarily for the education of sons of urban Spanish and Creole elites and propertied families.[11] Primary education as well as education at the University of San Carlos, the oldest university in Central America, was mainly religious. The typical primary school curriculum included elementary reading, catechism, Christian morals and ethics, Christian doctrine, writing, and basic arithmetic.[12]

Immediately after independence in 1821 President Galvez attempted to introduce a more positivist, empirically based curriculum into the schools, but the reforms were reversed by the conservative dictator Rafael Carerra (1839–1865). Carerra himself could not read or write. The Catholic Church regained control of education. The Pavon Law passed in Guatemala in 1852 reestablished the colonial era's religious-based primary school curriculum described above. Even during this period, however, liberal education reform was promoted by groups of intellectuals like those who founded the Sociedad Económica de Amigos del País de Guatemala.

A major attempt at education reform took place after Liberal dictator Justo Rufino Barrios (1865–1885) seized power. Barrios expelled the Jesuits and removed the Church from the education process. He promoted curriculum reform and encouraged education with three objectives: "progress, liberty, and scientific spirit."[13] He set up the Ministry of Public Instruction in 1873 and mandated free universal education for all children between the ages of six and fourteen. He encouraged the strengthening of primary school education and doubled primary school attendance from 8,074 (around 5 percent of the total population) in 1866 to 20,528 in 1874.[14] Barrios initially provided resources for teacher training but his budget did not stretch far enough to expand rural education to the Indian population. Instead his reforms had more of an impact on urban Ladino communities.

Barrios's reforms in education were short-lived. At the very time Costa Rica's primary education system was being expanded under the reform program of Mauro Fernández, Guatemala's new dictator Estrado Cabrerra (1898–1920) abolished wages for teachers and let the education budget deteriorate.

The next impetus for education reform came in the administration of José María Orellana in the 1920s. Orellana promoted the normal school movement, in which Indian teachers were trained to teach primary education in their villages. This effort fell into neglect during the Ubico administration (1931–1944). As a result, by the end of World War II rural educational infrastructure was still largely nonexistent and illiteracy was the norm.

Education reform again became a critical part of the Guatemalan agenda during the Arevalo and Arbenz administrations between 1944 and 1954. Dr. Arevalo, Guatemala's first freely elected president, was an educator who placed priority on what he called Guatemala's two orphans, "education and agriculture."[15] His successor, President Arbenz, succeeded in convincing the legislature to pass revolutionary legislation in Article 103 of the Organic Law on National Education, which decreed that

> every private enterprise of more than 100 employees that recruits seasonal workers is bound to provide education for children accompanying their parents, in schools functioning on the property of the enterprise concerned.[16]

Arbenz allocated resources for rural primary education, teacher training schools, and curriculum reform. The reforms stopped when Arbenz was overthrown in a counterrevolution partially financed by the CIA. As a result little changed in either the resource allocation or curriculum in nationwide education until the 1970s. In Latin America only Haiti spent less of its GNP on education between 1965 and 1980 than Guatemala.

The national plan for 1972–1978 again presented education reforms.[17] In Guatemala, as in many countries of the region, additional resources were potentially available as a result of the economic boom of the 1960s and 1970s described in Chapters 5 and 6. The education minister at that time proposed

> complete coverage of primary education, to make the first cycle of middle-level education compulsory, to give clear priority to adult education, to make use of new concepts and techniques for out-of-school education, to introduce polyvalent middle-level education in which there would be a wide range of specializations, to improve teaching by making use of a standard curriculum, to plan the development of human resources before the development of economic resources, to regard education not only as a government responsibility but also as a process involving the entire society, and last to stimulate lifelong education.[18]

As a result of the plan the government initiated three new programs: PEMEP, to improve primary education; EBR, to improve basic education for rural adults; and PEMEM, to improve middle-school education.[19] All three were financed with funds from external donors. All were experimental and limited in scope. In 1974 these programs were reinforced with a continuing education program for school dropouts and illiterate adults and with more attention to distributing resources equitably among rural areas. Guatemala's 1976 earthquake, however, brought an end to the emphasis on these programs when the government turned its attention to refugee relief and reconstruction. As a result the progress initially made in the programs slowed.

The economic crisis of the 1980s made it even more difficult for governments to invest in education. Although Venicio Cerezo and Jorge Serrano Elías, the first two freely elected presidents since the days of Arevalo and Arbenz, had an active interest in education reform, they had neither the resources nor the political support to bring such reforms to fruition. The Guatemalan public education system continues to be starved for resources while the Costa Ricans move ahead in an uncertain economic situation.

Underlying governance structures

Clearly the adoption of active policies to improve the health and educational status of the citizens of Costa Rica and Panama made a difference in the quality of their human capital base, particularly when compared with Guatemala and El Salvador. But to say that human development performance was different because social policies were different still does not explain why six nations with so much in common made such different choices. The different policies are in fact a reflection of differences in those nation's governance structures between 1965 and 1987. These differences are a reflection of the global differences we encountered earlier (see Table 7.6).

The high human development performers: Costa Rica and Panama   The governance structures of Costa Rica and Panama are similar to the two types displayed in other global high performers. Costa Rica, like about a third of the high human development performers, maintained an established democracy with high levels of political and civil rights. Panama, like two-thirds of the high human development performers, rarely used democratic forms to select top leaders, particularly between 1965 and 1987 but maintained at least medium levels of political and civil rights, which provided some avenues for other levels of popular feedback and participation. In these two governance structures the formal regime type—dictatorship or democracy—at the national level did not matter so much as the presence of at least medium levels of civil and political rights that permitted participatory mechanisms at the subnational level and guaranteed feedback to government.

TABLE 7.6 Governance Structures of the Central American Countries

	High human development performers			Medium human development performers			Low human development performers		
	Costa Rica	Panama	Summary	Honduras	Nicaragua	Summary	Guatemala	El Salvador	Summary
Democratic regime type (%)	100	22	61	51	0	26	22	18	20
Political rights[a]	1	5.5	3.3	4.1	5.1	4.6	4.1	3.8	4.0
Political instability (%)	0	57	29	64	62	63	71	52	62
Civil rights[a]	1	4.5	2.8	3	4.6	3.8	4.2	4	4.1
Government spending/GNP (%)	22	28	25	17	27	22	11	14	13
Health and education/GNP (%)	8.3	6.4	7.4	4.8	2.5	3.7	2.3	4.1	3.2
Military/health and education (%)	1	1	1	45	86	66	46	37	42
Fiscal deficit (%)	4	7	6	3	13	8	2	2	2
Debt/GNP (%)	50	61	56	39	85	62	11	19	15
Debt service/exports (%)	27	26	27	18	17	18	11	13	12
Market economy	Yes	No	Split	Yes	No	Split	Yes	Yes	Yes
Openness (%)	45	55	50	45	51	48	28	42	35
Export growth (%)	6	7	7	3	2	3	5	2	4

a. High political or civil rights 1-2, medium 3-5, low 6-7.
SOURCE: Compiled by the author based on data set.

Panama's initial commitment to a formal democratic process in the early 1900s was strengthened by the Panamanian leaders' distaste for the brutal warfare of Colombia's Liberal and Conservative parties.[20] The strong U.S. influence on Panama that began when Panama broke with Colombia and continues today supported that commitment by providing external pressure for at least formal participative traditions. Even under the military government of General Torrijos, and particularly after 1975, major reforms included open municipal elections and mechanisms of local participation in government problem solving.

Like other high human development performers, Costa Rica and Panama remained "promoter" rather than "producer" states; they spent 20–30 percent of GNP on public activities and played an active role in stimulating private sector initiative for much of the 1965–1987 period. Compared with their lower-performing neighbors, both pursued more export-promoting economic policies; maintained more open, market-oriented economies; and spent larger percentages of GNP on health and education, at least until the late 1970s.

These two nations, however, also had some important differences from other global high performers. Because neither country maintained high levels of defense spending, they were able to allocate more resources to social expenditures. Costa Rica disbanded its army in 1948. Panama abolished its military in 1904. Its national defense force was redeveloped, but spending was low compared with other nations because the U.S. military had assumed much of the responsibility for Panama's defense.

A second important difference was that Panama, particularly between 1965 and 1987, was not as politically stable as most of the global high human development performers. If it had followed the trends of other politically unstable nations, it would have stayed among the ranks of medium or low human development performers. It escaped low performance probably because it had several long periods of stability, in the early 1900s and between 1950 and 1968, when human development performance accelerated. Furthermore, major human development advances occurred during Torrijos's administration in the 1970s, a time of stable authoritarian continuity.

Finally, although both countries were promoter rather than provider states, both edged toward provider status in the late 1970s with disastrous consequences. Between 1975 and 1980 both countries raised government spending. As economic growth deteriorated and economic strategies in both countries became obsolete, each tried to maintain employment and social spending through borrowing and heightened fiscal deficits. While Costa Rica was able to reverse this process in the 1980s, Panama began to take on many of the worst vices of a producer state. Between 1975 and 1980 it expanded its public enterprise sector. Its government expenditures reached 35 percent of GNP. It provided wage and pension benefits and job security far in excess of the other Central American nations and developed large subsidies for its business community as well. One of Panama's many dilemmas in the 1990s will be how to restructure its state.

The low human development performers: El Salvador and Guatemala   The governance structures of El Salvador and Guatemala mirrored many of the characteristics of other low human development performers. They rarely used democratic forms for governance. They had lower levels of political and civil rights than their neighbors and few mechanisms for popular participation, even at lower levels of government. The levels of repression and violence in these nations were among the highest in the region.

They did maintain market economies and attain high levels of GDP growth for much of the period, but they operated small regulator states whose public spending averaged 11–14 percent of GNP. They spent little on health and education and, as described earlier, made little effort to reach their rural populations with services. Part of the profile of a regulator state included low fiscal deficits and low debt and debt-service levels.

Although both economies were open and export oriented, of the six nations Guatemala was the least open to international trade, primarily because of its large rural, indigenous subsistence sector. Because of the high population density and the scarcity of land in tiny El Salvador, the rural population was intimately connected to the export economy as plantation labor but tied to a system that made few social investments. This situation left labor and the poor highly vulnerable to world economic cycles.

The medium human development performers: Honduras and Nicaragua   The governance structures of Honduras and Nicaragua demonstrated many of the characteristics of medium human development performers. They used democratic forms less often than high performers and had substantial political instability. They maintained medium levels of political and civil rights but lower levels than their high-performing neighbors. The state in both nations was a regulator-promoter. After the 1979 Nicaraguan revolution, however, Sandinista policies established a provider state that spent more than 50 percent of GNP. This move gave Nicaragua much in common with other medium human development performers in the 1980s whose provider states acquired structural rigidities from which they are still trying to recover.

The Foundations of Governance Structures

It is not enough to say that the Central American high human development performers were more successful because they had different policies or that they had different policies because they had different governance structures. High human development performance depends on three factors:

- articulated human development policy values that have been translated into programs

- strong coalitions that emerge through changes in the social structure to provide support for the initial policy choices, resource allocation, and sustained commitment

- a solid institutional infrastructure for implementation

Building the foundation of governance for high human development performance is similar to nurturing a strong healthy plant. Policy ideas are the seeds that can germinate to produce strong performance. The institutional network provides the soil and nutrients to stimulate growth. The coalitions provide a lattice of support networks on which policies and programs can take hold and climb. Without these elements working together, high human development performance will not take place.

By 1965 these critical elements were in place in both Costa Rica and Panama but not in El Salvador, Guatemala, Honduras, or Nicaragua. A brief historical comparison of these elements in Costa Rica, one of the region's highest human development performers, and Guatemala, one of the lowest in the region (with occasional reference to Panama and El Salvador), helps provide possible explanations.

Policy values, coalitions, and institutions before 1840

Although all six of the Central American nations had a common Spanish colonial cultural heritage, the role of each nation within the empire produced different initial settlement patterns that resulted in important differences in policy values and norms, in the social structures that led to certain coalitions, and in the institutions that carry out policy.[21] I will examine how these foundations have emerged in Cost Rica and Guatemala since colonial times.

Costa Rica   If the Spanish settlers came to Costa Rica with visions of religious, political, and economic domination they must have been sorely disappointed. The province had few Indians to enslave or convert and no gold or minerals. If there were any soldiers, nobles, or passionate clerics, they must have left quickly, because only those willing to work hard for a living stayed alive. As a result there were only 330 Spanish immigrants (mostly from Andalusia) out of 17,479 inhabitants of that nation in 1611.

One prominent scholar suggests many of the original settlers were not passionate Catholics but rather were converted members of the Andalusian Sephardic Jewish community who fled the Inquisition.[22] He notes that the bishop of Nicaragua criticized the Costa Rican population in the early 1700s, saying that most tried to live as far away from towns with churches as they possibly could.

Even if the original settlers had been passionately committed to the policy values of political and religious domination and economic exploitation, the requirements of their physical survival forced them to develop a radically different social structure from that of their neighbors in other countries. The following excerpts from Spanish Governor Don Diego de la Haya Fernández to the king of Spain in 1719 shed light on this social structure:

> The capital [Cartago] has a church, a convent, two hermitages, and seventy adobe houses with tile roofs. Interspersed are about 300 houses of poorer families. These are made of straw. . . . On the outskirts of town are Indian villages with perhaps 114 families who have practically no clothes. In the city there is no barber, surgeon, doctor, or pharmacy. Nothing is sold in the streets or plazas. There are no small shops to get provisions. For this reason everyone including the Governor [Don Diego was referring to himself] must grow everything he wants to consume during the year. Anyone who does not do this will starve. . . . The money used here is the cocoa bean, no one uses Spanish silver reales. . . . I cannot understand why they call this place Costa Rica [Rich Coast] since it is so totally poor. . . . In the middle of this total poverty which I have come to know, I confess that I find Costa Rica's inhabitants to be quarrelsome, rebellious, and independent.[23]

As the quote reveals, there was little stratification among Spanish officials and between large and small landholders. There were virtually no tradesmen. A military caste is not in evidence, because there was little to conquer in this poor region.

Because of the absence of cheap Indian labor, settlers had to work the land themselves. As a result landholdings were smaller, and all citizens had to work hard to survive. Since it took more than three months for letters to reach Costa Rica from Guatemala, the Spanish administrative capital, citizens had to solve their problems on their own. Cooperative labor was necessary for roads and basic infrastructure. According to Spanish law trade had to be conducted through Panama or Peru. But the remoteness of Costa Rica from actual Spanish authority structures left room for contraband trade and promoted a certain disrespect for the rules of the empire. By 1800 Costa Rica had 50,000 inhabitants who were relatively homogeneous: about 70 percent mestizo; 10 percent Spanish; and the rest a combination of mulatto, Indian, and black. As late as 1800 the social structure was remarkably unstratified and homogeneous compared with the rest of Central America.

These economic conditions and the resulting social structure probably helped transform initial values of dominance and economic extraction to those of egalitarianism and independence moderated by necessary cooperation. The circumstances also gave rise to traditions of local self-governance and horizontal as opposed to vertical structures.

In contrast to other countries in Central America, Costa Rica's institutions were smaller, weaker, and more decentralized and partici-pative. Instead of the haciendas of Guatemala, one found individual small or medium-sized fincas. In contrast to Guatemala, the seat of the Spanish Central American empire, Costa Rica's capital Cartago had a rudimentary colonial administration with virtually no budget or tax base. Just as in Guatemala, one of the chief institutions was the church. But it was far from the central authority structure.

Central America declared independence from Spain in 1821. It briefly became part of Mexico (with the exception of Panama, which was part of Colombia), then formed a federation that collapsed in 1838, leaving each nation to follow its own path.[24]

Guatemala   The Guatemalan experience before independence provides a dramatic contrast to the pattern of values, social structure, and insti-tutions exhibited in Costa Rica. In Guatemala, El Salvador, Honduras, and Nicaragua a traditional hacienda-based society, founded on the policy values of religious and political domination and extraction of economic resources, developed during Spanish colonial rule. According to one scholar:

> The colonizers came principally from Spain and Portugal. They considered manual labor or any form of menial employment beneath them. Before colonizing the Americas Spain and Portugal had fought during eight centuries against the Moors, and as a result had glorified the soldier and priest and had looked down upon commercial and financial activities frequently in the hands of Jews and Muslims. Under these circumstances it was logical that there would be the constant pressure of a militant Catholic Church to christianize pagan populations, the necessity to morally justify the domination of inferior populations. It was natural to develop a mentality of rapid acquisition of wealth by the conquistadores. This was reinforced by efforts to discover sources of gold and precious metals and by the creation of latifundios as a predominant form of economic, social and political organization.[25]

Political domination was accomplished through the force of superior military technology and organization. The process is reflected in the letters of Pedro de Alvarado, one of the Guatemalan conquistadores:

> They [the Indians] hid in the bush and we had no way to damage them except to burn their village. Then I sent messangers to them and told them that if they gave obedience to our king, and to me in his name, they could return and cultivate their land. They returned and became vassals to our king.[26]

After the initial conquest the Spaniards set up more stable government institutions such as a tribunal, a mint, a post office, and a military, to insure the continuation of this domination.

Political domination permitted the development of institutions for economic domination and extraction of wealth. According to one Indian chronicle, upon conquest

> we began to pay tribute. . . . During that year they imposed terrible burdens. They forced tribute of gold. . . . They forced us to send four hundred men and women to go and wash [mine] gold. All of them wanted gold.[27]

In Guatemala, where gold and minerals were scarce, other means of economic extraction needed to be found. The subjugation of the local population permitted the Spanish Crown to assign Spanish settlers large tracts of land called haciendas. Since labor was needed to work in the haciendas, economic institutions were developed to provide a continued source of such labor. Simple slavery of the Indians was replaced by more sophisticated systems like *encomienda* (service and tribute). *Encomienda* was cheaper than slavery because the Indians had to support themselves through subsistence agriculture as well as supply labor to the Spanish hacienda owners. Later the system was replaced with an even more sophisticated system called *repartimiento*, which assigned Indians to specific tasks, usually public works. This system, with its abuses, became an equivalent to forced labor.

The strong church infrastructure pursued religious domination. At first the priests made forced conversions. Religious domination was reinforced through church control of the formal education system and school curriculum for the sons of the Spanish and Creole population. Although a limited number of people learned to read, write, and do basic arithmetic, education was predominately religious. Educators thought it unnecessary to teach the Indians anything but simple concepts of Catholicism.

The values and institutions described initially stimulated and later reflected a highly stratified social structure based economic, political, and ideological function. It was strongly reinforced in Guatemala by language and racial differences between Indians and Spanish colonial settlers.[28] At the top were Spanish-born bureaucrats, representatives of the church, and landowners. They shared top positions with the Central American–born pure-blooded descendants of the conquistadores called Creoles. In the middle was a tiny but growing group of Ladinos, frowned upon by the Spaniards because of their mixed blood. They served as merchants and tradesmen, and some had haciendas as well. Indians constituted the lower class and supplied labor. By 1800 Europeans were no more than 4 percent of the population of the region; 65 percent was Indian, and about 31 percent was Ladino.

Until independence the resources held by the tiny European coalition at the pinnacle of this social structure were sufficient to permit them to maintain the initial policy values of political and religious dominance and the extraction of wealth.

Policy values, coalitions, and institutions, 1840–1900

After independence important economic, social, and political developments produced major changes in the region's social structure. Coffee became Central America's major export. The Spanish, Creole, and indigenous populations were increasingly mixed. And the conflict between the political ideologies of liberalism, which advocated rapid economic development and social change, and conservatism, which attempted to slow the pace of development and maintain traditional values, dominated the political sphere.[29]

Between 1821 and 1838 the liberals held sway. They were imbued with the ideals of the American and French Revolutions. They attempted to establish free trade, abolish slavery, limit the powers of the Catholic Church, and integrate the Indians into mainstream Central American culture. They championed the ideals of public education, judicial reform, economic innovation, and investment in infrastructure. To carry out their programs they relied on the support of the emerging middle- and aspiring upper-class Ladinos and elements of the military. They rode to power in the backlash against the traditional elites connected with old Spanish colonial interests. The general population, largely mestizo in some countries, were a key element in the coalition that was responsive to these ideas in the immediate postindependence period.

The liberal programs required higher taxes and worked best during economic expansion. But the liberals made enemies of the Spanish-oriented upper class. Since resources were scarce and institutional infrastructure in the public sector was weak, their reforms were never far-reaching. Thus, their ideas were never fully translated into action, and a reservoir of frustration was left among the peasantry and lower class. In periods of economic downturn violent popular discontent rose and was normally squelched by more conservative elements of the military.

During one such period after 1838 the conservatives held sway. They rolled back the reforms, reestablished more traditional Spanish institutions, restored the church to its former preeminence, spoke out against foreign dominance, and pursued a more subsistence-oriented economic policy.

Costa Rica   Since coffee sales financed Costa Rica's human development achievements in the nineteenth and twentieth centuries, it is necessary to understand how this product system developed, affected social structure, and provided fertile soil for the flowering of human development policy values and the institutions to promote them.[30]

In light of Governor Don Diego de la Haya Fernández's description of Costa Rica's poverty and backwardness in the 1700s, it is hard to imagine how the inhabitants of this small nation developed the innovations that made coffee the region's major export for the next century and a half. It is also ironic that Costa Rica's practices and systems would be copied by other Central Americans, who had previously made Costa Ricans the butt of jokes and derision.

But this in fact happened. Between independence and the mid-1850s Costa Ricans, driven by economic stagnation and the continued threat of poverty, found methods for growing and harvesting coffee plants on a large scale that altered their social structure and government institutional network. They overcame major bottlenecks in the production system, like poor infrastructure, unreliable transportation, and inadequate credit. They established direct links with European markets, formed key alliances with European banks and marketing channels, and became the largest exporter of coffee in the region. And they laid the groundwork for major improvements in education that would form the foundation of later human development achievements.

The values reflected in this process of change are instructive. Interdependence and cooperation among producers continued. Later national initiatives favored the general population. The state actively encouraged private initiative, even in the colonial period, and experimental entrepreneurial responses. For example, the initial impetus for experimentation with coffee came from Costa Rican municipalities searching for an escape from poverty and stagnation.[31] The municipality of San José gave coffee plants to farmers in the 1820s. The municipality of Cartago encouraged people to grow coffee as well. The governor authorized tax holidays for those who experimented with a number of products, including coffee. Finally, in 1831 those cultivating products such as coffee on state lands were given the land free, and others who were willing to try coffee and other product experiments on state land for five years would receive title to that land.

A brief digression into the origins of coffee production in Costa Rica is useful. The first successful production and export of coffee to Chile was arranged in 1832 by Jorge Stipel, a German immigrant married to a Costa Rican.[32] By 1839 a growing group of Costa Rican farmers was following Stipel's lead.

The exports to Chile left the Costa Ricans at a real disadvantage. The transportation between Puntarenas, Costa Rica, and Chile was sporadic, and transport costs were high. Merchants in Chile then reexported the coffee as a Chilean product and made large profits. A major breakthrough took place in 1843 when an English ship put into Puntarenas for repairs. The captain

> took a mule and made the long and difficult trip [from Puntarenas to San José]. He was put in touch with Don Santiago Hidalgo, one of the principal coffee producers of that time. The captain offered to buy Don Santiago's coffee and take it directly to London at a good price. Unfortunately the captain did not have the money with him to pay Don Santiago. But because the coffee business was going so badly, Don Santiago let him take the coffee and that of many neighbors [whose losses he would reimburse if the captain did not return] on the promise that he would return and pay them. . . . The captain in fact returned after a highly profitable venture and the direct link in the coffee trade between London and Costa Rica began.[33]

There are many possible explanations for why a new product system developed first in Costa Rica. The nation's poverty may have placed special pressure on its government and on individuals to search for productive new options. Another possibility was that neither the government nor the citizens were bound by the rigid traditions or structures that were found in Guatemala. Some scholars argue that individual coffee farmers had more potential for innovation because they worked their land directly owing to labor shortages.[34] Thus, they were more inclined than the Guatemalans to experiment and learn from the results. Finally, some argue that the Costa Ricans' motivation to prove themselves came with being the most unsuccessful of the region's nations.[35]

The requirements of the new coffee production system resulted in greater social stratification among Costa Rica's racially homogeneous population. The increased demand for coffee motivated farmers to increase acreage and resulted in a new group of relatively large farmers. Because of labor shortages, however, there were limits to the size of farms. Although the coffee farms never grew to the size of Guatemala's haciendas, large coffee farmers did evolve into a new social group. At the same time the production of smaller farmers was needed to meet demand. Thus, the smaller farmers grew and prospered as well. Finally, some farmers who did not do well and could not repay their credits lost their land and became peons who provided labor for the others. Since certain technology and engineering were needed to maintain machinery in the coffee-processing areas and to build roads, a small class of professionals and technical people sprang up as well.[36]

While the social structure so eloquently described by Don Fernando in 1711 became more stratified in the 1800s as the result of coffee production, labor shortages helped to reinforce rather than destroy many of the previous values of interdependence and egalitarianism. Large farmers could hardly use threats, compulsion, or systems like *encomienda* to force peons to pick coffee. Thus, relations were based not only on wages but also on interpersonal relations, mutual obligations, and eventually the delivery of education and health programs. Small farmers were necessary to help Costa Rica keep its coffee production levels up and provide the economies of scale to make processing plants and transportation activities viable. Credit mechanisms had to be developed to reach both large and small farmers.

Labor shortages were sufficiently great that even large Costa Rican coffee farmers worked directly in their production as well as in other activities. As a result, they knew more about the problems of their workers than Guatemalan landowners. They also involved themselves directly in politics and civic organizations.

The new social structure that emerged under the expansion of the coffee product system continued to reinforce egalitarian values and mutual interdependence not because these were attractive abstract ideas, but rather because they were necessary for the production system to succeed. Since coffee production in Costa Rica was dependent on an outward trade orientation and harmonious interdependent class relations, it is easy to see why liberalism and positivism became easily accepted values for the policy agenda. Positivism and empirical experimentation fit well with the practical trial and error efforts necessary to keep the coffee production system moving. Liberalism, with its ideas of free trade and state stimulus, was a natural ideology for expanding coffee trade.

Coffee production could not have expanded without a healthy, motivated labor pool. Nor could it have functioned without small farmers who had enough education to manage their coffee operations. They needed not only agricultural skills but also basic literacy and math ability. It is not surprising therefore that legislators approved policies to improve primary education.

The policy values of economic development and liberal education and social reform benefited from the support of strong coalitions between 1870 and the early 1900s. These values were developed and refined by a generation of Costa Rican intellectuals and innovators called the Olympiad of 1888. The governments of that period took the first steps to consolidate national institutions that could build roads, improve ports, and deliver extensive primary school education. They provided sufficient state resources to turn the ideas into programs with functioning delivery systems. Their actions provided much of the initial stimulus that made Costa Rica's health and education policies and human capital base so different from Guatemala's by 1965.

Guatemala   The development of coffee production altered Guatemala's social structure, as it had in Costa Rica. In Guatemala, however, it served only to reinforce social stratification and the values of dominance and economic extraction that had prevailed earlier.[37] While liberal reforms helped benefit the growing Ladino population, they left the indigenous population relatively untouched.

The process of the introduction of coffee and its initial support by the Guatemalan government is similar to that which had begun twenty years earlier in Costa Rica. Although some farmers had cultivated coffee in Guatemala during the colonial period on a very small scale, the first serious proposal for large-scale coffee production appeared in a pamphlet by Manuel Aguilar in 1845.[38] Aguilar, a Guatemalan, visited Costa Rica and was tremendously impressed with the impact of coffee production on overall economic development. His pamphlet describes the technical details of planting, harvesting, and processing coffee. Aguilar's initial suggestions were disseminated by the Sociedad Económica de Amigos del País de Guatemala.[39] In 1855 the Guatemalan government established experimental farms to show growers how to grow coffee and offered incentives, like free plants, tax holidays, and technical assistance, to get the process started. In that year Guatemala exported 95 quintals of coffee. In contrast Costa Rica had already exported 29,000 quintals in 1843. But by 1880 Guatemala exported more than 325,000 quintals, which made up 92 percent of its total export earnings.

Since Guatemala's coffee production system was grafted onto the existing hacienda structure, it served to reinforce existing class divisions.[40] There was no reason for hacienda owners to change their pattern of detachment from production. Their role was to hire finca administrators who could copy a successful production system. As with other crops, the

Indian population was left to pursue subsistence agriculture for most of the year and then hired as a source of labor at harvest time. But labor shortages began to appear.

The Guatemalans' reaction to labor shortages was different from that of the Costa Ricans. Instead of relying on smaller fincas and cooperative strategies among larger and smaller farmers and laborers, the Guatemalan landowners and the government found new ways of extracting more cheap labor from the indigenous population.

At the suggestion of coffee growers, the administration of President Justo Rufino Barrios passed the Debt Peonage Act of 1877 and the Vagrancy Law of 1878.[41] Under the first law any debtor could be required to provide physical labor on the plantations for the value of his debts. A father's debts were transferable to his family. The second law allowed officials to assign people with no steady work to plantation activity. These two laws were used as a new means to extract labor from the Indian population.

Just as in Costa Rica, liberalism provided Guatemala with an ideology consistent with social reform and with the expansion of coffee production and international trade. During the Barrios administration the state provided incentives for economic production and improved the infrastructure. The ports were developed, a railroad was introduced, and roads were improved. Barrios and Cabrerra also made educational reforms described earlier.

In contrast to the situation in Costa Rica, however, the social reforms in Guatemala never attracted the political coalitions necessary to allocate enough resources for real national impact during periods of liberal rule. Then, in the periods of conservative rule, the policy ideas were reversed.

Policy values, coalitions, and institutions, 1900–1965

Costa Rica   By 1900 Costa Rica's peculiar dynamics of coffee production and its series of liberal administrations had strongly reinforced cooperative and egalitarian traditions. These values were translated into the key elements of a national democratic political system in the first half of the 1900s. In 1898 Costa Rica had its first free indirect presidential elections. Political reforms such as secret ballot, women's suffrage, direct elections, and the civil code followed. With two brief exceptions the country has maintained a democratic electoral process for the selection of national leaders.

At the same time some new elements in the international economy and political system stratified the social system. For example, the growth of foreign investment in the banana plantations created a new set of worker–foreign owner relationships based more on conflict than on collaboration. New unions for public workers and teachers also emerged.

Downturns in the international economy and the more competitive international coffee market made it more difficult for the system to produce sufficient benefits for peons as well as for small and large farmer-owners. With these new economic conditions and the Great Depression of the 1930s, new ideologies like socialism and communism became more attractive.

These circumstances helped to produce the crisis of 1944–1948, when the government of Rafael Angel Calderon Guardia allied itself with the Communist party and the church and pushed for a program of radical social reform. In 1948 the Calderon government refused to cede power after it had apparently lost the election.[42]

The response was the Costa Rican revolution of 1948, led by José Figuerez Ferrer. Figuerez abolished the army and ceded power to the elected president. He himself was elected in 1953. Although Figuerez's coalition included large coffee growers, it adopted many of the social reforms proposed by Calderon's group and expanded the role of the state through its social democratic National Liberation party. It moved to limit further social stratification based on wealth through nationalization of the banking and insurance systems and promoted more equitable allocation of credit to both large and small farmers. It championed both the education reforms and improvements in the health system already described. Finally, it substantially increased the state's role in economic as well as social development.

The Figuerez government allocated resources to develop new institutions to carry out such policies, including the social security institute, the electric company, the national petroleum company, the national banking system, and the insurance institute. The health and education ministries were strengthened considerably.

The new trends in social equity were sufficiently accepted by Costa Ricans that both the National Liberation party and its opposition agreed that human development policies would continue. They differed only on which policies to pursue and how much money to allocate for them.[43]

Guatemala   By the 1900s the governing coalitions and policy initiatives that had emerged in El Salvador, Guatemala, Honduras, and Nicaragua were substantially different from those in Costa Rica and Panama. In the first four countries government was controlled by traditional landowning families in alliance with key military leaders. The military was the best-organized institution in those nations, and its major function was not so much national defense as social control.

As shown in earlier chapters, shifts in leadership in Guatemala occurred in periods of economic collapse and social discontent. While these shifts were usually nothing more than realignments within the military and traditional upper class, they often signaled ideological shifts between the liberals and conservatives. Regardless of liberal or conservative dominance, however, there was insufficient commitment to democratizing the society or making major social investments. Thus, public delivery systems remained woefully inadequate while private systems functioned effectively for the small traditional elites.

In the early 1900s many of the same economic pressures that Costa Rica experienced helped to stratify Guatemala's social structure further.[44] The government gave major concessions to the United Fruit Company, which began banana production. A new group of rural workers sprang up. Urban workers unions and professional associations were formed. Socialist and communist ideologies became more attractive. Political instability mounted at the beginning of the Great Depression.

General Jorge Ubico (1931–1944) stepped into the vacuum and provided a typical realignment of landowners, the military, and foreign investors, a new element in the system. His economic policies were progressive.[45] He promoted private sector development. His fiscal policies were conservative. As a result he did not spend on substantial improvements in education or health. He abolished debt peonage but maintained the vagrancy laws under which every Indian had to work for wages 150 days a year. He maintained press censorship and prohibited union organization.

A combination of social pressure and U.S. support for anticolonialism and emerging democracies at the end of World War II permitted a new social coalition to form, resulting in the revolution of 1944. A postwar economic downturn made social grievances more acute. A coalition of young army officers, students, urban professionals, and trade unionists helped bring Ubico down when he refused to hold elections. A coup followed, a new constitution was drawn up in 1945, elections were held, and Dr. Juan José Arevalo was elected.

This new coalition promoted the health and education policies described earlier during both the Arevalo and Arbenz administrations. Arbenz followed more nationalist policies than his predecessor. He nationalized the United Fruit Company's railway and plantations. He passed a land reform act and promised a series of additional reforms. His domestic opponents as well as the United States feared what they believed was communist infiltration in the hemisphere during the height of the new cold war with the Soviet Union. As a result the CIA backed a coup led by Castillo Armas in 1954.[46] Armas and his successors steered a course of economic development with few social investments, which continued until the late 1960s.

*Policy values, coalitions, and performance
in Central America, 1965–1978*

While the Central American nations all followed the new highly successful strategy for economic growth described in Chapters 5 and 6, which included export product diversification, industrial import substitution, and the development of a regional common market in the 1960s and 1970s, they adopted radically different social policies, expanding the gap between the high and low Central American human development performers. As we saw earlier, Costa Rica and Panama made major commitments to expanding rural primary health care and improving rural health and education conditions. They allocated additional resources from the economic boom of the 1960s and 1970s to do so. The Costa Rican social democrats during the administration of Daniel Oduber had the coalitions to permit this. In Panama Torrijos's administration and his Democratic Revolutionary party (PRD) favored the improvement of rural conditions. His government therefore had the coalitions to support progressive social policy. The existence of adequate political support in each country assured the passage of the Costa Rican Social Development Law and the design of the Panamanian health expansion program. Both nations substantially increased the health budget, built rural health infrastructure, and strengthened the ministries whose work would be essential to deliver the services. During the 1970s Panama doubled the number of its teachers and extended its rural education system as well. The improvements in human development performance in both nations are documented in Tables 7.1 through 7.5.

Guatemala also made formal commitments to new health and education policies. El Salvador actually developed an educational reform strategy. But the Guatemalan process was halted by the diversion of resources owing to the earthquake of 1976, and in El Salvador the revolution, coups, and countercoups brought the process to a halt.

So El Salvador, Guatemala, Honduras, and Nicaragua entered the late 1970s without the three elements necessary to ensure high human development performance—articulated policy values, sustained coalitions to support them, and strong human development implementing institutions. My final task is to examine whether the 1980s have changed anything fundamental in these nations.

Central American Double-Shock Transitions in the 1980s

In 1978 a new transition period began in Central America. Triggered by the worst world recession since the Great Depression of the 1930s, it was accompanied by tremendous violence and disruption in all nations. Revolutions took place in El Salvador and Nicaragua, and the U.S. military invaded Panama to overthrow General Manuel Noriega. Guatemala undertook a political opening while fighting a counterinsurgency war, and Honduras began a democratic transition with less violence. Eventually all Central American governments responded with double-shock policies of economic adjustment and political opening, which were very difficult to implement. Were these upheavals simply another stage for rotating elites in the region (Costa Rica excluded) or did a more profound shift in the foundations for human development governance structures take place?

An assessment of the transitions of the 1980s leads one to cautious optimism that four of the six Central American nations—Costa Rica, El Salvador, Nicaragua, and Panama—may have crossed the threshold where stronger, more lasting human development governance structures can be put into place (if, of course, appropriate actions continue to take place).

A closer examination shows three patterns of transition (see Figure 7.1). The first type of transition, a regime-led one with a high degree of social consensus, was begun in Costa Rica. Its challenge is to further define a successful new economic strategy and to modernize Costa

FIGURE 7.1   Central American Regime Transitions, 1978–1990

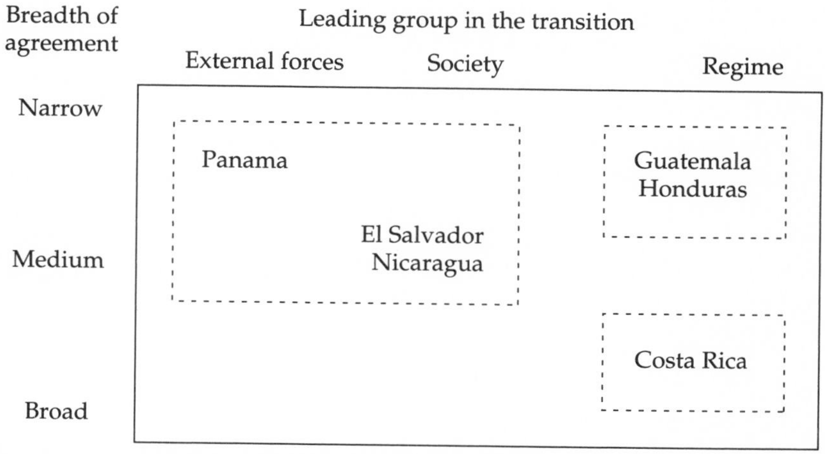

SOURCE: Author's summary of participant perceptions, Harvard conference on Central American transitions sponsored by the World Peace Foundation, 1991.

Rica's model of democratic participation. This modernization, however, continues to take place on a solid foundation forged particularly after the 1948 revolution.

In Nicaragua and El Salvador new governance structures emerged through negotiated agreements among key coalitions representing a relatively broad spectrum of ideologies and social groups. Societal-led movements overturned earlier governments, but no single internal group proved capable of imposing its will on the others. Power relations were altered precisely because these military stalemates led to negotiated political settlements with broad support. Property relations were substantially changed because of land reform. Finally, the Guatemalan and Honduran transitions were military regime–led adjustments negotiated with a narrow spectrum of groups, which left elements of the traditional business, civil elite in a predominant position. These transitions may do nothing more than repeat the old cycle of Central American military and civil realignment. For example, key participants in the Guatemalan transition of the 1980s lament that their nation again postponed a social realignment that would allow for more power and participation from below.[47] Former Honduran and Guatemalan military leaders warn of the continued independence of the armed forces in their societies.[48] Let us look at these transitions in more detail.

Costa Rica: Fine tuning a transition in process

The Costa Ricans have made major headway in the economic and political transition that began in 1982. Their nation has achieved successful economic stabilization and several phases of an adjustment program. The basic parameters of the outwardly oriented strategy were accepted by both political parties and the general population. Although there was disagreement about the speed of this transition, broader consensus had been built through intensive dialogue among government, business, labor, and community groups. As a result the basic direction of economic policy remained unchanged even when the National Liberation party was replaced by the Social Christian party in the elections of 1988. Furthermore, the nation survived the temptation to restrict basic rights and drastically increase its police budget during the heightened tensions with Nicaragua and Panama.

The two biggest challenges to Costa Rica's continued transition are consolidating the outwardly oriented economic growth and fine tuning the democratic process. There are five barriers to consolidating the new outwardly oriented economic model. First, vested economic interests still pose weak resistance to opening the economy. Members of business chambers and community groups continue to fight the reduction of specific subsidies. A second threat is the reaction of low-income groups to perceived losses in their real wages as a result of the new policies. A third barrier is the slow pace of the transformation of the state into a smaller, more dynamic catalyst of economic and social activity. This change implies a reduction in the role of public enterprises and a search for new private or mixed alternatives in banking and insurance. But such systems have proved extremely difficult to dismantle. A fourth dilemma is to how protect Costa Rica's human capital base during the adjustment process. The Costa Ricans want to maintain quality health and education programs without large fiscal deficits. Finally, according to leaders in both major political parties, the education system will need to be completely reoriented to help citizens work in a competitive environment and to help public sector employees change from a bureaucratic to a service-oriented mentality.

The Costa Ricans' second major challenge is remedying the "vices" of democracy. This requires creative responses to four basic problems. First, many Costa Ricans decry the excessive time and attention both parties gave to political campaigning as opposed to governing effectively. Often candidates begin campaigning within a year of the last election. Second, both political parties need to overhaul their internal rules to permit more democratic control and participation. Third, the older generation of political leaders who played important roles in the revolution of 1948 are reluctant to surrender key positions to the younger generation. Finally, opinion polls show that the public believes there has been a serious increase in corruption in both public and private life. This may heighten cynicism about the value of democratic government.

El Salvador, Nicaragua, and Panama: Consolidating fragile but important beginnings

Salvadorans, Nicaraguans, and Panamanians express optimism about the transition process. They point to the negotiated agreements between the Sandinistas and the government of Violeta Chamorro and between the FMLN and the Cristiani government as first steps in setting tentative new rules of the game. Important new institutions and political parties have emerged, but political consolidation and the development of dynamic new institutions are important unfinished tasks.

The barriers to economic reform are formidable. In contrast to Costa Rica, which began its economic stabilization in 1982, these three nations were beginning such efforts ten years later and after a series of aborted attempts. Furthermore, unlike Costa Rica none has yet found a model that provides growth, employment, and substantial investments in human capital to help overcome major problems of health and education.

This has been a major factor in the region's past political instability. Panama appears to have taken larger strides in achieving an outward orientation and in achieving this balance. But its interoceanic canal provides an extra economic motor that neither El Salvador nor Nicaragua has.

Another barrier to economic reform is that strong vested interests oppose adjustments. Nicaraguan observers differ about whether the traditional business community presents as much of a barrier to efficient outwardly oriented production as Sandinista unions and new economic groups accused of enriching themselves through the "piñata" in the last days of Sandinista rule. (The piñata, say critics, was the process through which friends of the Sandinistas received property before the Sandinistas left power. The Sandinistas argue that there was no piñata.) An additional threat is the thinness of expertise in economic policy making in new political parties, in government, and in civic groups. Furthermore, attempting to resurrect economies on a base of poverty, after war, with minimal external resources is no easy task under any circumstances. Finally, modernizing the state and making it an efficient promoter of economic and social development will take decades.

Strengthening the new democracies will not be possible without further work on the rules of the game. New legislation, pacts, and dialogues will be needed to provide the social glue to hold the transitions together. Nicaraguans lament the sporadic outbreaks of violence by what they called *recontra* and *recompa* groups (demobilized former contra and Sandinista soldiers) dissatisfied with the outcomes of the transition and backed by political extremists on both ends of the spectrum. New formal government institutions like legislatures, executive staffs, and judiciary must build competent staff and sound procedures. The new political parties, unions, civic organizations, and business chambers need considerable strengthening to represent their constituents effectively. A deep change in political culture through massive education and by the example of efficient, fair government is needed if democracy is to have a chance. Finally, the boundaries between military and the new civilians in government remain ambiguous. For example, the minister of defense in the new Chamorro government in Nicaragua continued to be Humberto Ortega, one of the nine Sandinista commanders and the brother of former president Daniel Ortega. In El Salvador it is not clear how well the agreements for establishing a new police force and civilian control of the military will actually work. While the abolition of Panama's National Guard provides a real opportunity for a new organization under civilian control, the task of developing such a new group is not easy.

In summary the Salvadoran, Nicaraguan, and Panamanian transitions demand further articulation of human development policy values and consolidation of new institutions on a fragile but important foundation of radically changed political coalitions.

Guatemala and Honduras: Initiating a more lasting transition

Most of the threats to the transitions in El Salvador, Nicaragua, and Panama also plague Guatemala and Honduras. But there are two additional serious concerns. First, the reassertion of power by traditional groups may again postpone needed social transformation. For example, the former Guatemalan defense minister stated that business pressure groups in Guatemala almost brought the Cerezo government down over the issue of increased taxation and social expenditures. They not only protested, he said, but encouraged elements within the military to try two unsuccessful coups. The postponement of social transformation may lead to a bloodier transition later.

Finally, in the absence of real countervailing pressures, the military will keep its predominant role. The Honduran military still maintains a high level of formal, structural independence from civilian control. Although Guatemala's new constitution permits executive oversight, civilians have been unwilling and afraid to take the reins.

Is Speeding Up Transition Processes for High Human Development Performance Really Feasible?

At the end of Part II of this book, I offered an optimistic message: I said that policies did make a difference in human development performance and that nations could at least loosen their contextual bonds to promote human development performance. A closer examination of the Central American nations reveals a more somber message. In fact high-performance human development governance structures are built upon values, coalitions, and institutions that take years, and even centuries, to form. Some of the most perceptive students of democratic transitions believe that the process is an evolutionary one that may be impossible to rush. For example, Robert T. Putnam argues that today's relatively effective democratic infrastructure in Northern Italy was built upon a base of civic organizations formed centuries earlier.[49] The lack of a similar infrastructure in Southern Italy, he believes, can be traced to the absence of this earlier civic base. Samuel Huntington argues that democratization is intimately related to a more complex, long-term process of economic development and modernization.[50] More recent work (including Chapters 3 and 4 of this book) on the management of simultaneous economic transition and political opening in the 1980s provides evidence on the difficulties of speeding up managed change.[51]

For better or worse Central America and the world are in the midst of important economic and political transitions. Policy makers cannot afford to wait while scholars sort out exactly what might help consolidate the transition process. Recent work by the World Bank and other institutions shows convincingly that policies do matter and that economic change can be accelerated.[52] While acknowledging how little is known about consolidating democratic transitions, Graham Allison and others have attempted to identify key interventions to promote democracy.[53] Although there are no rules for speeding up transitions, one can at least identify the barriers and suggest the policy interventions that might help overcome them. Each nation, however, must identify its own problems and craft solutions based on its own situation.

Barriers to transition

Although my analysis in this chapter shows that every nation has a different set of barriers to transition, it is possible to cluster them into five areas based on their origin in (1) the institutional context; (2) civic organizations; (3) political parties; (4) legislative, executive, or judicial institutions; or (5) the ministries and government policies (see Figure 7.2). Such an organizing framework is useful because it helps identify where reform programs might be more specifically directed even though each nation must find its own road to transition.

Barriers in the institutional context   The institutional context may be thought of as the cluster of complex rules that govern the interactions among civil society, political society, and the state. Nonexistent or imprecise rules of the game continue to be a serious barrier to transition. The presence of formal rights and the absence of real, enforceable civil, political, and economic rights result in low levels of confidence. For example, unclear property rights after a decade of revolution and reform in Nicaragua made it difficult to attract foreign investors and to convince Nicaraguans to invest as well. In addition the lack of experience with dialogue and negotiation as opposed to violence, confrontation, and repression made consolidating the transitions a real problem.

Barriers in civil society   Although civil society did not flourish in Central America under authoritarian rule, citizens were permitted to form business, labor, and private associations to promote their civic interests. The state permitted nongovernment media to operate as well. The terms under which civic groups were permitted to function fluctuated.

FIGURE 7.2   Barriers to Consolidating Transitions

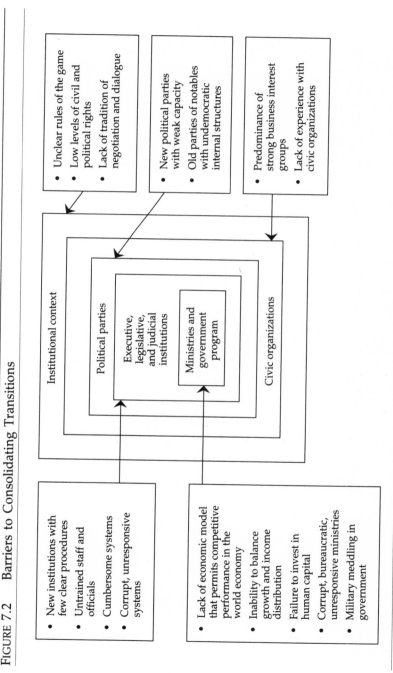

- Unclear rules of the game
- Low levels of civil and political rights
- Lack of tradition of negotiation and dialogue

- New political parties with weak capacity
- Old parties of notables with undemocratic internal structures

- Predominance of strong business interest groups
- Lack of experience with civic organizations

Institutional context

Political parties

Executive, legislative, and judicial institutions

Ministries and government program

Civic organizations

- New institutions with few clear procedures
- Untrained staff and officials
- Cumbersome systems
- Corrupt, unresponsive systems

- Lack of economic model that permits competitive performance in the world economy
- Inability to balance growth and income distribution
- Failure to invest in human capital
- Corrupt, bureaucratic, unresponsive ministries
- Military meddling in government

SOURCE: Author.

Sometimes groups were permitted to operate freely, but when governments felt threatened they generally imposed press censorship and states of emergency.

Liberalization in the 1980s permitted an expansion of civil society, but not without some serious problems. First, when the government restricted opposition political parties, civic organizations like business chambers filled the vacuum. They not only defended specific sectoral interests, but also engaged in broad-based political action. With the opening of political life, leaders of these civic groups had difficulty accepting a more restricted role and a less confrontational style. In addition, civil society had been strongly dominated by powerful business chambers. Their resources and expertise put new labor and civic groups at an extreme disadvantage. Furthermore, new organizations lack the skills and experience to develop strategies, structures, and processes to allow them to be self-sustaining and to have real impact. Most groups, including the business pressure groups, have yet to serve as a source of policy ideas, legislation, and debate.

Barriers in political society   The new democratic transformations permitted an expanded role for political parties but created a new set of problems. In societies where a strong political party, like the National Sandinista Liberation Front (FSLN) in Nicaragua or the Democratic Revolutionary party (PRD) in Panama, dominated political life for a decade, it was hard for new parties to compete on a level playing field. In addition, many of the old political groups like the National Liberation Movement (MLN) or the Democractic Institutional party (PID) in Guatemala had been parties of notables that really functioned only at election time. Still others were totally dependent upon a single charismatic figure. Modernizing old parties has been a major bottleneck in the transition.

Old minority parties and new parties have special problems building professional organizations capable of contesting power and then staffing an effective government. The Christian Democrats in El Salvador, Guatemala, and Panama, for example, had operated under severe legal restrictions in the past. Their leaders were under constant threat, and in El Salvador and Guatemala assassinations were not infrequent. One Guatemalan participant noted that his party had had to spend so much effort simply mounting a successful election campaign that they had little chance to think seriously of what policies they would pursue if they won. He added that they had problems even staffing the new government with talented people. A final problem for all parties was the democratization of internal procedures and the development of a professional staff capable of developing policy positions.

Barriers within the state: New legislatures, executive branches, and judicial institutions   The assignment of more dynamic roles to legislatures and the judiciary put tremendous strains on these antiquated institutions. For example, many newly elected officials had virtually no experience in the legislative process, critical analysis of national priorities, or evaluation of programs and budgets. Furthermore, procedures for conducting government business had to be invented as democratization advanced. One Panamanian leader noted that in the first public legislative budget hearings neither the legislators nor the executive officials knew quite what to do. In addition, there was no tradition of legislative staff work on policy issues. The vice president of the Salvadoran Assembly said he had no staff for policy analysis. He felt it had been easier to operate clandestinely than as a key player in a legislative assembly. Finally, many Central Americans noted that the pressures of guaranteeing a fair, open civil and political process put special strains on the judiciary. Systems were cumbersome. Judges were paid poorly and were susceptible to threats, intimidation, and corruption.

Barriers within the state: The ministries and government programs   The transitions will only be as successful as the ability of new governments to define coherent plans for economic and political development and to carry them out efficiently and fairly. With the exception of Costa Rica, new governments have not been effective in defining an economic strategy to generate growth, employment, and more equal income distribution. Key ministries did not have the talent to perform policy analysis or implement programs effectively. The ministries had ambiguous objectives. They were overstaffed with underpaid and unmotivated officials. Finally, the lack of clear rules for civil-military relationships left the door open for the return of "a firm hand in government" should the civilians prove incapable of providing effective government.

Policies for strengthening transitions

Each nation faces different problems in its transition process, and no single set of actions will consolidate the transitions in every country. It is possible, however, to talk about the potential ways that particular barriers can be overcome. The list that follows is meant as a device to stimulate leaders and policy makers who believe their nations have particular transition problems (see Figure 7.3). They are motivated by the spirit that one should not mention problems without being willing at least to think about solutions. Each nation, however, must craft its own solutions based on its particular situation.

FIGURE 7.3   Policies for Consolidating Transitions

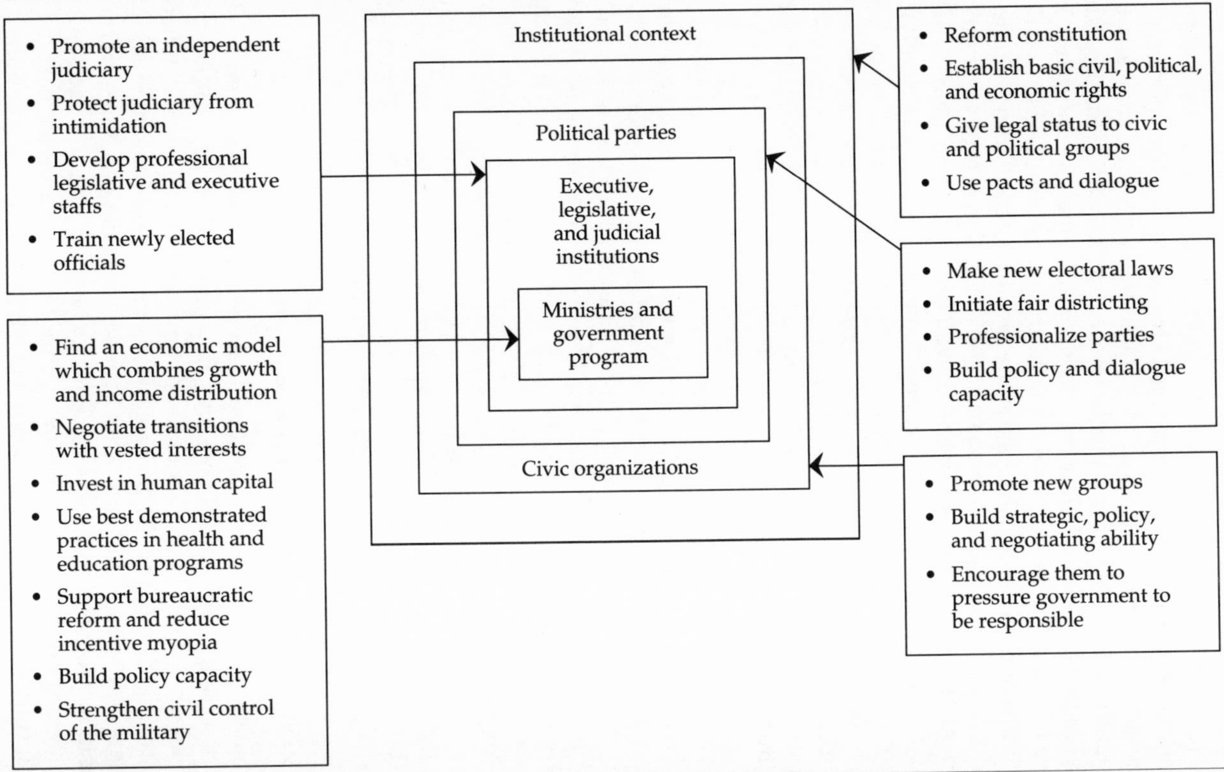

Reform constitution
Establish basic civil, political, and economic rights
Give legal status to civic and political groups
Use pacts and dialogue

Make new electoral laws
Initiate fair districting
Professionalize parties
Build policy and dialogue capacity

Promote new groups
Build strategic, policy, and negotiating ability
Encourage them to pressure government to be responsible

Institutional context

Political parties

Executive, legislative, and judicial institutions

Ministries and government program

Civic organizations

Promote an independent judiciary
Protect judiciary from intimidation
Develop professional legislative and executive staffs
Train newly elected officials

Find an economic model which combines growth and income distribution
Negotiate transitions with vested interests
Invest in human capital
Use best demonstrated practices in health and education programs
Support bureaucratic reform and reduce incentive myopia
Build policy capacity
Strengthen civil control of the military

Source: Author.

Institutional context

1. Complete the constitutional reforms that establish the separation of powers and the basic rules for democratic government.

2. Formalize the guarantee of basic civil, political, and economic rights.

3. Insure the legal recognition of new civic and political groups.

4. Promote the resolution of conflicts through pacts, dialogue, and discussion rather than through violent conflict.

5. Keep international attention focused on regional advances and also on abuses.

6. Use the United Nations and regional organizations to help monitor peace agreements and the transition process.

7. Promote education reforms that favor problem solving and awareness of basic rights. Promote basic education.

Civil society and civic organizations

1. Stimulate the formation of new civic organizations and community-based problem solving.

2. Provide training and technical assistance to help new organizations define strategy and programs and to build their capacity to be dynamic, self-sufficient organizations.

3. Encourage civic organizations to put pressure on government to be responsive.

4. Stimulate civic and private organizations to provide programs that force government to be competitive and more service oriented.

Political society and political parties

1. Support electoral laws that make the election process clear, transparent, and efficient. Rely on international experience and monitoring when fairness may be an issue.

2. Encourage redistricting to ensure fair representation of citizens by politicians.

3. Promote the professionalization of political parties. Rely on world experience in party development.

4. Provide technical assistance to build capacity within the parties to define policy options and debate these options publicly.

The state: New legislatures, executive staffs, and the judiciary

1. Use best demonstrated world practices to design executive, legislative, and judicial procedures.

2. Provide training in policy design, budgeting, program evaluation, and the legislative process to newly elected officials.

3. Promote the establishment of professional analytical executive and legislative staffs.

4. Support an independent judiciary. Protect judges from intimidation.

5. Combat corruption.

The state: Ministries and government programs

1. Encourage the search for economic strategies that stimulate balanced growth, generate employment, and invest in the human capital base.

2. Promote public sector reform to help develop a smaller but more dynamic client-responsive public sector.

3. Strengthen civilian control of the military.

4. Identify and implement the best demonstrated practices in social service delivery systems.

While there is no road map for successful transitions, adoption of some of these proposals, where they apply to specific country situations, might increase the probability of reaching the destination.

Conclusions

We have seen that the roots of human development performance differences in one region, Central America, lie deep beneath the actual differences in health and education policies and the governance structures that helped produce them. These governance structures are built on a foundation of slowly evolving policy values, key political coalitions, and implementing institutions built over centuries. In spite of the almost glacial evolution of these foundations, it is possible to identify critical periods like the transition periods of the 1980s and 1990s when large irreversible changes take place and when it is possible to help speed the transitions along and consolidate them with sound policies to promote human development.

PART IV

CONCLUSION

Lessons for Achieving High Human Development

I have invited readers to watch the race for human development that took place between 1965 and 1987. The race can be better described as the struggle of developing nations to improve their citizens' chances to lead a long and healthy life, to acquire knowledge, and to gain access to resources needed for a decent level of living.

As ninety developing countries crossed the finish line readers were asked to consider a basic dilemma. Why might two countries, such as South Korea and Liberia, which began the race in the middle of the pack with relatively similar per capita incomes, achieve such fundamentally different performances? Korea won the silver medal. It had the second-highest level of human development improvement. In contrast, Liberia actually lost ground and finished in the bottom twelve.

I have attempted to identify the special characteristics of nations that finished the human development race at the top of the pack. Specifically, the book asked six questions:

1. What were the characteristics of the developing countries that showed high human development performance?

2. Did policies play as important a role in high human development performance as contextual factors like external economic shocks, size, and natural resource endowment?

3. What role did the state play in mobilizing high human development performance, and how important were regime type and basic political and civil rights in attaining high performance?

4. How and why did the wave of rapid economic and political liberalization take place in the 1980s?

5. Did countries that rode this wave improve their performance substantially during the human development race?

6. What lessons might be drawn for development policy for the next decade?

Readers were asked to observe the development race with two different sets of field glasses. The first set permitted a general view of all ninety developing country participants. The second set allowed a more penetrating focus on six Central American nations. The basic conclusions follow.

What Were the Characteristics of the Developing Countries That Showed High Human Development Performance?

The high human development performers shared six important characteristics. They began the human development race in 1965 with a relatively high-quality human resource base. They were more likely to be in East or Southeast Asia. They were less linguistically and ethnically diverse than their neighbors. During the actual race (1965–1987) they were more politically stable. They used more outwardly oriented economic policies. They spent substantially more on health and education as a percentage of gross national product (GNP) than low and medium performers.

Did Policies Play as Important a Role in High Human Development Performance as Contextual Factors Like External Economic Shocks, Size, and Natural Resource Endowment?

Developing countries were not prisoners of their context. High performers in the human development race proved to be no more handicapped than low performers by contextual constraints like population density, natural resource endowment, or external shocks.

Appropriate economic and social policies were a key ingredient in high human development performance. The economic and social policy choices of the winners of the human development improvement race were quite different from those of the losers. For example, high human development performers spent an average of 1.7 percent more of their GNP per year on education and health than low performers every year between 1965 and 1987.

Although it is impossible to establish clear causality, there is strong evidence of the relationship between policy choice and improvements in human development status. For example, Costa Rican and Panamanian investments in rural health, education, water, and infrastructure programs coincide with the disappearance of intestinal parasites from the list of the top five causes of death in those nations by the mid-1970s. This same disease remains a major killer even in the 1990s in El Salvador and Guatemala, where similar investments were not made.

So policy choices provided a substantial part of the explanation for achieving high human development status. In fact of the six key characteristics of high human development performance, only a country's geographic location is not subject to policy intervention. As already noted, there is no way to move Chad to Asia. If region is a surrogate for important but little understood cultural characteristics, however, then it may one day be possible to learn more about how to speed human development by using key elements of local culture.

Optimism about the role of policy in human development must be tempered with a heavy dose of realism. Paradoxically, the factors most easily subject to policy intervention like exchange rates and social spending provided less human development disparity reduction per unit than factors like political instability or linguistic diversity. Unfortunately less is known about how to strengthen political institutions and increase ethnic harmony than about devaluing currencies and increasing social spending. Furthermore, the factors that were least subject to policy intervention, like a country's location or previous human development status, at least in theory, would have yielded the largest human development gains per unit of change had it been possible to influence them. But no one can turn back the clock, for example, to 1950 and increase Chad's education and health spending so that its population enters the the development race in 1965 with a stronger human capital base.

Although policies matter, the process of policy reform is much slower than optimists would hope. Stable political environments and consistent long-term policy commitments proved to be much more important than quick doses of economic and social reform. For example, Costa Rica's high human development status by 1987 was strongly dependent on past policies to build the human capital base, which can be traced back to at least the 1880s.

These general findings were reinforced by a more focused look through the stronger lens at the Central American high and low human development performers. This lens enabled us to pinpoint interactions between context and policies that were invisible at a more general level. We could see, for example, how external shocks created waves of political instability and set the stage for leadership rotation through coups. We uncovered a complex and messy process of change in which new leaders established key coalitions, experimented with new economic strategies to diversify products, markets, and sectors and searched for appropriate social policies.

What Role Did the State Play in Mobilizing High Human Development Performance, and How Important Were Regime Type and Basic Political and Civil Rights in Attaining High Human Development Performance?

The search for the underpinnings of high human development performance described above began with an exploration of the role of regime type in mobilizing these achievements. To the disappointment of ideologues of all persuasions, the list of high performers gives no edge to either formal democracies or nondemocracies. The economies of formal democracies, however, grew seven-tenths of a percent faster annually between 1973 and 1987. But such growth was no guarantee that governments would allocate more resources for human development.

While the formal existence of democracy or nondemocracy at a national level did not matter much in high human development performance, the winners and losers in the human development race had substantially different underlying governance structures. Governance structures were defined as "the combination of institutions and rules that manage the relations within and among civil society, political society, and the state."

The governance structures of most high human development performers showed certain similarities. They were active promoter states (as opposed to producer or regulator states) that pursued outwardly oriented growth based on market mechanisms. They had strong leadership and high levels of resource commitment and innovation in the area of social policy. Their government spending was between 20 and 30 percent of GNP. They had at least medium levels of political and civil rights regardless of regime type. They promoted mechanisms for two-way communication between citizens and governments even when formal democracy did not exist. Finally, they had high policy continuity and low political instability for long periods of time.

Medium human development performers typically had larger, more interventionist producer states with lower levels of political and civil rights. Low human development performers had smaller regulator states that left large segments of the population out of their sphere entirely. They used rigid, top-down mechanisms with low levels of civil and political rights to dominate the population within their reach. This governance style helped contribute to high levels of political instability and regime turnover.

At the core of high performance governance structures were a triangle of prevailing policy values, key political coalitions, and implementing institutions. This core, however, evolved over decades. A look, for example, at the origins of the critical triangle in Central America requires a journey back to the colonial period. Cooperation was necessary for human survival in Costa Rica in the 1500s, while in Guatemala a hierarchical, authoritarian culture emerged based on political, economic, and religious domination. These initial structures helped condition the reactions of key groups to the organization of new product systems, the choice of economic strategy, and the willingness to make social investments.

How and Why Did the Wave of Rapid Economic and Political Liberalization Take Place in the 1980s?

In light of the evidence that high human development performers implemented consistent policies over a longer period of time, under conditions of low political instability and relatively clear rules of the game, it is hard to imagine why the push for rapid political and economic liberalization became popular in the 1980s. It is equally hard to understand what double-shock policies have to do with the human development story.

Yet the discussion of double shock is a key element in the human development race because it was a policy response to the strong external shocks caused by the second oil price hike of 1978 and the global recession of 1982. These shocks affected the conditions under which the last ten years of the human development race under review here was run. Every runner had to adjust its strategy in the last laps of the race to these new conditions.

The wave was not an illusion created by the media or politicians, but rather a tidal wave with three different currents: political liberalization, economic reform, and double shock—simultaneous economic and political reform. As a result of the first current, political liberalization, the number of democratic regimes in developing countries grew from seventeen of ninety (19 percent) in 1973 to thirty-eight (41 percent) by 1989. Furthermore, the number of countries with at least medium levels of civil and political rights (measured by the Gastil index) increased from 57 percent in 1980 to 68 percent in 1989.

As a result of the second current, economic liberalization, thirty nations participated in World Bank–sponsored structural adjustment loans between 1982 and 1989. Swept along by the third current, double shock, all of the Eastern European nations began a difficult process of political liberalization and economic transition to the market. Furthermore, between 1982 and 1988 at least thirteen developing nations took double-shock medicine as well—eight with assistance from the World Bank and five without. In the 1980s the number of developing countries adopting double-shock policies was more than thirty.

Although it is tempting to blame aid donors for imposing double shock, in reality many countries acted far in advance of the donors to correct serious imbalances exacerbated by the external shocks described earlier. The wave began in different ways in each region. For example, in Latin America early double-shock policies in Argentina, Brazil, and Uruguay were regime led, not externally imposed, and heterodox in their application of economic theories. These adjustments were triggered by a combination of shocks, international events like the Falklands War, and the popular rejection of authoritarian regimes that had presided over economic and political collapse. The shape of the second wave in the mid-1980s in Bolivia, Costa Rica, and Guatemala was more orthodox. It was formed through a combination of internal responses to donor pressure, learning based on observation of other processes of reform, and political pressure for democratization from the United States. The Eastern European variant began in the later 1980s. It accelerated not because of pressure from the International Monetary Fund (IMF) and the World Bank, but because of the inability of totalitarian regimes to stave off economic collapse. It was carved out of the political space ceded to the opposition by Moscow's policies of glasnost and perestroika. In Asia the market-oriented nations substituted single- for double-shock policies. They streamlined their economies and engaged in controlled political openings, for example, in Taiwan and Korea. The formerly centrally planned economies in Asia like China and Vietnam also tried single-shock economic reform without major political transition. Finally, the African version of double shock began in the late 1980s, almost ten years after the first Latin American experiments. It was brought on by international ripple effects and donor pressure.

Did Countries That Rode This Wave Improve Their Performance Substantially During the Human Development Race?

Few nations were able to maintain the pace of their human development improvements in the 1980s. The world recession of 1982 and the oil price shocks of 1978 changed the nature of the human development race. Every runner had to slow down and make corrections. The struggle was about who lost less ground.

The healthier runners made the corrections more easily. For example, the Asian nations whose imbalances were less serious could afford to embark on single-shock policies. They restructured their economies and streamlined their public sectors. In Latin America some countries used single shock as well. For example, Chile's earlier economic restructuring allowed it to concentrate on political opening. Costa Rica, whose democratic political institutions were quite healthy, was able to focus on economic restructuring. The weaker runners who developed serious imbalances during the race, like Bolivia and Argentina, were forced to consider double-shock policies. Finally, the slowest runners like Ethiopia, Chad, and Somalia stumbled under the burdens of war and political instability.

There is a strong indication that high human development performers found it less necessary to take double-shock medicine in the final phase of the human development race. In fact only 25 percent of the high human development performers used double-shock policies, while 50 percent of the medium and 60 percent of the low performers had to do so.

Although the 1980s were a somber period, those who embarked on economic and political reform did achieve some positive results. Countries that adopted World Bank adjustment programs did reverse serious economic collapse. Many nations like Bolivia, Nicaragua, and Mexico brought hyperinflation under control. Others reduced the size of the state and made it more efficient. A few nations made the transition from stabilization to adjustment. They changed the composition of their export base through diversification of products, markets, and sectors. On the political side new feedback channels were opened and mechanisms other than coups were developed for changing top leadership.

Unfortunately the single- and double-shock policies also had their negative consequences. Some nations stopped inflation by wrenching their economies into deep recession from which they have yet to recover. Most managed effective stabilization without fostering a real structural adjustment. Narrow-minded policy advisers sometimes led an indiscriminate attack on the state that left it too weak to promote either adjustment or human development. Initial studies by the U.N. Educational, Scientific, and Cultural Organization (UNESCO) indicated that the social costs of adjustment on high-risk groups like young children and pregnant women were high.

Although the data on social performance in the late 1980s are not yet available, there is an indication that education and health levels in developing countries deteriorated. For example, Costa Rica, whose data base is quite good, reports a rise in infant mortality in the early 1990s.

Reduced expenditures for health coincide with a resurgence of malaria, tuberculosis, and other diseases that had been under control. In former socialist economies macroeconomic policy now provides market signals in a vacuum chamber. Few individuals and institutions know how to respond to them. Adjustment fatigue has led to the potential for backlash. Finally, the disinvestment in education and health may sacrifice several generations of people and slow down future human development improvement decades from now.

While circumstances forced many nations to adopt double-shock policies in the 1980s, performance improvements have been slow in coming. New democracies are not as economically strong as old ones. The economic performance track record of the thirteen double-shock nations I could identify in the 1982–1988 period was worse than the other nations in the sample.

It is too early to say exactly who lost less in the 1980s. The list of countries reputed to have achieved successful economic or political adjustment in this difficult period, however, has a disproportionate number of high human development achievers from the 1965–1980 period. Perhaps they were more capable of living off the social margins created by their earlier high human development policies.

What Lessons Might Be Drawn for Development Policy for the Next Decade?

Policy makers facing the next decade might ponder the following summary conclusions. First, developing nations are not prisoners of their context.

Second, economic and social policies and policy makers do make a difference in the human development race. There are plenty of specific policy lessons to learn from countries that have reduced infant mortality, increased literacy, and restructured their economies successfully.

Third, policies to reduce political instability and cultural impediments to development have the potential to yield great benefits if they can be designed realistically. Policies must, however, be crafted based on individual circumstances.

Fourth, the postponement of human development investments has serious consequences for human development performance decades in the future.

Fifth, behind the successful human development performers in the past were high-performance governance structures that included elements like active promoter rather than producer states, outwardly oriented economic strategies within a market context, an active role in social policy, at least medium levels of political and civil rights, and low levels of political instability. It is worthwhile to consider how such structures might be built elsewhere.

Sixth, beware of simple recipes like liberalizing or reducing the role of the state. In cases where the state has been a weak regulator it will be necessary to strengthen its capacity. Tailor solutions based on current human development status, governance structure, and the existing barriers to reform.

And finally, achieving high human development performance takes time and patience. Double-shock policies have not normally been part of the portfolio of high human development performers. Instead the process from which high human development policies have emerged was a gradual one, often involving decades. It included both the managed as well as evolutionary formation of a triangle of values, coalitions, and institutions that formed the foundation of high performance governance structures. These structures, in turn, proved capable of selecting and implementing creative human development policies.

This last conclusion is meant to serve as a warning for those enamored of quick fixes and rapid policy impact. This book shows convincingly that policies cannot even reach the agenda for approval without solid political coalitions that have a strong commitment to human development policy values. They cannot be successfully implemented without the institutional infrastructure necessary to make them work. In Central America these foundations emerged through a slow evolutionary process over the course of centuries.

Thus, the economist's idea as expressed in regression analysis that for every increment in x policy you get an increment of y human development performance is simplistic. Underneath these transformations are living and breathing human beings who form coalitions, express values, and develop institutional infrastructures that can take generations to fall into place.

This final conclusion has two serious implications for development professionals. First, the failure to consider the institutional foundations of development can lead to some gross, humanly costly miscalculations about strategies for policy reform. This is the biggest risk for those who think that getting macroeconomic policy right is the exclusive leading-edge solution to the development dilemma. This view is evident in many who provide policy advice to governments in Eastern Europe and the former Soviet Union, as well as in the developing world. They often fail to see the texture of the institutional fabric completely and the complex threads of interactions that must be woven together underneath to make policies work.

Blind macroeconomic policy proponents appear surprised when people and institutions do not respond, for example, to the market forces supposedly unleashed by their reforms. They are even more surprised when citizens throw the reform governments they advised out of office. These advisers often blame everyone but themselves when their policies do not work. They need to incorporate a greater emphasis on institutional reform and political coalition building into their approach to change. They should not mislead themselves or others into thinking that social change is easy.

The second unfortunate response to the insights in this book would be extreme pessimism. Pessimists would argue that since successful reforms are so deeply imbedded in the glacially slow, evolutionary development of civic culture and governance structures, nothing can be speeded up. They ignore the evidence that between 1965 and 1987 and before, many successful governments did in fact think systematically about how to overcome barriers to more rapid change and that they built upon their understanding of their cultural and institutional context to speed reforms. While macroeconomic and social policy changes such as adjustments in exchange rate policy or increases in social spending had less potential impact on human development performance than immutable factors and than we might have hoped, they still can and do make an important difference.

The pessimists need to learn more about successful mobilization of policy to promote change. They should focus on the triangle of values, coalitions, and institutions that provide the foundations of high-performance governance structures. They can identify the barriers to change and suggest how to overcome them, as I began to do in Chapter 6 and as many policy makers and citizens in developing countries are doing today. Such an approach attempts to build upon context and culture to increase the probability that policy reform will be more successful. We have the capacity and the responsibility to use what we know to help improve people's life chances.

Calculating the Modified
Human Development Index

This book uses a modified version of the 1990 UNDP human development index to construct country baseline data.[1] A country's human development index (HDI) score (between 0 and 100) is based on its performance on three equally weighted variables: (1) PPP-adjusted real GDP, (2) literacy, and (3) life expectancy. The index expresses a country's human development status as a percentage of the best industrial-country human development performance. In other words Chad's 1987 HDI score of 23 was about a quarter of that achieved by the best industrial country in that year.

The score is computed in four steps. First, a deprivation scale range is defined for each variable based on the lowest and highest attainable score for any country. Second, a formula is used to convert a country's raw score to a deprivation index score between 0 and 100. Third, the country's deprivation scores on each variable are given equal weight and averaged. Fourth, the average deprivation score is subtracted from 1 so that high HDI scores indicate high performance. The UNDP's 1990 method is modified, however, to make 1965 and 1987 data comparable within a 0 to 100 range. The modification is achieved by setting parameters using the lowest and highest scores for whole 1965–1987 data set, not just for the year to be measured. Thus, no index scores are greater than 100 or less than 0.

Here are the steps for computing HDI:

Step 1: Upper and lower limits are determined from the data set (based on 1965–1987 raw scores).

Step 2: A country deprivation score is computed for each indicator, where

life expectancy = $X1$
literacy = $X2$
log of real GDP per capita = $X3$

$$I_{ij} = \frac{(\max_j X_{ij} - X_{ij})}{(\max_j X_{ij} - \min_j X_{ij})}$$

Step 3: A simple average is taken of the three indicators (the indicators have equal weight).

$$I_j = \sum_{i=1}^{3} I_{ij}$$

Step 4: The human development index (HDI) is 1 minus the average deprivation index.

$$(HDI)_j = (1 - I_j)$$

To compute an HDI score for Liberia, the following steps are taken:

Step 1: Determine upper and lower scale limits.
       Maximum life expectancy: 78.4 (Japan 1987)
       Minimum life expectancy: 33 (Ethiopia 1965)
       Maximum literacy rate: 100.0 (Norway 1987)
       Minimum literacy rate: 3.0 (Niger 1965)
       Maximum PPP-adjusted real GDP log: 3.68
         (log of average official "poverty line" income of nine industrial countries—Australia, Canada, Federal Republic of Germany, Japan, Norway, Sweden, Switzerland, United Kingdom, and United States—adjusted by purchasing-power parities, of US$4,861)
       Minimum PPP-adjusted real GDP log: 1.54 (log of Bhutan's 1965 PPP-adjusted real GDP of US$35)

Liberia's life expectancy in 1965: 44
Liberia's literacy in 1965: 10.0
Liberia's real GDP per capita (log) in 1965: 2.75

Step 2: Compute individual deprivation scores.

Liberia's life expectancy deprivation score
$(78.4 - 44)/(78.4 - 33) = .757$

Liberia's literacy deprivation score
$(100 - 10.0)/(100 - 3.0) = .927$

Liberia's GDP deprivation score
$(3.68 - 2.75)/(3.68 - 1.54) = .434$

Step 3: Average Liberia's deprivation scores.
$(.757 + .927 + .434)/3 = .706$

Step 4: Find Liberia's human development index (HDI).
$1 - .706 = .294$

Although the United Nations modified its 1991 index to differentiate more effectively among the very highest HDI performers, I have not used these modifications for two reasons. First, missing data in my time series, particularly for 1965, do not permit me to use the new measure called educational attainment (a combination of literacy and years of schooling). Second, the new UNDP adjusted income measure, which provides refined discrimination among the thirty industrial countries, is not necessary since my topic is the ninety developing countries.

Calculating the Disparity Reduction Rate

There are many ways to measure human development improvements between 1965 and 1987. One can study, for example, (1) absolute increments of change, (2) average annual rates of change, or (3) disparity reduction rates. As Tables A2.1 and A2.2 show, each method leads to a very different interpretation of high and low HDI performance.

The *Human Development Report 1991* uses the first method—absolute increments of change. The problem with the use of absolute gains is that they are considered equally easy to make regardless of whether

TABLE A2.1	Three Methods for Calculating HDI Change, 1970–1985				
	HDI (%)		Absolute	Average annual	Average annual
Country	1970	1985	change (%)	change (%)	DRR (%)
Costa Rica	75.9	86.5	10.6	0.9	3.8
Nigeria	18.9	24.3	10.4	3.7	0.46
Niger	5.4	15.8	10.4	12.8	0.8
Soviet Union	82.1	92.5	10.4	0.8	5.6

SOURCE: HDI scores and absolute change data come from U.N. Development Programme, *Human Development Report 1991* (New York: Oxford University Press, 1991) pp. 96–97. Average annual change and DRR calculations were made with methods described by James Grant, *Disparity Reduction Rates in Social Indicators*, Overseas Development Council, Monograph no. 11 (Washington, D.C.: 1978), pp. 11–30; and Morris Morris, *Measuring the Condition of the World's Poor* (New York: Pergamon Press, 1978) pp. 74–78 and 121.

TABLE A2.2   Graphic Presentation of Three Methods for Calculating HDI Change

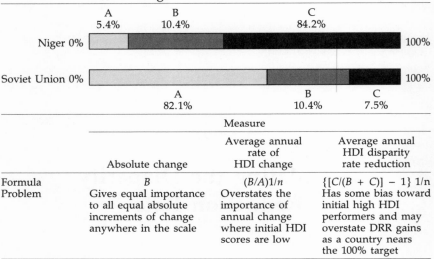

	Measure		
	Absolute change	Average annual rate of HDI change	Average annual HDI disparity rate reduction
Formula	B	$(B/A)1/n$	$\{[C/(B + C)] - 1\} 1/n$
Problem	Gives equal importance to all equal absolute increments of change anywhere in the scale	Overstates the importance of annual change where initial HDI scores are low	Has some bias toward initial high HDI performers and may overstate DRR gains as a country nears the 100% target

A = 1970 HDI score.
B = absolute increase in the score between 1970 and 1985.
$A + B$ = 1985 HDI score.
C = the disparity between the 1985 HDI score $(A + B)$ and a perfect scale score.
$B + C$ = the disparity between the 1970 HDI score (A) and a perfect scale score.
n = number of years.

SOURCE: Author's calculations.

countries have high or low initial HDI scores. This is like assuming that a runner will find it as easy to jump three-foot hurdles on the top of Mount Everest as at sea level. In fact, it may be easier for Niger to improve its very low HDI score (5.4) by ten percentage points, than for Costa Rica to make the same ten-point HDI gain from its relatively high initial HDI score of 75.9. This would be the case if, for example, public health investments for countries like Niger, with low levels of life expectancy, yield quicker absolute improvements than for countries like Costa Rica which already have relatively high levels of life expectancy.

One escape from the dilemma of absolute increments might be to compare annual rates of change in the HDI. But as can be seen in Table A2.1 this second method also understates the importance of change for countries like the former Soviet Union with higher initial HDI scores. For example, although both Niger and the former Soviet Union jump the same 10.4 percent absolute HDI hurdle between 1970 and 1985, Niger, with an initial HDI score of 5.4, shows a giant 12.8 percent rate of average annual improvement since it did not jump HDI hurdles well before, and the former Soviet Union shows only a tiny 0.8 percent gain because of the mechanics of the calculation method.[1]

A third method, called the disparity reduction rate (DRR), treats percentage rates of change among high and low initial performers in a more uniform fashion. It is the method of choice in this book. The DRR, developed by Morris Morris for tracking improvements in the physical quality of life, measures the rate at which the disparity between a country's current and possible performance is reduced over time. Possible performance is equivalent to that of a typical industrial country. The DRR helps reduce the distortions in the average annual percentage changes between lower initial HDI performers like Niger and higher initial HDI performers like the former Soviet Union, even though the absolute increment of improvement is the same for these two countries.

The formula for calculating the DRR is

$$\left(\frac{t + n}{t}\right) = \left(\frac{xt + n}{xt}\right)\frac{1}{n} - 1$$

where x is the disparity between social indicator performance in time t and 100 and time $t + n$ and 100. This calculation yields a negative rate when the disparity is being reduced. For ease of exposition Grant and Morris recommend that this rate be expressed as a rate of gap reduction.[2]

NOTES

Chapter 1, "The Human Development Dilemma"

1. For a good overview of recent trends, see World Bank, *World Development Report 1987* (New York: Oxford University Press, 1987), Chapter 1, and *World Development Report 1988*, Chapter 1. For a more popular account of the post–World War II development experience, see "The Third World: Trial and Error," *The Economist*, September 23, 1989, pp. 1–53.

2. This problem shows up in any time-series analysis of the growth of per capita gross domestic product (GDP) between 1970 and 1988. See, for example, Inter-American Development Bank, *Economic and Social Progress in Latin America* (Washington, D.C., 1988), pp. 423–24; or World Bank, *World Development Report 1987*, pp. 202–3.

3. For one of the most detailed accounts of the effects of the adjustment efforts of the 1980s on income distribution, high-risk populations, and the quality of life, see Giovanni Andrea Cornia, Richard Jolly, and Frances Stewart, eds., *Adjustment with a Human Face*, Vols. 1 and 2 (Oxford: Oxford University Press, 1987).

4. Some examples are John Fei, Shirley Kuo, and Gustav Ranis, *The Taiwan Success Story* (Boulder, Colo.: Westview Press, 1981); Jaime de Melo, "Sources of Growth and Structural Change in the Republic of Korea and Taiwan: Some Comparisons," in Victorio Corbo et al., eds., *Export-oriented Development Strategies: The Success of Five Newly Industrialized Countries* (Boulder, Colo.: Westview Press, 1985); and Lawrence Lau, ed., *Models of Development: A Comparative Study of Economic Growth in South Korea and Taiwan* (San Francisco: ICS Press for the International Center for Economic Growth, 1986).

5. A representative example of this popularization is "The Third World: Trial and Error," *The Economist*, pp. 1–53.

6. See Gustav Ranis, "The NICs and Near NICs and the World Economy," in Silvio De Franco, ed., *Estrategias de Crecimiento y Orientación Hacia Afuera* (San José: Editorial Universitario Centroamericano (EDUCA), 1988), pp. 173–209.

199

7. Stephan Haggard, "Institutions, Policy, and Economic Growth: Theory and a Korean Case Study," paper presented at the annual meeting of the American Political Science Association, May 1986. See also Silvio De Franco, "Políticas Macroeconómicas y Dimensiones Político-Institucionales en el Crecimiento Económico: El Caso de Corea del Sur," in De Franco, ed., *Estrategias de Crecimiento*, pp. 421–65.

8. Discussion of stabilization and adjustment policies adopted at the IMF and World Bank can be found in Constantine Michalopoulos, "World Bank Programs for Adjustment and Growth," paper presented at the World Bank Symposium on Growth-Oriented Adjustment Programs, Washington, D.C., February 1987; Armeane M. Choksi and Demetris Papageorgiou, eds., *Economic Liberalization in Developing Countries* (Oxford: Basil Blackwell, 1986); and World Bank, *World Development Report 1987*, Chapter 5. An easy-to-read, more popular description of the approach can be found in Vinod Thomas and Ajay Chhibber, eds., *Adjustment Lending: How It Has Worked, How It Can Be Improved* (Washington, D.C.: World Bank, 1989).

9. Between 1986 and 1989 General Manuel Noriega of Panama survived repeated attempts to remove him as head of the Panamanian Defense Forces. He actually consolidated his control of the military and his party, rather than losing it. In Paraguay, although General Alfredo Stroessner was removed through a coup d'état in 1989, the structure of power remained remarkably similar in the new government.

10. Charles Radin, "Prophet Recalls Prediction of Marxism's Fall," *Boston Globe*, November 13, 1989, p. 3.

11. George Bush, "Remarks to Citizens of Hamtramck, Michigan, April 17, 1989," *Presidential Documents* (Washington, D.C.: Government Printing Office, 1989), p. 563.

12. *The Times*, London, October 19, 1989, p. 1.

13. Ruyard Kipling, "Epitaphs of the War," *Rudyard Kipling's Verse: Definitive Edition* (London: Hodder and Stoughton, 1940).

14. There is now an extensive literature on the problems of industrial import-substitution strategies. See particularly C. H. Kilpatrick and F. I. Nixon, *The Industrialization of the Less Developed Countries* (Manchester: Manchester University Press, 1982), Chapter 1. See also Albert O. Hirschman, "The Political Economy of Import Substituting Industrialization in Latin America," *Quarterly Journal of Economics* 82, no. 1 (1968). For a review of the origins of the approach, see Raúl Prebisch, *The Economic Development of Latin America and Its Principal Problems* (New York: United Nations Economic Commission for Latin America, 1950). Also see Gustav Papanek, *Development Policy: Theory and Practice* (Cambridge: Harvard University Press, 1968).

15. *New York Times*, November 14, 1989, p. 4, shows a typical example of the coverage carried in 1989 about the reaction to liberalization in the People's Republic of China.

16. Examples are Hollis Chenery, Sherman Robinson and Moshe Syrquin, *Industrialization and Growth* (New York: Oxford University Press, 1986); World Bank, *World Development Report 1987*, Chapter 5; Moshin S. Khan, "Macroeconomic Adjustment in Developing Countries: A Policy Perspective," *World Bank Research*

Observer 2, no. 1 (January 1987), pp. 23–42; and Gerald Scully, "Foreign Trade Regimes, Efficiency, and Economic Growth," paper presented at the Liberty Fund Conference on the Political Economy of Neo-Mercantilism and Free Trade, Big Sky, Montana, June 9–11, 1988.

17. Samir Amin, *Accumulation on a World Scale* (New York: Monthly Review Press, 1974), Immanuel Wallerstein, *The Modern World System* (New York: Academic Press, 1974); and Fernando Henrique Cardoso and Enzo Faletto, *Dependency and Development in Latin America* (Berkeley: University of California Press, 1979).

18. Bimal Jalan, ed., *Problems and Policies in Small Economies* (London: Croom Helm, 1982); "Islands," Special Issue, *World Development* 8 (December 1980); and Simon Kuznets, "The Economic Growth of Small Nations," in E. A. G. Robinson, ed., *Economic Consequences of Size of Nations* (London: Macmillan, 1960).

Chapter 2, "Measuring Human Development"

1. Calculations are based on data from World Bank, *World Development Report 1991* (New York: Oxford University Press, 1991), pp. 196–97. The figures are not based on the real GNP data adjusted for purchasing-power parity presented later in this chapter.

2. For a discussion of the physical quality of life index, see Morris Morris, *Measuring the Condition of the World's Poor* (New York: Pergamon Press, 1979).

3. United Nations Development Programme, *Human Development Report 1990* (New York: Oxford University Press, 1990), particularly p. 10.

4. Charles Taylor and Michael Hudson, *World Handbook of Political and Social Indicators* (New Haven, Conn.: Yale University Press, 1972) p. 271.

5. Robert Klitgaard, "On Culture" (Department of Economics, University of Durban, 1992, mimeographed).

6. Hollis Chenery, Sherman Robinson, and Moshe Syrquin, *Industrialization and Growth* (New York: Oxford University Press, 1986).

7. See, for example, David Korten, *Getting to the 21st Century* (Hartford: Kumarian Press, 1991); and World Bank, *World Development Report 1992*.

8. See World Bank, *World Development Report 1991*, statistical annex, pp. 181–269.

9. U.N. Development Programme, *Human Development Report 1990*, p. 10.

10. Per capita GNP growth rates are the appropriate way to tie these two ideas of growth and personal access to resources together. In my own data the simple correlation between the GNP growth and GNP per capita growth is quite high (0.80).

11. World Bank atlas method is described in World Bank, *World Development Report 1989*, pp. 229–30.

12. The best-known work of the IPC was that of Irving B. Kravis, Zoltan Kenessey, Alan Heston, and Robert Summers, *A System of International Comparisons of Gross Product and Purchasing Power* (Baltimore: Johns Hopkins University Press, 1975), and "Real GDP Per Capita in More Than One Hundred Countries,"

Economic Journal 88 (June 1978), pp. 215–42. More recent applications of the concepts appear in U.N. Development Programme, *Human Development Report 1990*, particularly pp. 1–15 and 104–15.

13. See Kravis, Kenessey, Heston, and Summers, *A System of International Comparisons* and "Real GDP Per Capita in More Than One Hundred Countries."

14. Ibid.

15. See Morris, *Measuring the Condition of the World's Poor.*

16. One logical reason might have been to avoid the problem of assigning relative weights to economic and social variables. Another might have been the desire not to violate interval scale assumptions, which would treat 1-point gains in per capita income on a scale of 1 to 100 as if they were really on equal footing with 1-point gains in literacy or life expectancy.

17. See note 16 and Appendix 1 for a detailed discussion of the index.

18. See U.N. Development Programme, *Human Development Report 1992* for a discussion of refinements in the index.

19. See U.N. Development Programme, *Human Development Report 1990*, p. 10.

20. See Appendix 1 for a detailed description of the index and its mathematical computation.

21. An excellent early discussion of the problem and the concept of disparity reduction rates can be found in James P. Grant, *Disparity Reduction Rates in Social Indicators*, Monograph 11 (Washington, D.C.: Overseas Development Council, 1978), particularly pp. 11–28. See also Morris, *Measuring the Condition of the World's Poor.*

22. The DRR is a good choice for this analysis. Although it overstates the importance of the DRR for countries nearing 100 percent HDI, the developing country set used here contains few of those countries. Finally, as Grant and Morris note, the DRR provides policy makers with a tool for setting targets for disparity reduction across countries. For the formula for calculating the DRR and more on why it was selected for use here, see Appendix 2.

23. Analysis by country performance allows those with methodological objections to the HDI as a composite interval scale index to analyze performance based on more stringent assumptions of ranked performance groups. Special attention is paid to these country performance groups since they allow us to look for common characteristics of high versus low HDI performers. This method also permits those comfortable with the HDI as an interval scale index to use it that way to look at stepwise regressions with HDI DRR gain scores as the dependent variable.

24. U.S. Department of Commerce, *Statistical Abstract of the United States* (Washington, D.C., 1976), p. 866. Although the United Nations statistics include more countries, their economic data are not as complete. The world population in 1989 was 5.2 billion according to the U.S. Department Commerce, *Statistical Abstract of the United States* (Washington, D.C., 1990), p. 831.

25. The Pearson's correlations between PPP-adjusted real per capita GDP in 1965 and literacy and life expectancy are .74 and .78, respectively. The correlation between 1965 literacy and life expectancy is .94. An example of the argument linking per capita GDP, literacy, and life expectancy appears in U.N. Development Programme, *Human Development Report 1990*, pp. 13–16. Morris Morris has a more

careful and interesting treatment of the same problem in *Measuring the Condition of the World's Poor*, pp. 52–56. He noted that there was little direct relationship between a country's per capita GDP and its PQLI in any given year. For example, Sri Lanka might have a higher PQLI (69) than Brazil (52) in a given year like 1965 but a lower per capita GDP (US$157 compared with US$229). He argued that GNP and GDP measures did not account for either improved income distribution or social investments that could be made independent of a country's per capita income level. The current data for 1965, 1980, and 1987 partially support his initial conclusion. However, they also support an analysis that Morris did not attempt showing that early PQLI and HDI status may be a key indicator of future economic and social performance and status and that growth is necessary to have resources to use for social investments.

26. Since I am dealing with population rather than sample data, statistical treatment using analysis of variance is unnecessary. However, the F scores and probability values are given so that the reader can see what they would have been like had I been trying to generalize from a sample to a population. The analysis of variance data in Table 2.1 shows that the four income groups have significantly different levels of literacy, life expectancy, and HDI performance.

27. See note 26 for a discussion of the limitations of using analysis of variance here.

28. See note 26 for the limitations of using analysis of t-tests here. Within each income group the countries were divided into those with lower and higher HDI scores for 1965. T-tests were run to look at differences within each income group between those countries with higher and those with lower 1965 HDI scores over the period 1965–1987: GDP growth, growth in PPP-adjusted real per capita GDP, literacy DRR gain, life expectancy DRR gain, and HDI DRR gain. For the very low-income group the higher initial HDI countries performed significantly better (at the .001 level) on all measures except literacy (where there was no difference). For the low-income countries those with higher initial HDI scores performed significantly better (at the .001 level) on GDP growth, life expectancy, and HDI. The results were not significant for literacy or PPP-adjusted real per capita GDP. For the medium-income group, the higher HDI countries performed significantly better (at the .01 level) in all cases except PPP-adjusted real per capita GDP.

29. Developing-country performance groups were selected by dividing the ninety developing countries into three equal groups based on their 1965–1987 HDI DRR score. There is little difference in the final list of countries in each performance category when an alternative selection method based on country ranks on each of the three HDI components was used.

Because of insufficient data for some countries, the performance groups have only twenty-four countries each. The problem of missing data is greatest in the countries with very low per capita GDP like Afghanistan, Bhutan, and Laos, largely because of a lack of 1965 baseline data to compute an index. The countries affected are mainly in Asia and the Middle East, causing the African countries to be over-represented. Since many of the very poorest countries with the weakest 1965–1987 development performance have been excluded, the differences between the very low GDP income group and the other country groups may be understated. Thus, if the group differences are still statistically significant when the weakest performers are excluded, we can be fairly comfortable with the strength of these differences.

30. Ethnic scale data come from Taylor and Hudson, *World Handbook of Political and Social Indicators.*

31. Gastil's indexes of political and economic context are described in Raymond Gastil, *Freedom in the World* (Westport, Conn.: Greenwood Press, 1983), pp. 3–9 and 51–90.

32. The correlation matrix for all contextual variables yielded no evidence of multicollinearity. Problems related to non-normal distributions of data in 1965 HDI status and 1965–1987 HDI disparity performance were reduced by using log data. Distributions for the other variables showed no serious abnormalities.

The high Durban Watson statistics indicated that there were no serious problems of autocorrelation. Examination of scatterplots of the residuals in initial regressions showed some problems in overpredicting HDI performance of African countries and underpredicting the performance of some key East and Southeast Asian nations. The risk of heteroskedastity due to these prediction areas was reduced by introducing dummy variables for Africa and for East and Southeast Asian nations. The regressions on the variables reported here produced statistically significant F and t statistics.

33. The results did not differ substantially from those presented here.

34. These policies are considered more short term in nature than some of the contextual institutional factors.

35. Because of the large number of policy variables, a two-step process was used for developing the regressions. First, all ten policy variables were added to an OLS multiple regression. Then the variables with the highest t values significant at the .05 level scores were kept for a second regression. At this second stage a stepwise regression was run to look at the incremental r squared contributed by each variable.

The correlation matrix for all variables yielded no evidence of multicollinearity. Problems related to non-normal distributions of data in average military, health, and education expenditures as a percentage of 1965–1987 GDP were reduced by using log data. Distributions for the other variables showed no serious abnormalities.

The high Durban Watson statistics indicated that there were no serious problems of autocorrelation. Examination of scatterplots of the residuals in initial regressions showed no serious problems. The regressions on the variables reported here produced statistically significant F and t statistics.

36. For the high human development performers four variables—political liberty, export growth, higher education and health expenditures, and lower fiscal deficits—accounted for 0.218 of the adjusted r squared. The F and t statistics were significant at the .001 level, and the Durban Watson statistic of 1.79 indicated no serious autocorrelation. For the low human development performers only two variables proved to be significant: political liberty and health and education expenditures. They combined to predict about 0.199 of the adjusted r squared.

37. The same procedure described in note 35 was used in the regressions of policy variables on GDP growth. The results were significant; the correlation matrices and the Durban Watson statistics indicated no serious anomalies.

38. See, for example, World Bank, *World Development Report 1990*.

39. John Fei, Shirley Kuo, and Gustav Ranis, *The Taiwan Success Story* (Boulder, Colo.: Westview Press, 1981).

40. The same procedure described in note 35 was used in the regressions of external influences on human development performance. The results were significant; the correlation matrices and the Durban Watson statistics indicated no serious anomalies.

41. The results for high and low performers were similar to those reported here.

42. The same procedure described in note 35 was used in the regressions of external influences on GDP growth. The results were significant; the correlation matrices and the Durban Watson statistics indicated no serious anomalies.

43. Because of the large number of variables, a two-step process was used for developing the regressions. First, all significant internal, external, and policy variables were added to an OLS multiple regression. Then the variables with the highest t values significant at the .05 level scores were kept for a second regression. At this second stage a step-wise regression was run to look at the incremental r squared contributed by each variable.

The correlation matrix for all variables yielded no evidence of multicollinearity. Problems related to non-normal distributions of data in average military, health, and education expenditures as a percentage of 1965–1987 GDP were reduced by using log data. Distributions for the other variables showed no serious abnormalities. The high Durban Watson statistics indicated that there were no serious problems of autocorrelation. Examination of scatterplots of the residuals in initial regressions showed no serious problems. The regressions on the variables reported here produced statistically significant F and t statistics.

44. For the top third of human development performers there are four significant variables that entered the stepwise regression with significant t values. They predicted 34 percent of the adjusted r squared. The Durban Watson statistic of 1.96 showed no evidence of autocorrelation among variables. The variables that entered the equation were nonprogrammed change of presidents ($3.45F$ r squared 0.205), HDI in 1965 ($9.141F$ r squared 0.288), export product diversification in 1965–1987 ($2.678F$ r squared 0.318), and location in Asia ($2.713F$ r squared 0.340).

For the lower third of human development performers there are four significant variables that entered the stepwise regression with significant t values. They predicted 44 percent of the adjusted r squared. The Durban Watson statistic of 2.004 showed no evidence of autocorrelation among variables. The variables that entered the equation were nonprogrammed change of presidents ($4.42F$ r squared 0.346), HDI in 1965 ($6.435F$ r squared 0.390), log of health and education expenditures in GNP in 1965–1987 ($5.171F$ r squared 0.420), and location in Africa ($2.792F$ r squared 0.440).

45. Table 1.9 helps show that statistically significant effects on human development performance do not always produce the same level of policy effects. For example, exchange rate policies contributed 0.030 in incremental r squared to the statistical explanation of the HDI disparity reduction rate. Social policies (education and health expenditures) contributed only 0.005 in incremental r squared. However, moving Chad's policy performance in each of these areas to

the developing country average produced a slightly larger human development gain from the social expenditure policy change (1987 HDI of 26.26) than from the exchange rate policy change (1987 HDI of 26.10).

Chapter 3, "Regime Type and Economic Performance"

A shorter presentation of the ideas in this chapter appears in Marc Lindenberg and Shantayana Devarajan, "Prescribing Strong Economic Medicine," *Comparative Politics* 25, no. 2 (January 1993). Forrest Colburn, Jorge Domínguez, Robert Klitgaard, Jack Montgomery, Dwight Perkins, and Dani Roderik contributed helpful comments. The data analysis could not have been completed without the assistance of Veronica Marseillan, Diemar Smith, and Julie Stanton and the help of a grant from the Ford Foundation.

1. See for example, Barbara Stallings and Robert R. Kaufman, eds., *Debt and Democracy in Latin America* (Boulder, Colo.: Westview Press, 1989); Thomas E. Skidmore, "The Politics of Economic Stabilization in Postwar Latin America," in James M. Malloy, ed., *Authoritarianism and Corporatism in Latin America* (Pittsburgh: University of Pittsburgh Press, 1977), pp. 149-90; Robert R. Kaufman "Democratic and Authoritarian Responses to the Debt Issue: Argentina, Brazil and Mexico," *International Organization* 39 (Summer 1985), pp. 473-503; and James M. Malloy and Mitchell A. Seligson, eds., *Authoritarians and Democrats: Regime Transition in Latin America* (Pittsburgh: University of Pittsburgh Press, 1987).

2. Skidmore, "The Politics of Economic Stabilization in Postwar Latin America," p. 181.

3. See Joan Nelson and contributors, *Fragile Coalitions: The Politics of Economic Adjustment* (New Brunswick, N.J.: Transaction Books, 1989); Stephan Haggard, "The Politics of Stabilization: Lessons from the IMF's Extended Fund Facility," in Miles Kahler, ed., *The Politics of International Debt* (Ithaca, N.Y.: Cornell University Press, 1985), pp. 157-86; Karen Remmer, "The Politics of Economic Stabilization: IMF Standby Programs in Latin America, 1954-84," *Comparative Politics* 19, no. 1 (October 1986), pp. 1-24; idem, "Democracy and Economic Crisis: The Latin American Experience," *World Politics* 42, no. 3 (April 1990), pp. 315-35.

4. Remmer, "Democracy and Economic Crisis," p. 318. This article has an excellent discussion of the literature and the key issues.

5. While the research driving this debate is much more comprehensive today than in the past, recent studies are still incomplete. First, economic performance is defined with relatively few variables. For example, Remmer provides a sound foundation but does not offer the more comprehensive economic analysis using measures of growth, internal and external balance, and debt burden provided, for example, by Ricardo Faini, Jaime de Melo, Abdel Senhadji-Semlali, and Julie Stanton, "Macro Performance under Adjustment Lending," *Policy, Planning, and Research Working Paper 190* (Washington, D.C.: World Bank, 1989). Second, reform is limited largely to stabilization rather than structural adjustment, which dominated the economic efforts of the 1980s. Haggard and Remmer, for example, concern themselves almost entirely with stabilization. Nelson initiates an interesting discussion of the politics of adjustment rather than simply stabilization. Haggard's most recent work continues these discussions in "The Politics of

Stabilization and Structural Adjustment," in J. Sachs, ed., *Developing Country Debt and Economic Performance* (Chicago: University of Chicago Press, 1989). Third, most of the published research does not yet assess the experience of the 1980s. Fourth, the few studies that have been completed on simultaneous economic and political liberalization during the 1980s have focused principally on Latin America, since the majority of political openings in the decade occurred there. Finally, regime type has been crudely defined, often considering only democratic forms—that is, whether or not the government permits regular competitive elections. Other important variables, such as the presence or absence of basic political, civil, and economic rights, have been neglected.

6. Faini, de Melo, Senhadji-Semlali, and Stanton were kind enough to share their extensive data base and their measures.

7. There are many ways to classify regime types. For example, see D. Berg-Schlosser, "African Political Systems: Typology and Performance," *Comparative Political Studies* 5, no. 2 (1984), p. 17; or K. Bollen, "Dimensions of Democracy," *American Sociological Review* 46 (1981). Preference, however, was given to maintaining consistency with the most recent studies of regime type and economic performance, particularly with Remmer, "Democracy and Economic Crisis," p. 322. To summarize the method, regimes are coded as democratic if they came to power on the basis of popular and competitive elections as noted in Arthur Banks, Thomas Muller, Sean Phelar, and Elaine Talman, *Political Handbook of the World* (Binghamton, N.Y.: CSA Publications, State University of New York, 1991). The discussion was broadened to include the country scores on Gastil's indexes of civil, political, and economic rights from 1973 to 1989, Wright's index of economic rights, and Gastil's economic system classifications, all of which appear in Raymond D. Gastil, *Freedom in the World: Political Rights and Civil Liberties, 1982* (Westport, Conn.: Greenwood Press, 1982), particularly pp. 9–48 and 51–89, and *Freedom in the World: Political Rights and Civil Liberties, 1988–1989* (New York: Freedom House, 1989).

8. A country was considered an established democracy if it had a score of 51 on the percentage democratic rule measure for both 1973–1981 and 1982–1988. It was considered newly democratic for 1982–1988 if it had a score of less than 50 percent between 1973 and 1981 and greater than 50 percent between 1982 and 1988.

9. George Bush, "Remarks to Citizens of Hamtramck, Michigan, April 17, 1989," *Presidential Documents* (Washington, D.C.: Government Printing Office, 1989), p. 563.

10. When the countries are placed in a two-by-two matrix with "democratic" and "other" on one axis and "regime collapse" (yes or no) on the other, the chi square value for the period 1973–1980 is 3.565, significant at the .16 level. In the 1981–1989 period the chi square value of 0.917 is significant at the .63 level.

11. The equation used, based on an error-components framework, is

$$Yit = B0 + B1\, Di + B2\, DiT + Uit$$

where:

Yit = the logarithm of GDP of country i in year t
$D1$ = dummy variable which equals 0 if country i is authoritarian and 1 if it is democratic
T = time trend
Uit = composed error term

12. We estimate the following equation to control for the effects of shocks using a control group framework:

$$Yij = aoj + Xi'ai + SHia2j + a3jDi + Eij$$

where:

Yij = performance indicator j for country i
Xi = lagged values of these indicators for country i
SHi = changes in the country i's external environment
D = dummy variable (0 if authoritarian and 1 if democratic)

13. Although the raw numbers show that about 20 percent of the democratic regimes and 33 percent of the nondemocratic ones initiated structural adjustment loan (SAL) programs, the chi square value of 2.273 (.13 probability level) shows no significant difference in SAL initiation by democratic and authoritarian regimes. Once programs are initiated, the chi square value of .001 (.91 probability level) shows no difference in collapse rates by regime type.

14. The SAL-participating countries undergoing regime collapse or transition were Bolivia, Brazil, Nigeria, Panama, the Philippines, Sudan, Turkey, and Uruguay. Non-SAL countries undergoing regime collapse or transition in the same period were Argentina, Bangladesh, Burma, El Salvador, Fiji, and Guatemala.

15. See Faini, de Melo, Senhadji-Semlali, and Stanton, "Macro Performance under Adjustment Lending."

16. There are three serious limitations to comparing the economic performance of the SAL and non–SAL participants engaged in simultaneous regime transitions in the 1980s. First, only a small number—eight of the thirty SAL participants and six of the sixty-three non–SAL participants—were involved in simultaneous transitions. Statistical testing is of limited utility with such small numbers. Second, owing to the use of period averages rather than time-series data geared to the actual phasing of transitions, it is impossible to determine whether economic results deteriorated before regime transition and continued to do so during the transition or whether performance improved once the transition began. A third problem is that the aggregate statistics group a number of dissimilar transitions together. For some regimes like the Philippines, the process of simultaneous transition was neither intentional nor orderly. President Ferdinand Marcos had no intention of surrendering power but was thrown out of office by a broad-based popular movement. In other transitions, such as in Guatemala, the process was led by the regime itself during worsening economic conditions but not total collapse.

17. See, for example, Gerald W. Scully, "The Institutional Framework and Economic Development," *Journal of Political Economy* 96, no. 3 (1988), pp. 652–62.

Chapter 4, "Governance Structures and Human Development"

1. Governance structures may be thought of as specific encompassing relationships by which people organize themselves for collective life. The origins of the idea can be found in Aristotle, *The Politics*, bk. 1, ch. 1, sec. 6–7. The broad definition is useful because it permits a better discussion of the relation of elements of the polity like civil society, the state, and political society. The narrower definitions recently used by donor agencies—for example, "the management of a country's economic and social resources for development" (World Bank, "Managing Development: The Governance Dimension," Discussion paper, Washington, D.C., 1991), p. 1—do not specifically highlight the potential relationships between citizens and political institutions.

2. Alfred Stepan, *Rethinking Military Politics* (Princeton: Princeton University Press, 1988), pp. 3–12.

3. Ibid.

4. There are many more complicated and varied categorizations of these structures, but for the purposes of this argument they will not be discussed.

5. The time-series data at this level of aggregation are not good enough to establish which features of the governance structure developed in what order or how they interacted with overall economic development. Samuel Huntington explores these interrelationships in *The Third Wave: Democratization in the Late Twentieth Century* (Norman: University of Oklahoma Press, 1991). More detailed empirical treatment of the phasing of institutional development will have to be continued by others.

6. There were differences in the styles of the democratic and nondemocratic regimes. The eight democratic regimes had higher levels of political and civil rights than the fifteen nondemocratic ones. They also had larger public sectors than their nondemocratic counterparts. But both maintained medium or high levels of political and civil rights.

7. See, for example, Huntington, *The Third Wave*, and Robert D. Putnam with Robert Leonardi and Raffella Nanetti, *Democracy and the Civic Community: Tradition and Change in an Italian Experiment* (Princeton: Princeton University Press, 1992). For a more optimistic vision, see Graham Allison and Robert Beschel, "Can the United States Promote Democracy?" *Political Science Quarterly* 106, no. 4, (1991–92).

8. Ricardo Faini, Jaime de Melo, Abdel Senhadji-Semlali, and Julie Stanton, "Macro Performance under Adjustment Lending," Policy, Planning, and Research Working Paper 190 (Washington, D.C.: World Bank, 1989).

9. Michael Bruno, "Stabilization and Reform in Eastern Europe: A Preliminary Evaluation" (Discussion paper presented at a Harvard seminar series on transitions in Eastern Europe and the former Soviet Union organized by Janos Kornai, Faculty Club, March 1992). Bruno's insights about this problem came out in the question-and-answer session after he delivered his paper.

Chapter 5, "Context, Policies, and Human Development in Central America"

1. These findings are partially reported in Marc Lindenberg, "Central America: Crisis and Economic Strategy: Lessons from History," *Journal of Developing Areas* 22, no. 2 (January 1988) pp. 155–78.

2. Belize is not included because it is a former British colony normally thought of as having more in common with the English-speaking countries.

3. Of the nine regions of the world, only three have ethnic diversity index scores lower than Central America's 0.25. They are the Middle East 0.22, Europe 0.21, and the Caribbean 0.16. When Guatemala is excluded, Central America's low ethnic diversity index is second only to the Caribbean.

4. A number of authors have treated the problem of external shocks and small economies. See, for example, Nathaniel Leff and Kazuo Sato, "Macroeconomic Adjustment in Developing Countries: Instability, Short-run Growth and External Dependency," *Review of Economics and Statistics* 62, no. 2 (May 1980). Also see B. F. Massell, "Export Instability and Economic Structure," *American Economic Review* 60, no. 4 (September 1970); and G. K. Helleiner, "Balance of Payments Problems and Macro-economic Policy in Small Economies," in B. Jalan, ed., *Problems and Policies in Small Economies* (London: Croom Helm, 1982), pp. 165–85. See also S. Kuznets, "The Economic Growth of Small Nations," in E. A. G. Robinson, ed., *Economic Consequences of Size of Nations* (London: Macmillan, 1960); Boris Blazic-Metzner and Helen Hughes, "Growth Experience of Small Economies," in B. Jalan, ed., *Problems and Policies in Small Economies* (London: Croom Helm, 1982), pp. 85–103; and "Islands," *World Development* 8, no. 12 (December 1980).

5. See Antonio Colindres, Marc Lindenberg, and Rodrigo Valverde, "Economic Trends in Central America and Panama since 1900," INCAE Technical Note (San José: Instituto Centroamericano de Administración de Empresas (INCAE), 1986). Because GDP data for Central America were not collected before 1950, data on the percentage growth and decline of total trade (imports plus exports) were used as a surrogate for 1930–1950 GDP growth rates. For an interesting discussion of Central American economic history and business cycles, see Hector Pérez Brignoli, "Growth and Crisis in the Central American Economies 1950-80" *Journal of Latin American Studies* 15, no. 2 (November 1983), pp. 365–98. Some of the most complete and creative work is that of Victor Bulmer-Thomas. Bulmer-Thomas has built some of the best time-series GDP data. His insights on trend periods and economic strategy are particularly useful as a cross check on my work. See, for example, "Central American Integration, Trade Diversification and the World Market," in George Irvin and Xavier Gorostiaga, eds., *Towards an Alternative for Central America and the Caribbean* (London: George Allen and Unwin, 1985), pp. 194–213; "Central America in the Inter-War Period," in Rosemary Thorp, ed., *Latin America in the 1930's* (London: Macmillan, 1984), pp. 279–314; and "World Recession and Central American Depression: Lessons from the 1930s for the 1980s," in Esperanza Duran, ed., *Latin America and the World Recession* (Cambridge: Cambridge University Press, 1985), pp. 130–51. Also see John Weeks, "An Interpretation of the Central American Crisis," *Latin American Research Review* 21, no. 3 (September 1986), pp. 31–53.

6. For a good discussion of the typical problems of small economies, see Percy Selwyn, "Smallness and Islandness," *World Development* 5, no. 12 (December 1980), pp. 945–51.

7. Ibid.

8. For the purposes of this study, five kinds of economic periods were identified: (1) a *strong contraction* is defined as either three consecutive years of declining GDP growth in which each year has a rate of growth of less than

3 percent annually or three years of nonconsecutive declining growth but where each year the growth rate is negative; (2) a *weak contraction* is defined as either three years of nonconsecutive declining growth with annual averages of between 2 and 3 percent per year or one to two years where growth drops from one year to the next by more than 3 percent and under the total of 3 percent per year; (3) a *recovery* is defined as the first two consecutive years of positive growth after a period of strong or weak contraction; (4) *mild sustained growth* is defined as the period of two or more years after recovery of average growth between 0.1 and 3.9 percent; and (5) *strong sustained growth* is defined as the period of two or more years after recovery where GDP growth on an annual basis is above 4.0 percent.

Since I am interested in how Central America responds to contractions and recovery, I have regrouped these five trend periods into four for analytical purposes: *major crisis,* which combines a strong contraction and its recovery period; *minor crisis,* which combines a weak contraction and its recovery period; *weak sustained growth;* and *strong sustained growth.*

9. For an excellent discussion of these and other historical periods in the world economy, see W. W. Rostow, *The World Economy: History and Prospect* (Austin: University of Texas Press, 1978).

10. See Pedro Belli, "An Inquiry Concerning the Growth of Cotton Farming in Nicaragua" (Ph.D. dissertation, University of California at Berkeley, 1966).

Chapter 6, "Regime Type, Political Instability and Human Development in Central America"

A summary of the results presented in this chapter appear in Marc Lindenberg, "World Economic Cycles and Central American Political Instability," *World Politics* 42, no. 3 (April 1990), pp. 397–421.

1. Ekhart Zimmerman, *Political Violence, Crises and Revolution* (New York: Schenkman, 1983) provides an extensive review of the literature on causes of political instability. Four perspectives of particular interest are modernization theory, psychological theories of relative deprivation, perspectives derived from Marxist political economy, and those derived from more conventional economics. For an explanation of modernization theory, see Samuel Huntington, *Political Order in Changing Societies* (New Haven: Yale University Press, 1968). Examples of the psychological approach are I. Feierabend and R. Feierabend, "Systemic Conditions of Political Aggression: An Application of Frustration-Aggression Theory," in I. Feieraben, R. Feierabend, and T. Gurr, eds., *Anger, Violence and Politics* (Englewood Cliffs, N.J.: Prentice Hall, 1972), 136–83; and T. Gurr, *Why Men Rebel* (Princeton: Princeton University Press, 1970). Representative presentations of the Marxist perspective can be found in Samir Amin, *Accumulation on a World Scale,* vols. 1 and 2 (New York: Monthly Review Press, 1974); and Immanuel Wallerstein, *The Modern World System* (New York: Academic Press, 1974). For a more conventional approach see Gunnar Myrdal, *Rich Lands and Poor* (New York: Harper, 1958); and Albert O. Hirschman, *The Strategy of Economic Development* (New Haven: Yale University Press, 1962).

2. See, for example, Amin, *Accumulation on a World Scale,* and Wallerstein, *The Modern World System.*

3. For an explanation of modernization theory, see Huntington, *Political Order in Changing Societies.*

4. Examples of contributions from a Marxist perspective are Paul Baran, *The Political Economy of Growth* (New York: Monthly Review Press, 1957). Baran's work was further developed by Andre Gunder Frank, *Latin America: Underdevelopment or Revolution* (New York: Monthly Review Press, 1969). See also Celso Furtado, *Economic Development of Latin America: A Survey from Colonial Times to the Cuban Revolution* (London: Cambridge University Press, 1970). One of the most interesting reformulations of dependency theory is Fernando Henrique Cardoso and Enzo Faletto, *Dependency and Development in Latin America* (Berkeley: University of California Press, 1979). For non-Marxist perspectives see Guillermo O'Donnell's *Modernization and Bureaucratic-Authoritarianism,* Institute of International Studies, Politics of Modernization Series, no. 9 (Berkeley: University of California Press, 1973), pp. 291–93; David Collier, ed., *The New Authoritarianism in Latin America* (Princeton: Princeton University Press, 1979); and David Becker, Jeff Frieden, Sayre Schatz, and Richard Sklar, *Postimperialism* (Boulder, Colo.: Lynne Rienner, 1987).

5. The word dependency is derived from the Spanish word *dependencia.* Advocates of this viewpoint see *dependencia* not as a theory but rather as a world view that asserts that the economic growth of peripheral economies is conditioned by the fluctuations and growth of the dominant industrial economies. The historic development of *dependencia* is discussed in Ronald Chilcote and Joel Edelstein, *Latin America: Capitalist and Socialist Perspectives of Development and Underdevelopment* (Boulder, Colo.: Westview Press, 1986), ch. 3 and 4; and Juan Eugenio Corradi, "Cultural Dependence and the Sociology of Knowledge: The Latin American Case," in June Nash, Juan Corradi, and Hobart Spalding, Jr., eds., *Ideology and Social Change in Latin America* (New York: Gordon and Breach, 1977), pp. 7–30. For specific works see Baran, *The Political Economy of Growth,* and Frank, *Latin America: Underdevelopment or Revolution.*

6. Cardoso and Faletto, *Dependency and Development in Latin America.* See also Bill Warren, *Imperialism, Pioneer of Capitalism* (London: New Left Books, 1980).

7. See, for example, Guillermo O'Donnell, Philippe Schmitter, and Laurence Whitehead, *Transitions from Authoritarian Rule* (Baltimore: Johns Hopkins University Press, 1986), or Alfred Stepan, *Rethinking Military Politics* (Princeton: Princeton University Press, 1988). See also Myrdal, *Rich Lands and Poor,* and Hirschman, *The Strategy of Economic Development.*

8. The concept of bureaucratic authoritarianism was first presented in O'Donnell, *Modernization and Bureaucratic-Authoritarianism.* See also O'Donnell, "Reflections on Patterns of Change in the Bureaucratic-Authoritarian State," *Latin American Research Review* 13, no. 1 (1984), pp. 3–38, and "Tensions in the Bureaucratic-Authoritarian State and the Question of Democracy," in David Collier, ed., *The New Authoritarianism in Latin America* (Princeton: Princeton University Press, 1979), pp. 285–318. For a critique see Karen Remmer and Gilbert Merkx, "Bureaucratic-Authoritarianism Revisited," *Latin American Research Review* 17, no. 2 (1982), pp. 3–40.

9. See Becker, Frieden, Schatz, and Sklar, *Postimperialism.*

10. O'Donnell, *Modernization and Bureaucratic-Authoritarianism*, p. 11. O'Donnell specifically excludes Central America from his analysis and focuses on the larger economies. The closest he comes to discussing regime types in the smaller Latin American states is to classify them as traditional authoritarian (p. 114). Cardoso and Faletto, in *Dependency and Development in Latin America*, pp. 122–24, also provide no more than a brief analysis of the effects of international economic forces on class relations in Central America. They argue that the system continues to be based on dominance by traditional agricultural exporters, enclave foreign interests, and the military. They make no attempt to trace the dynamics of change in those relationships and treat the region as a unit.

11. This part of the thesis most closely parallels the discussions of global economic forces in Frank, *Latin America: Underdevelopment or Revolution*, and Cardoso and Faletto, *Dependency and Development in Latin America*; the regional discussions in Daniel Camacho and Rafael Menjivar, *Movimientos Populares en Centro América* (San José: Editorial Universitario Centroamericano (EDUCA), 1985); and Robert G. Williams, *Export Agriculture and the Crisis in Central America* (Chapel Hill: University of North Carolina Press, 1986); and the country analysis, for example, in Rafael Menjivar, *Formación y Lucha del Proletariado Industrial Salvadoreño* (San Salvador: UCA, 1979); or Rene Poitevin, *El Proceso de Industrialización en Guatemala* (San José: Editorial Universitario Centroamericano (EDUCA), 1977).

12. External economic crisis can be thought of here as the element that stimulates frustration, setting off the dynamics of aggression and social discontent described in Feierabend and Feierabend, "Systemic Conditions of Political Aggression," and Gurr, *Why Men Rebel*.

13. This argument runs counter to Huntington's modernization theory in *Political Order in Changing Societies*. It fits O'Donnell's general idea that economic stagnation initiates a cycle of discontent that results in repression. According to O'Donnell, however, for the large Latin American countries the source of stagnation is the end of the easy stage of industrial import substitution. In small, highly open, export economies like those found in Central America, the source is more clearly international economic instability. O'Donnell, *Modernization and Bureaucratic-Authoritarianism*.

14. This part of the thesis builds upon Cardoso and Faletto's contention that in Central America in the twentieth century there has been no regime change but only leadership or government change as the coalition of military, traditional agricultural, and enclave forces reestablish themselves. It supports O'Donnell's general contention that until the 1980s at least five of the Central American countries might be classified as traditional authoritarian regimes.

15. One interesting hypothesis that will have to be explored elsewhere is that the 1986–1989 period can be viewed as a unique change from traditional authoritarian to democratic regimes as opposed to simply the continued unprogrammed rotation of military leaders and governments. This shift may be due to the demands of the larger urban middle and working classes that developed as a result of import substitution stimulated through Central America's common market between 1960 and 1978. Certainly levels of urbanization increased from 1965 (37.5 percent) to 1983 (45 percent).

16. See, for example, Daniel Rapport, "American Foreign Policy in Central America: A Method of Analysis and Results" (John F. Kennedy School of Government, Harvard University, 1988, unpublished paper).

17. For discussions of the problems of population density and ethnic diversity on political discontent and repression, see Richard Adams and Michael Stone, "Memorandum on Relations between Native Americans and the State in Central America" (paper prepared for the International Commission for Central American Recovery and Development, April 1988). Specific country examples are "Los Pueblos Indigenas ante el Mundo," *Revista de la Escuela Nacional de Antropología e Historia* 1, no. 1 (June 1980), pp. 2–5; Mexico and CIDCA, Development Study Unit, "Ethnic Groups and the Nation State: The Case of the Atlantic Coast in Nicaragua" (Department of Anthropology, University of Stockholm, 1987). For more general sources see Cepal Fao Oit, *Tenencia de la Tierra y Desarrollo Rural en Centroamerica* (San José: Editorial Universitario Centroamericano (EDUCA), 1980); and Tom Barry, *Roots of Rebellion: Land and Hunger in Central America* (Boston: South End Press, 1987). For excellent treatment of the development of the class structures in Guatemala and Costa Rica and the different treatment of indigenous groups, see Severo Martínez Pelaez, *La Patria del Criollo: Ensayo de Interpretación de la Realidad Colonial Guatemalateca* (San José: EDUCA, 1985); and Samuel Stone, *La Dinastia de los Conquistadores* (San José: EDUCA, 1982).

18. The accentuated effects of economic crisis on countries with dense population and indigenous groups whose traditional relationship to the land has been broken is noted by Menjivar, *Formación y Lucha del Proletariado Industrial Salvadoreño.*

19. See notes 17 and 18.

20. Although these two factors are extremely important, it was difficult to get accurate regionwide data. The best recent source in this matter is the International Commission for Central American Reconstruction and Development at Duke University. See the background papers to the commission forthcoming from Duke University Press.

21. Leadership instability is distinguished here from government, regime, and political instability. Helpful definitions of terms can be found in David Sanders, *Patterns of Political Instability* (New York: St. Martin's, 1981), pp. 49–69; J. Blondel, *An Introduction to Comparative Government* (London: Weidenfeld and Nicholson, 1968); and David Easton, *The Political System* (New York: Knopf, 1953). Using Sanders's definitions, leadership instability refers to higher than normal levels of nonprogrammed changes of the chief executive; government instability, to high levels of nonprogrammed changes of the chief executive and cabinet. Regime instability refers to high levels of nonprogrammed changes in goals, norms, and authority structures—for example, moving from oligarchic to democratic participation in elections or decisions. Political instability might be defined as higher than normal levels of peaceful or violent social discontent that challenges or replaces presidents, governments, or regimes.

22. Governments engage in official repression through formal decrees of censorship, suspension of the right to strike, suspension of constitutional guarantees, denial of rights of assembly, states of emergency, martial law, and war. In addition to studying formal decrees, I could have looked at the number

of political prisoners, deaths by torture, or arrests and injuries in confrontations with government security forces. The latter measures are so difficult to document that I confined this study to formal measures of government repression—decrees that appear in the official government records called *Gazettas*, which have been published since the early 1900s. The index is grouped in five categories: censorship, interventions and nationalization, militarization, limits on organizational meetings and assembly, and others. The governments' stated reasons for each repressive measure taken paint a fascinating historical picture of the formal justification for their actions and the individuals, groups, and social classes against which the measures were directed. The data on repression that appear in this book are based on a review of all *Gazettas* for all Central American countries and Panama since 1930.

23. The intensity of social discontent might be measured by the number of people involved or the frequency or seriousness of their actions. It is equally useful to try to establish the source of such discontent, which may be rural or urban, or upper, middle, or lower class in its origins. It may come as well from mainstream or from ethnic minorities, from men or from women. The data on social discontent since the 1930s are among the hardest to amass for Central America. There are no accurate records of the number of strikes, confrontations, combats, and deaths and no systematic evidence about the origins of social action. In addition to using traditional historical sources, this study developed a random sample of 28 percent of Central American newspapers between 1930 and 1985. Researchers selected two papers per week per country for every week in the study period and then analyzed their contents to identify the numbers of stories, editorials, and opinion articles about strikes, demonstrations, sabotage, armed confrontations, and combats. Each action was classified according to its sector of origin (such as, urban or rural) and by the kind of group involved (such as, political party, interest group, or paramilitary group).

Of all the data sources developed, the newspaper material on social discontent is the weakest. The newspaper data required the most time and effort and netted the fewest results, because of the problems of censorship and changes in the formats of the newspapers themselves during the study period. Precisely when historical sources indicate that discontent is highest, evidence on the volume of that discontent disappears in countries whose newspapers are censored. While data on discontent are higher in crisis periods than in periods of military rule, the data appear to understate the volume and intensity of that discontent. The newspaper data are a better source to establish who was protesting or fighting and what their social origin was.

24. Nonprogrammed presidential turnover is a building block in Sanders's definitions of government instability and regime instability; see Sanders, *Patterns of Political Instability*, chapter 3 and p. 62.

25. One potential problem in using the population density data over a fifty-year period is that country ranks may change. For example, Honduras could be less dense than Costa Rica in 1940 but more dense in 1980. An analysis of population data since 1950 shows that rankings for Central American countries did not change. El Salvador and Guatemala retain the highest densities, Costa Rica and Honduras medium, and Nicaragua and Panama low.

Central American ethnic populations are of two types: Indians of Mayan and other stock who populate northern Guatemala, parts of El Salvador, and Honduras and Panama, including its islands, and Negro groups that settled the east coast areas of Central America.

Data on urbanization are from World Bank, *World Development Report 1985* (New York: Oxford University Press, 1985), p. 216.

26. Daniel Rapport's unpublished paper "American Foreign Policy in Central America: A Method of Analysis and Results" generates some interesting hypotheses about why Central American economic cycles appeared to be more weakly related to political instability than to world economic cycles. Rapport's content analysis of Central American cable traffic, which appears in *Foreign Relations of the United States between 1930–49*, indicates that shifts in U.S. policy toward Central American governments might have been sufficient either to override political instability that normally accompanied economic crisis (1934–1943) or to exacerbate political instability in spite of economic growth (1944–1949). For example, between 1934 and 1943, a period of economic collapse in Central America, U.S. diplomatic recognition of Central American military governments was more lenient than in the previous or subsequent periods. It recognized all new governments without hesitation, whereas in 1930–1934 it recognized only 18 percent without hesitation and in 1944–1949 only 50 percent. The United States might have been more concerned with reliable Central American allies against the Axis powers in World War II than with the tendencies of Central Americans toward dictatorship. In late 1944 the United States altered its criteria for recognition of new governments in Latin America. Cable traffic reflected active support for democratic openings and elections, new sympathy in U.S. policy circles for the end of colonialism, and a new policy of U.S. recognition of newly independent, democratic governments.

27. Although it would have been useful to look at accurate data on the volume of overt expressions of social discontent in the 28 percent sample of Central American newspapers, the data proved to be unreliable because of changes in newspaper format and reporting style. Earlier newspapers report fewer total incidents than later newspapers. The volume of discontent in newspaper accounts often falls in crisis periods because of censorship laws. The data on the types and origins of discontent (violent or less violent, rural or urban), however, appear to show a consistent pattern related to crisis.

28. El Salvador, *Gazetta Oficial*, August 22, 1930.

29. Ibid., February 2, 1932; February 25, 1932; July 25, 1932; July 30, 1932; and July 29, 1933.

30. See, for example, Nicaragua, *Gazetta Oficial*, November 3, 1931, on the state of siege in Litoral Atlántico, Nueva Segovia, Jinotega, Estelí, and Matagalpa; and November 25, 1931, on the state of siege in León and Chinandega.

31. Honduras, *Gazetta Oficial*, December 31, 1932, and December 14, 1932.

32. El Salvador, *Gazetta Oficial*, December 5, 1941; Guatemala, *Gazetta Oficial*, December 8, 1941; Nicaragua, *Gazetta Oficial*, December 23, 1941.

33. For example, Costa Rica, *Gazetta Oficial*, December 18, 1941.

34. For example, El Salvador, *Gazetta Oficial*, August 9, 1941; and Guatemala, *Gazetta Oficial*, December 12, 1941.

35. Costa Rica, *Gazetta Oficial*, December 11, 1941; and Honduras, *Gazetta Oficial*, June 10, 1943.

36. For example, in Costa Rica public servants affiliated with the Calderonistas or communists were dismissed; *Gazetta Oficial*, December 17, 1948. In Guatemala the goods of ex-president Ubico and functionaries of his government were seized; *Gazetta Oficial*, November 28, 1944.

37. In Guatemala Aero-vias was nationalized; *Gazetta Oficial*, February 6, 1945. In Costa Rica the banks were nationalized; *Gazetta Oficial*, June 21, 1948.

38. Costa Rica, *Gazetta Oficial*, March 12, 1948.

39. Honduras, *Gazetta Oficial*, February 3, 1956.

40. Ibid., January 5, 1960. In El Salvador the military school was founded; *Gazetta Oficial*, June 24, 1955.

41. Costa Rica, *Gazetta Oficial*, January 6, 1960.

42. Guatemala, *Gazetta Oficial*, all of 1954 and 1955.

43. Ibid., July 16, 1954, August 20, 1954, September 11, 1954, September 30, 1954, and June 6, 1955.

44. The only notable exception was the 1968 coup by Omar Torrijos in Panama. He then controlled that country for fifteen years.

45. Costa Rica, *Gazetta Oficial*, October 29, 1962, and October 26, 1962; Guatemala, *Gazetta Oficial*, November 10, 1963.

46. Costa Rica, *Gazetta Oficial*, June 10, 1974.

47. Nicaragua, *Gazetta Oficial*, October 16, 1978, and September 19, 1978.

48. Guatemala, *Gazetta Oficial*, April 4, 1983, July 5, 1982, March 25, 1982, October 7, 1981, and November 12, 1982.

49. Costa Rica, *Gazetta Oficial*, November 12, 1982.

50. On nationalization of the banking system, see El Salvador, *Gazetta Oficial*, March 7, 1980; and Nicaragua, *Gazetta Oficial*, August 24, 1979. On other nationalizations, see Nicaragua, *Gazetta Oficial*, November 3, 1979.

51. El Salvador, *Gazetta Oficial*, March 5, 1980; and Nicaragua, *Gazetta Oficial*, August 21, 1981.

52. Nicaragua, *Gazetta Oficial*, August 22, 1979, and July 22, 1981,

53. Ibid., July 22, 1981, February 21, 1980, April 12, 1983, and December 22, 1981.

54. The Arias Peace Plan was signed by the Central American presidents on August 7, 1987. The complete text appears in *La Nación*, San José, Costa Rica, August 8, 1987, p. 1.

55. Rank order correlations between the percentage of indigenous population, population density, the percentage of urban population, and political instability, repression, and social discontent were all statistically insignificant with one exception. There was a positive (.80) rank order correlation between the percentage of indigenous population and social discontent during economic crisis. The lack of consistent income and land distribution data prohibited their inclusion in the analysis.

Chapter 7, "Historical Roots of Human Development Performance in Central America"

1. Guatemala's performance was similar enough to the group of poorest performers that I will treat it here as a low performer along with El Salvador.

2. Some of the best sources on comparative health policy are Leonardo Mata and Luis Rosero, *National Health and Social Development in Costa Rica* (Washington, D.C.: Pan American Health Organization, 1988); Pan American Health Organization, *Health Conditions in the Americas* (Washington, D.C., 1980–1990); J. Jaramillo, *Los Problemas de la Salud en Costa Rica* (San José: Litografia Ambar, 1983); B. Castro, P. Jiménez, L. Mata, M. Vives, and M. E. Garcia, "Estudio de Puriscal, Morbilidad Infecciosa de Niño," *Revista Medico Hospital Nacimiento de Niños* (Costa Rica) 17 (January 1984), pp. 49–56; L. Mata, *The Children of Santa María Cauque: A Prospective Field Study of Health and Growth* (Cambridge, Mass.: MIT Press, 1978); "Políticas Públicas de Salud en Centro América," *Revista Centroamericana de Administración Pública*, no. 15 (special edition, June/December 1978); José Rómulo Sánchez López, "Seguridad Social en Guatemala," *Revista Centroamericana de Ciencias de la Salud*, no. 15 (January–April 1980), pp. 103–20; José Rómulo Sánchez, "Consideraciones Generales de la Salud en Guatemala," *Revista Centromericana de Ciencias de la Salud*, no. 4 (May–August 1976), pp. 97–120; Ludwig Guendell, "Enfoque sobre el Análisis de las Políticas Estales de Salud," *Revista Centroamericana de Administración Pública*, no. 17 (1978), pp. 5–27 and 105–14; Dierdri Strachan, "Marketing an Unpopular Idea: Rural Health Technicians in Guatemala," in Marc Lindenberg and Benjamin Crosby, eds., *Managing Development: The Political Dimension* (New Brunswick, N.J.: Kumarian Press and Transaction Books, 1980), pp. 109–44.

3. Mata and Rosero, *National Health and Social Development in Costa Rica*, p. 74.

4. Ibid., pp. 138–64.

5. Ibid.

6. For the most useful sources comparing educational policy in Costa Rica and Guatemala, see Sylvain Lourie, *Education and Development: Strategies and Decisions in Central America* (Stoke on Trent, England: Trendham Books, 1989); Conferencia sobre la Familia, la Infancia y la Juventud de Centroamérica y Panamá, *Las Sociedades Centroamericanas Actuales* (Guatemala City: Editorial José de Pineda Ibarra, 1972); Primera Conferencia Regional sobre Educación y Desarrollo, *Coordinación Educativa Centroamericana* (Guatemala City: Editorial José de Pineda Ibarra, 1977); A. Guttierez-Renon, *La Desegualidad de Opportunidades Educativas de la Niñez Guatemalteca* (Guatemala City: UNESCO, 1977); Severo Martínez Pelaez, *La Patria del Criollo* (San José: Editorial Universitaria Centroamericana (EDUCA), 1976); A. Guttierez-Renon, *Informe Final sobre la Misión: Proyecto de Apoyo al Plan de Desarrollo Educativo de Guatemala* (Guatemala City: United Nations Development Programme (UNDP)/UNESCO, 1978); Oficina de Planeamiento Integral de la Educación, *Plan Nacional de Educación para la República de Guatemala, 1972–78* (Guatemala City, 1973); Monica Toussaint, *Guatemala: Textos de la Historia de Centro América y el Caribe* (Guadalajara: Universidad de Guadalajara, 1988), pp. 602–79; L. Alfaro Monge and F. Rivas Rios, *La Educación: Fragua de una Democracia* (San José: Editorial Universidad de Costa Rica, 1978); L. F. Azofiefa, *Don Mauro Fernández: Teoria y Práctica de Su Reforma Educativa* (San José: Editorial Fernández Arce, 1975); Ministerio de Educación Pública, *Planeamiento del Desarrollo Educativa*, Vol. 1, (San José: Diadonisto, 1971).

7. Alfaro Monge and Rivas Rios, *La Educacion*, p. 15.

8. Lourie, *Education and Development*.

9. Azofiefa, *Don Mauro Fernández*.

10. Ministerio de Educación Pública, *Planeamiento del Desarrollo Educativa*, p. 25.

11. Lourie, *Education and Development*.

12. Carlos González Orellana, "Retroceción de la Educación durante el Regimen Conservador de los 30 Años," in Toussaint, *Guatemala*, p. 610.

13. Toussaint, *Guatemala*, p. 603.

14. Ibid., pp. 613–14.

15. Lourie, *Education and Development*.

16. Guatemala, *Organic Law on National Education*, Article 103 (1950).

17. Oficina de Planeamiento Integral de la Educación, *Plan Nacional de Educación para la República de Guatemala*, p. 5.

18. Ibid.

19. Lourie, *Education and Development*, pp. 139–50.

20. For a discussion of the origins of Panama's governance structures, see the chapters by Nicolás Ardito-Barletta and Eduardo Vallarino in Marc Lindenberg and Jorge Domínguez, eds., *Central American Transitions of the 1980s* (Boulder, Colo.: Westview Press, 1993).

21. For discussions of the origins of Central American social structure, see Tom Barry, *Roots of Rebellion: Land and Hunger in Central America* (Boston: South End Press, 1987); Victor Bulmer-Thomas, *Studies in the Economics of Central America* (New York: St. Martin's Press, 1988); Marc Lindenberg, "World Economic Cycles and Central American Political Instability," *World Politics* 42, no. 3 (April 1990), pp. 397–421; Rafael Menjivar, *Formación y Lucha del Proletariado Industrial Salvadoreño* (San Salvador: UCA Editores, 1979); Fred Weaver, *Political Economy of Development in Central America* (Boulder, Colo.: Westview Press, 1993); and Robert G. Williams, *Export Agriculture and the Crisis in Central America* (Chapel Hill: University of North Carolina Press, 1986).

22. Samuel Stone, *La Dinastía de los Conquistadores* (San José: EDUCA, 1982), has an excellent treatment of the origins of Costa Rican social structure. See particularly pp. 68–71 for his discussion of the possible Jewish origins of the original settlers.

23. León Fernández Bonilla, *Documentos para la Historia de Costa Rica*, Vol. 5 (Paris, 1886), pp. 475–97.

24. Panama's social structure developed initially around its role as a goods transshipment point (from Peru and the Orient to Mexico and Spain) rather than around a hacienda structure. Until independence Panama's elites were urban-based commercial families with rural landholdings. Although they did not espouse democratic values, they were outwardly focused and more open to information about international commerce than other Central Americans.

25. Seymour Martin Lipset, "Elites, Education and Entrepreneurship," in Seymour Martin Lipset and Aldo Solari, eds., *Elites and Development in Latin America* (Buenos Aires: Paido, 1971), p. 21.

26. Francisco Andonio de Fuentes y Guzman, *Ecordación Florida, Discurso Historical y Demonstración Material, Militar y Política del Reyno de Guatemala*, Vol. 2 (Guatemala City: La Sociedad de Geografía y Historia de Guatemala, Tipografia Nacional de Guatemala, 1932), p. 227.

27. Severo Martínez Palaez, *La Patria del Criollo* (San José: Editorial Universitario Centroamericano (EDUCA), 1983), p. 33.

28. See Jorge Domínguez and Marc Lindenberg, *Central America: Current Crisis and Future Prospects* (Washington, D.C.: U.S. Foreign Policy Association, 1984).

29. For a more detailed discussion of the historical roots of policy values in the region, see Ralph Lee Woodward, Jr., *Central America: A Nation Divided*, 2nd ed. (New York: Oxford University Press, 1985); and Domínguez and Lindenberg, *Central America: Current Crisis and Future Prospects.*

30. Stone, *La Dinastía de los Conquistadores*, is an excellent source on the development of coffee and its implications for Costa Rican social structure.

31. Ibid.

32. Ibid.

33. Costa Rica, Archivos Nacionales, Sección Hacienda, No. 6658, 1843.

34. Stone, *La Dinastía de los Conquistadores.*

35. Ibid.

36. Between 1870 and 1890 the military was also a factor in the Costa Rican social structure. There were three military presidents, the first of whom seized power after conflicts between civilian leaders proved impossible to settle. These presidents, Tomas Guardia Gutierrez, Prospero Fernández Oreamuno, and Bernardo Soto Alfaro, came from the upper class and had income from coffee fincas and cattle, unlike the military leaders in the rest of the region. They had less professional military training than those of other nations. They were steeped in the values of liberalism and supported major improvements in education and commerce. They paved the way for civilian, democratic government at the turn of the century.

37. Some of the best sources on this period in Guatemala are Miguel Angel Austurias, *Guatemalan Sociology* (Tempe: Arizona State University, 1977); Monica Toussaint, *Guatemala, A Short History* (Guadalajara: Universidad de Guadalajara, 1988); Monica Toussaint, *Guatemala: Textos de la Historia de Centro América y el Caribe* (Guadalajara: Universidad de Guadalajara, 1988); García Laguardia, *El Pensamiento Liberal de Guatemala* (San José: EDUCA, 1977); and John Dombrowski, Elinor Betters, Howard Blutstein, Lynne Cox, and Elery Zehner, *Area Handbook for Guatemala*, (Washington, D.C.: U.S. Government Printing Office, 1968).

38. Toussaint, *Guatemala, A Short History.*

39. Sam A. Mosk, "Economía Cafetalera de Guatemala durante el Periodo 1850–1918," in Jorge Lujan Munos, ed., *Economía de Guatemala 1750–1940: Antología de Lecturas y Materials*, vol. 1 (Guatemala City: Universidad de San Carlos, 1980), pp. 347–66. The original pamphlet was prepared by Licenciado Don Manuel Aguilar and printed by the Consulado de Comercio de Guatemala, Guatemala City, 1845. It appears in the Archivo General del Gobierno de Guatemala, Various pamphlets, 1845–1847.

40. In El Salvador, because of land scarcity, the emergence of coffee as a potentially profitable crop increased social stratification even more. The pressure to increase the size of haciendas drove the rural small farm and subsistence population off the land and converted a large group into a rural prolateriat. See Eduardo Colindres, *Fundamentos Económicos de la Burguesía Salvadoreña* (San Salvador: UCA Editores, 1977).

41. *Revista, Periodico Semianuario de la Sociedad Económica de Amigos del Estado de Guatemala* 10, no. 2, (December 10, 1846), pp. 6–7.

42. Stone, *La Dinastía de los Conquistadores*.

43. In Panama the foundations for successful human development policy emerged in the 1900s as well. At the time of independence from Colombia in 1903, Panamanian liberal and conservative leaders

> wary of the violent conflicts of Colombia's past, decided to accept the existence of diversity in unity and to that extent institutionalize some crucial aspect of democratic procedure. In this case it was the peacefully contested sharing of power. Habituation to the working of those rules was made possible through the disbanding of the army in 1904 and the country's focus on a new priority, the building of the Panama canal. (Eduardo Vallarino, "Panama," in Lindenberg and Domínguez, eds., *Central American Transitions of the 1980s*).

The development of the canal and further commerce allowed for more growth of the middle class and aided the transition from oligarchy to polarchy, or a government based on multiple groups. From 1903 to 1968 the Panamanian government was selected through periodic elections. While there were accusations of fraud on more than one occasion, power was often transferred from one freely elected government to another. This transition was reinforced by strong U.S. influence through the canal zone. The United States helped subsidize general education and health programs.

44. Dombrowski et al., *Area Handbook for Guatemala*, and Toussaint, *Guatemala: Textos de la Historia de Centro América y el Caribe*.

45. Ibid.

46. North American Congress on Latin America (NACLA), *Guatemala* (New York, 1984).

47. Comments of Rodolfo Paíz, minister of finance during the Venicio Cerezo government in Guatemala, Harvard Central American Transitions Workshop discussion notes, 1991.

48. Comments of General Hector Gramajo, minister of defense during the Venicio Cerezo government in Guatemala, and General Walter López, former minister of defense of Honduras, Harvard Central American Transitions Workshop discussion notes, 1991.

49. Robert T. Putnam with Robert Leonardi and Raffella Nanetti, *Democracy and the Civic Community: Tradition and Change in an Italian Experiment* (Princeton: Princeton University Press, 1992).

50. Samuel Huntington, *The Third Wave: Democratization in the Late Twentieth Century* (Norman: University of Oklahoma Press, 1991).

51. Marc Lindenberg and Shantayana Devarajan, "Prescribing Strong Economic Medicine: Revisiting the Myths about Structural Adjustment, Democracy, and Economic Performance in Developing Nations," *Comparative Politics* 25, no. 2 (January 1993).

52. World Bank, *World Development Report 1992* (New York: Oxford University Press, 1992).

53. Graham Allison and Robert Beschel, "Can the U.S. Promote Democracy?" *Political Science Quarterly* 106, no. 4 (March 1991-92).

Appendix 1, "Calculating the Modified Human Development Index"

1. See U.N. Development Programme, *Human Development Report 1990* (New York: Oxford University Press, 1991), pp. 108–9.

Appendix 2, "Calculating the Disparity Reduction Rate"

1. Because the Soviet Union begins with a relatively high HDI (82.1), the relatively large size of that score (the denominator in the percentage calculation) in relation to the smaller increment of change (10.4—the numerator in the calculation) means that the actual average percentage improvement is quite small in contrast to Niger, whose low initial HDI score results in a small denominator (4.6) relative to the large numerator (10.4) in the same calculation.

2. James Grant, *Disparity Reduction Rates in Social Indicators*, Monograph 11 (Washington, D.C.: Overseas Development Council, 1978), p. 12.

INDEX

About the Author

Marc Lindenberg is currently the senior vice president for programs of CARE, an international nongovernmental organization, which provided more than $400 million in emergency relief and human development programs in 41 developing countries in 1992. To join CARE he took a leave of absence from his position as a lecturer in public policy at Harvard's John F. Kennedy School of Government, where he received the Manuel Carballo Award for Excellence in Teaching in 1989. He is the author of numerous books on problems of international development, such as *Managing Adjustment in Developing Countries* (with Noel Ramírez), *Central America: Current Crisis and Future Prospects* (with Jorge Domínguez), *Managing Development: The Political Dimension* (with Benjamin Crosby), and *Public Budgeting* (with Fremont Lyden) as well as many articles. From 1981 to 1987 he was the rector of the Central American Institute of Business Adminstration (INCAE) in Costa Rica. He completed his B.A. degree in political science at Oberlin College (1967) and his M.P.A. and Ph.D. in comparative and development administration at the University of Southern California.

ICEG Academic Advisory Board